The College History Series

The University of Maine

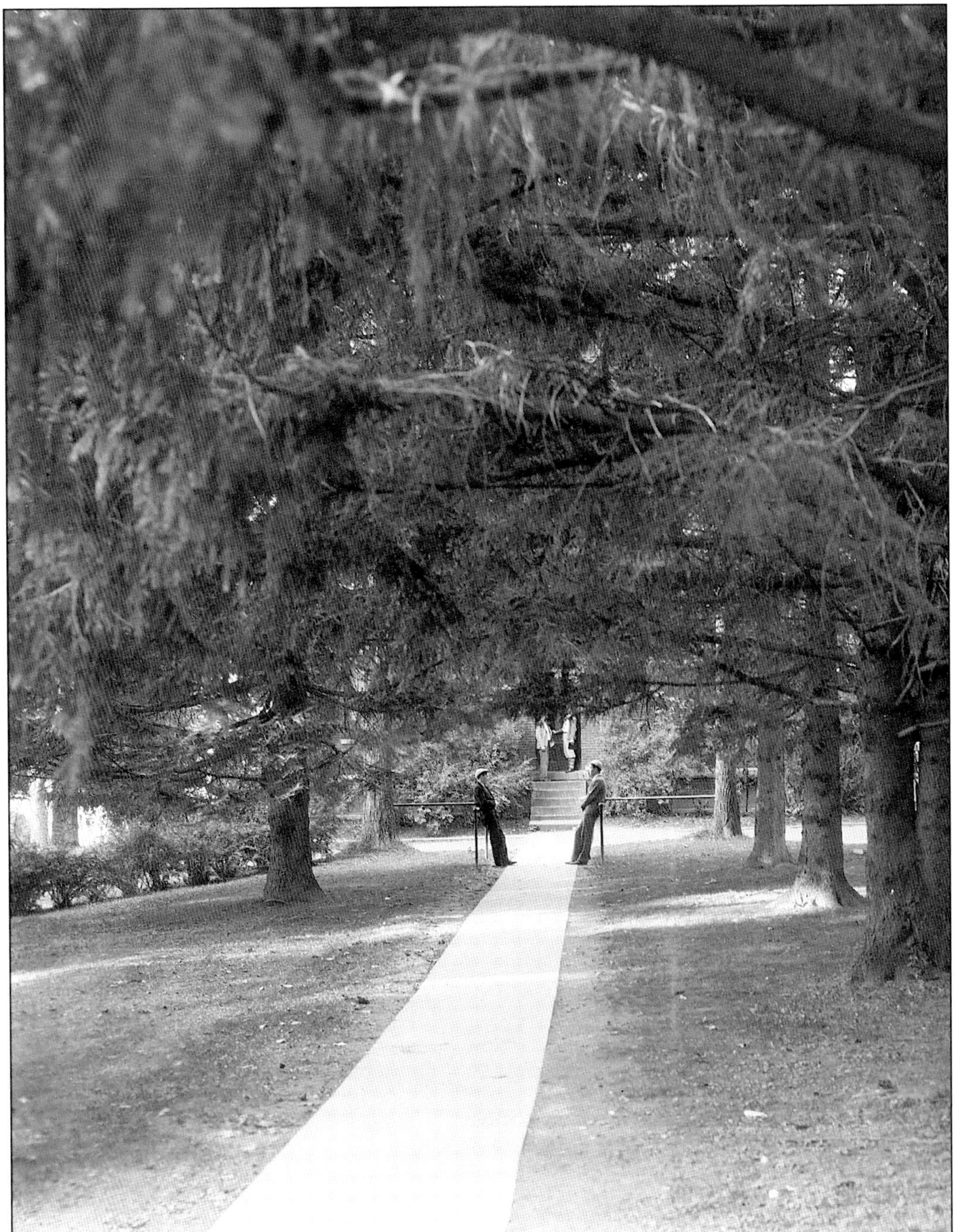

LOOKING DOWN THE FOOTPATH LEADING TO OAK HALL C. 1890.

The College History Series

THE UNIVERSITY OF MAINE

BOB BRIGGS & DEBRA WRIGHT

ARCADIA PUBLISHING

ISBN 978-0-7385-0175-8

Published by Arcadia Publishing
Charleston, South Carolina

Printed in the United States of America

Library of Congress Catalog Card Number: 99-63939

For all general information contact Arcadia Publishing at:
Telephone 843-853-2070
Fax 843-853-0044
E-mail sales@arcadiapublishing.com
For customer service and orders:
Toll-Free 1-888-313-2665

Visit us on the Internet at www.arcadiapublishing.com

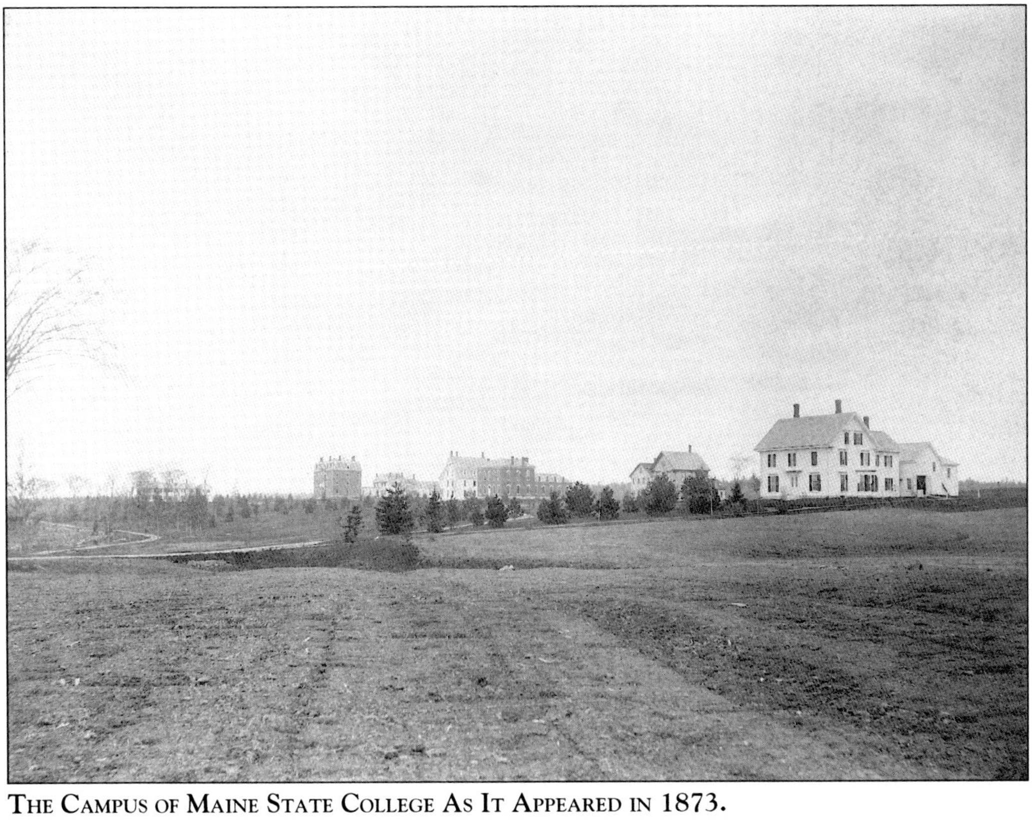

THE CAMPUS OF MAINE STATE COLLEGE AS IT APPEARED IN 1873.

CONTENTS

Dedication

This volume is dedicated to the memory of Dr. Merritt Caldwell Fernald—professor, pioneer, and president—without whose efforts no book on the history of the University of Maine would be necessary.

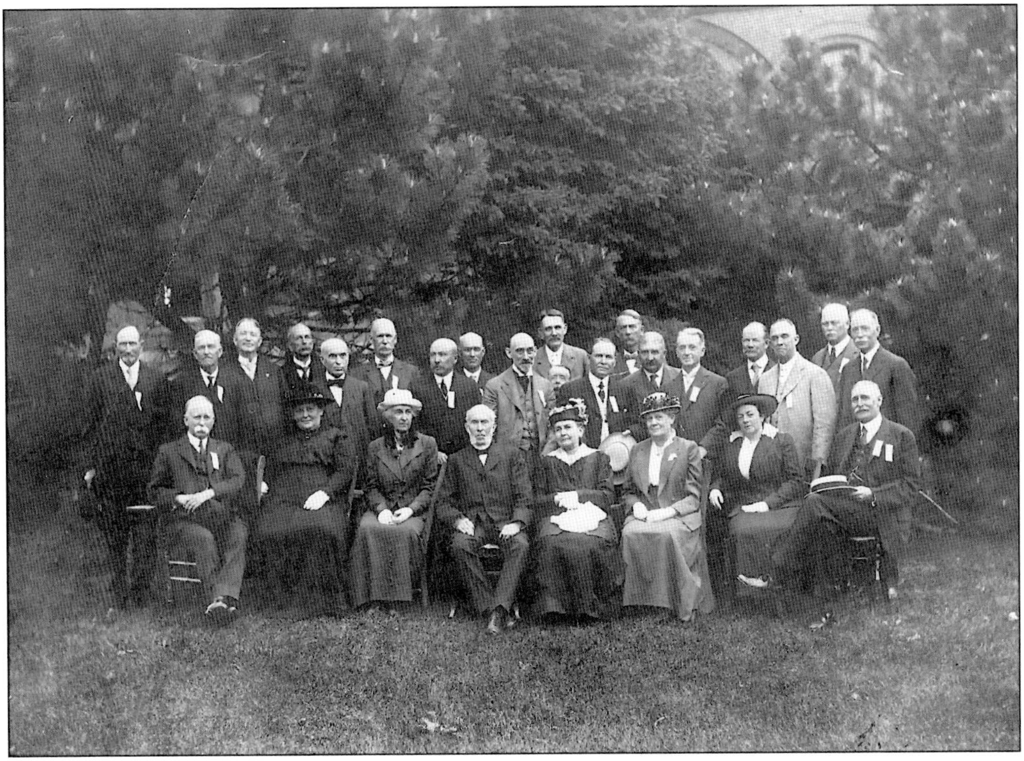

DR. FERNALD (SEATED FRONT AND CENTER WITH HIS WIFE, MARY LOVEJOY FERNALD, TO HIS RIGHT). With death approaching, Dr. Fernald was asked about the resting place of his remains. He replied, "I shall be buried on the hill in the cemetery across the river from the University in sight of the buildings which I love and where I have lived and worked." Such was the case.

". . .And through faith, though he is dead, he still speaks." *Hebrews 11:4.*

Introduction
by Maine Governor Angus S. King

STATE OF MAINE
OFFICE OF THE GOVERNOR
1 STATE HOUSE STATION
AUGUSTA, MAINE
04333-0001

ANGUS S. KING, JR.
GOVERNOR

Maine people have a lot to be proud of in their university. For more than 120 years, the University of Maine at Orono has served as the crown jewel of publicly funded higher education in Maine and, more recently, as the centerpiece of an outstanding multi-campus system. The young men and women who have passed through the halls and dormitories of the Orono campus have gone on to make their mark in law, business, politics, science, sports, the arts – not just in Maine but across the country and around the world.

That the University of Maine has had such a significant impact on Maine life is a testament to the people of this state who have supported the university with their tax dollars. Their investment has paid off. The University's Forestry Department's graduate program, for example, is ranked one of the top five in the nation. Research programs at the university have developed new products and better processing equipment for the state's blueberry and lobster industries. The School of Marine Sciences has helped nurture Washington County's aquaculture industry by developing new and better treatments for fish diseases. University researchers recently came to the rescue of Maine's important lobster industry when a deadly virus threatened it. And because of university-based research, Maine is using recycled materials in road construction and developing materials for composite-reinforced timber bridges that are more durable and cost effective than existing steel and concrete bridges.

That's just a few examples of how the university has helped shape the natural resource-based economy of Maine. But its contributions don't stop there. The Orono campus serves as the cultural center of northern Maine. Its world-class sports teams have generated excitement and pride throughout Maine. And if anyone needs confirmation that UMO's arts and literature courses can prepare one for greatness, here it is: Stephen King, a UMO graduate.

From its humble beginnings – as this book documents – the University of Maine at Orono has become a symbol of education excellence. In the process, it has raised the aspirations of thousands of Maine students and challenged them to aim high and follow their dreams. Our state is better for it.

Angus S. King, Jr.
Governor

PHONE: (207) 287-3531(Voice)
PRINTED ON RECYCLED PAPER
(207) 287-6548 (TTY)
FAX: (207) 287-1034

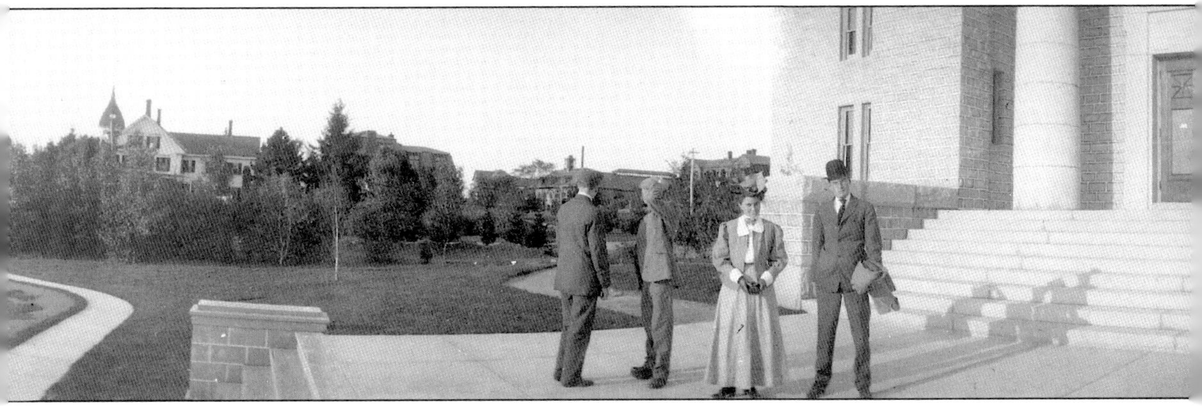

ACKNOWLEDGMENTS

We are grateful for the opportunity to acknowledge the efforts and kind intentions of the many people who helped make this volume a reality.

Our first thanks is to the very helpful staff of the Special Collections Department of Folger Library at the University of Maine at Orono. Many thanks to Muriel Sanford, Betsy Paradis, and Kathy Corridan, who have graciously borne with our perusal of the many resources available in special collections. You made the research for the book easy and enjoyable.

Our thanks go once again to Earle Shuttleworth and the Maine Historic Preservation Commission for use of their photographs and Mr. Shuttleworth's graciousness to help out whenever and wherever he can.

Special thanks to Miss Cheyan Costigan, who helped in the typing of the manuscript, and also to Miss Chelsie Smith, who helped in the final layout of the pages.

We also acknowledge our indebtedness to those who labored to preserve the history of the university in volumes much more informative and complete than this work. Dr. David Smith's book *The First Century: A History of the University of Maine, 1865–1965*, was of particular help and interest.

A final thanks to Gov. Angus King for taking time to write a forward for this work and for sharing his thoughts on the need for and benefits of higher education in our great state.

One

Beginnings

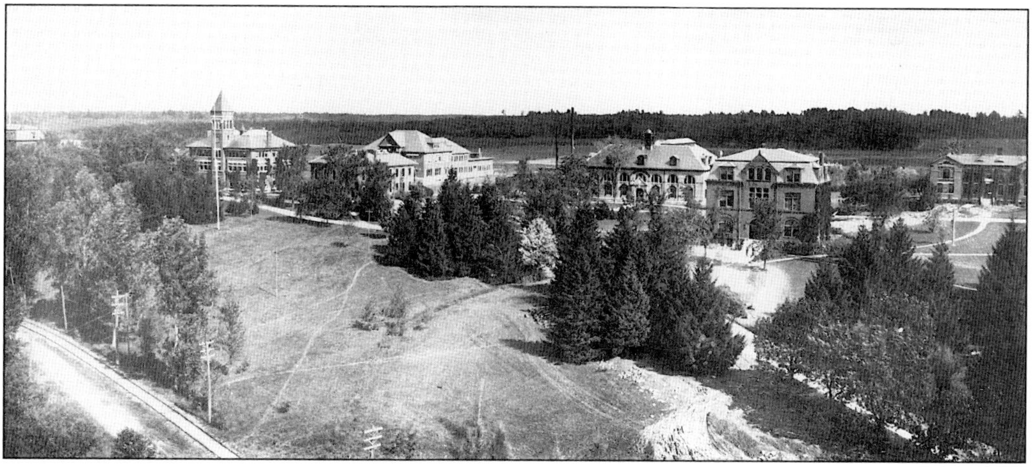

The University Campus c. 1910. Note the trolley tracks heading toward nearby Old Town. Prominent buildings, from left to right, are Wingate Hall, Lord Hall, Alumni Hall, and Coburn Hall. In September of 1862, Congress, with the approval of President Lincoln, enacted the Morrill Land Grant College Act for the purpose of establishing colleges across the nation "to promote the liberal and practical education of the industrial classes." The act granted each state 30,000 acres of land per senator and representative in Congress, thus entitling Maine to 210,000 acres. Acres were sold by the state anywhere from 52¢ to $1 per acre. The endowment fund resulting from the entire sale of the land script was $118,300. Maine State College officially opened its doors in Orono on September 21, 1868, with a pioneer class of 12 men. They sat under the instruction of two paid faculty members: Merritt C. Fernald, acting president and professor of mathematics; and Samuel Johnson, farm superintendent. From such humble origins, Maine State College (later the University of Maine) has endured to become a first-rate institution of higher education. Its history has witnessed student involvement in two world wars, times of student unrest and protest, and showdowns with governors and legislators not always amenable to its cause and existence.

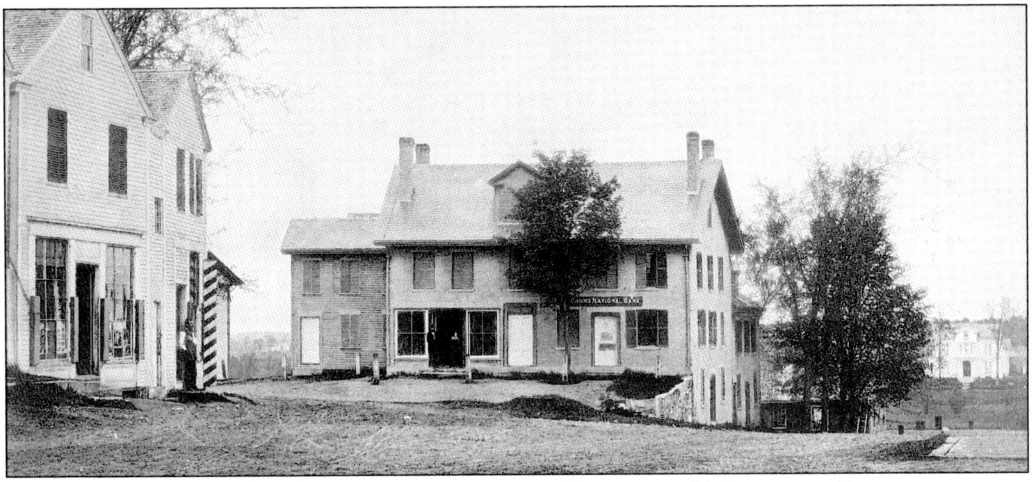

The Orono Post Office and Orono National Bank, c. 1875, with a Storefront and Barbershop to the Left. Orono's location (approximately halfway between Kittery, the state's southernmost boundary, and Fort Kent, the northernmost boundary) gave it favor with the board of trustees appointed by the state legislature in 1865 to determine where to establish the college. Also under consideration were Togus, Topsham, Fairfield, and Bangor. Bowdoin and Colby Colleges made offers to take Morrill funds and carry out the provisions of the act without having to build another college. The trustees finally settled on building in Orono by a slim eight-to-seven margin.

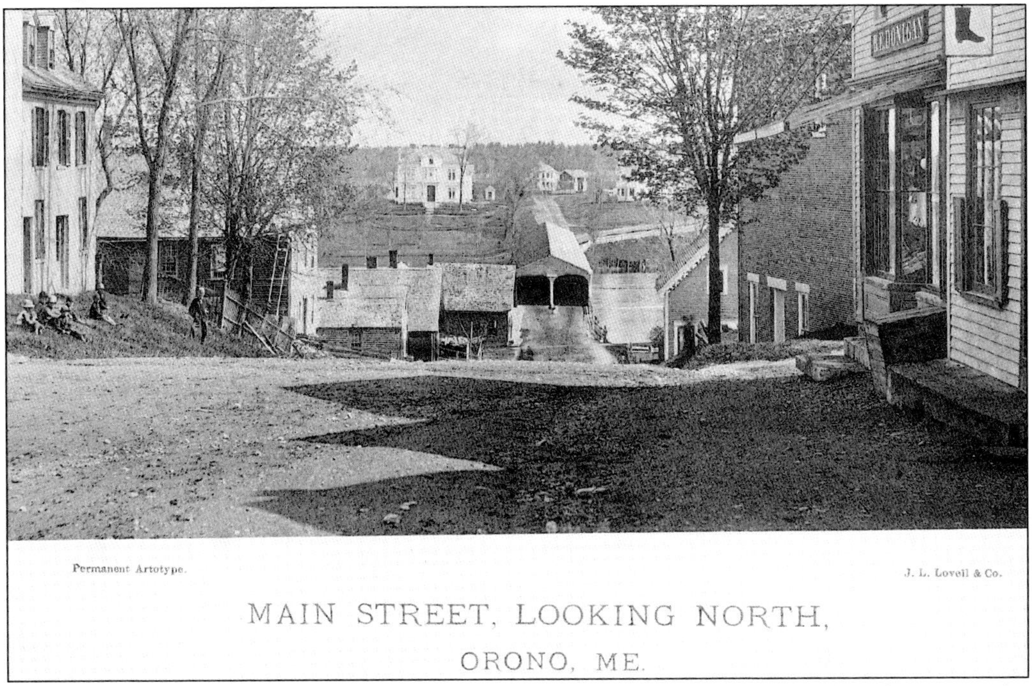

Main Street in Orono, Looking North, c. 1880. Note the covered bridge that spans the Stillwater River. Located one mile from the village of Orono and nine miles from Bangor, trustees settled on a 370-acre tract of land that bordered the Stillwater River. The parcel was purchased for $11,000 by the towns of Orono and Old Town and given to the State. Two working farms, the White and Frost Farms, were included in the transaction.

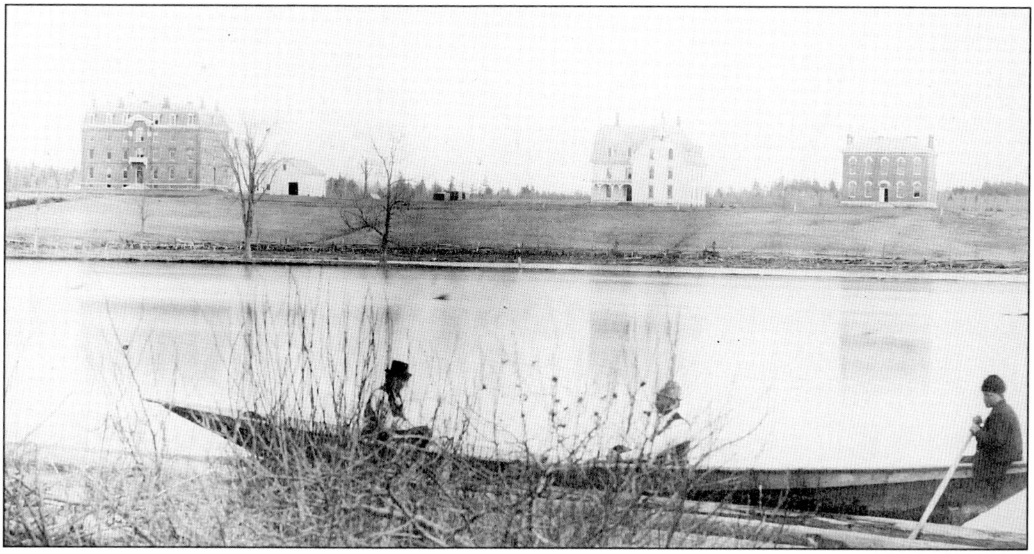

RIVER VIEW OF THE FLEDGLING COLLEGE IN 1873. Buildings seen here, from the far left to the right, are Brick Hall (later renamed Oak Hall), White Hall, and Chemical Hall (later renamed Fernald Hall). Maine State College was not the state's first endeavor in providing higher education to the non-professional classes. The Gardiner Lyceum, founded in 1822, was an unsuccessful forerunner that folded when state aid was revoked. The Kents Hill School in Readfield made efforts to combine shop and farm work with academic offerings, to enable students to pay a portion of their expenses by manual labor.

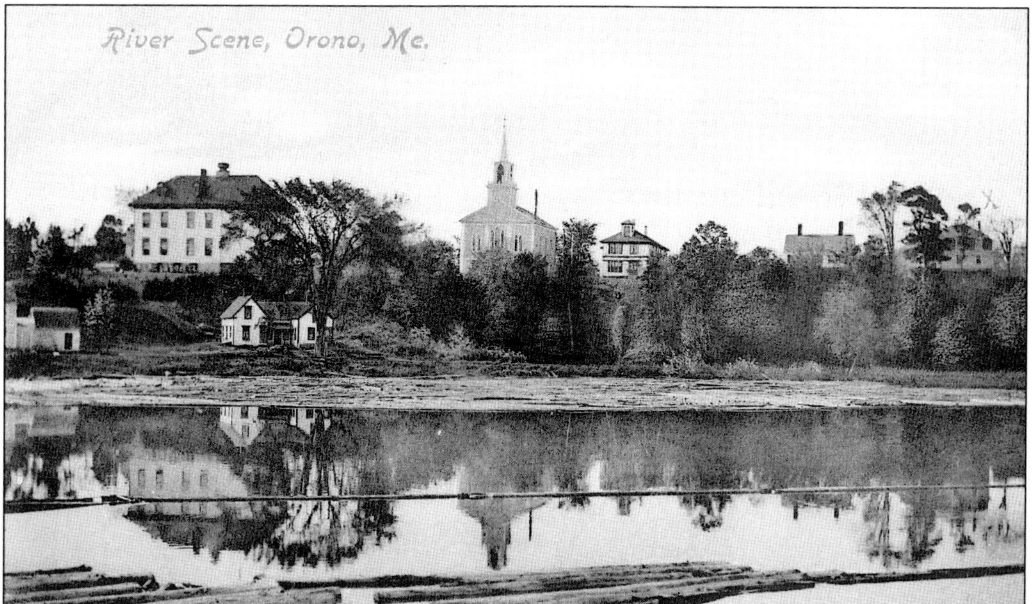

A RIVER SCENE OF THE VILLAGE OF ORONO, C. 1880. Note the log-sorting booms on the shore. Buildings in this photograph include the back side of the post office and the Orono Congregational Church. The establishment of the university was greatly encouraged by Orono and its environs, as it brought notoriety and increased business to merchants, boardinghouses, and other local industry.

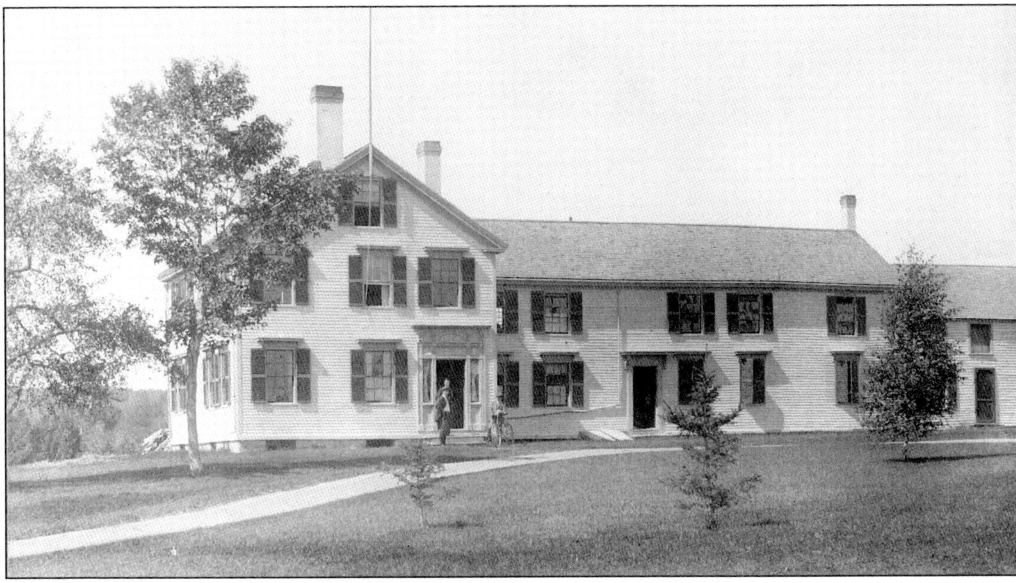

An Image of the White Farm, c. 1885. Built in 1833, this was for many years the oldest building on campus. Farm superintendent Charles Johnson first occupied the building in July of 1868. A working farm, Johnson used it to give instruction in agriculture, horticulture, and also to provide food for the student body and administration. In 1898, the building was remodeled, converted into a dorm for women students, and renamed Mount Vernon. It was destroyed by fire in 1933.

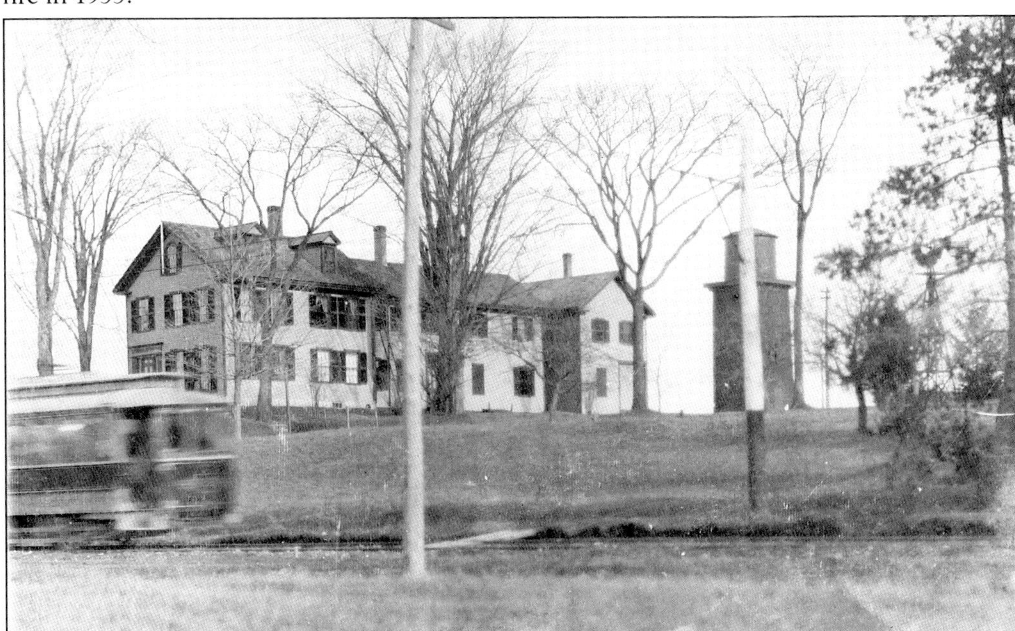

A Trolley Passing by Frost Farm, c. 1890. Note the water tower and the windmill in the background. The historic building, once part of the Goddard Farm complex, has served the university as a faculty residence, infirmary, and fraternity house. It was moved in 1904 and became known as North Hall. First President Fernald and his family took up residence in the house before the President's House was built in 1873.

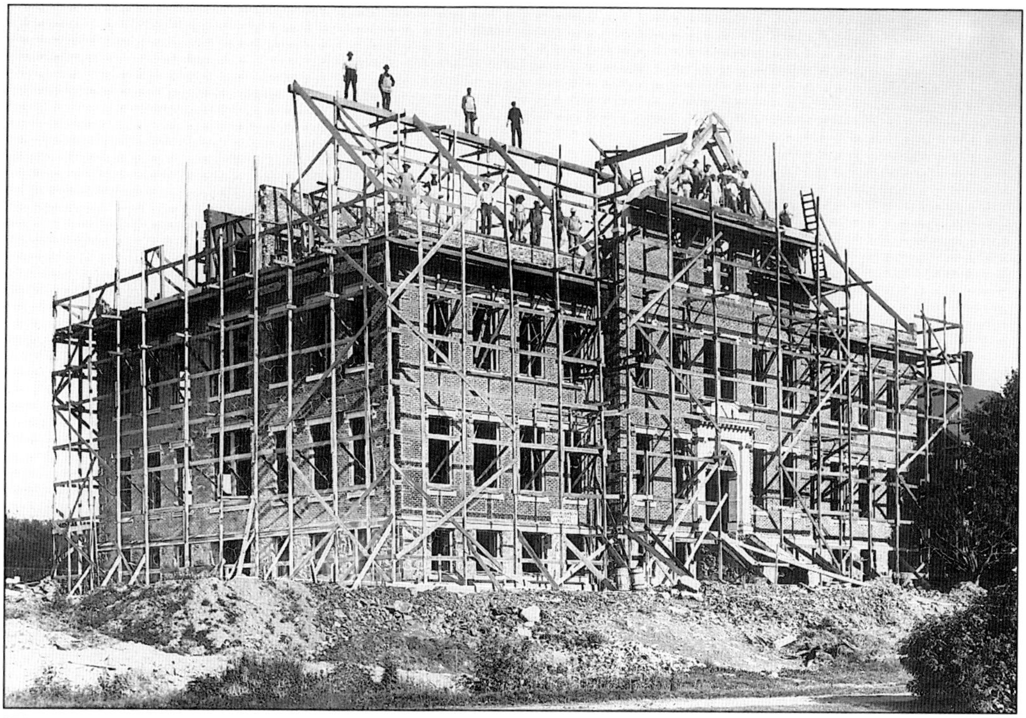

Workers atop Winslow Hall in 1908. Obtaining revenues for erecting new buildings and maintaining the older ones was a constant battle for trustees and university presidents. Monies raised from the two Morrill Acts, gifts and endowments from private benefactors, and allotments from the Maine Legislature allowed the campus to move forward in the early years.

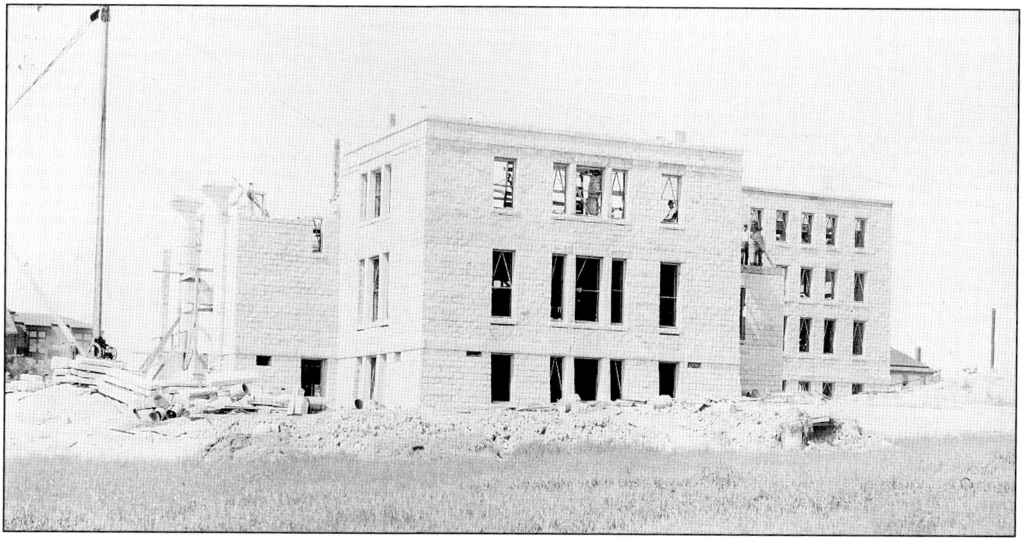

Carnegie Hall under Construction in 1906. Not all of the early buildings erected on campus were dependent on federal or state funding. The benevolence of philanthropists and alumni enabled the building of several buildings, including Alumni Hall and Carnegie Hall. Carnegie was enabled by a $55,000 gift from steel magnate Andrew Carnegie, with granite supplied at cost by the Hallowell Granite Works. Alumnus A.B. Houghton, class of 1887, provided architectural plans for the interior of the building.

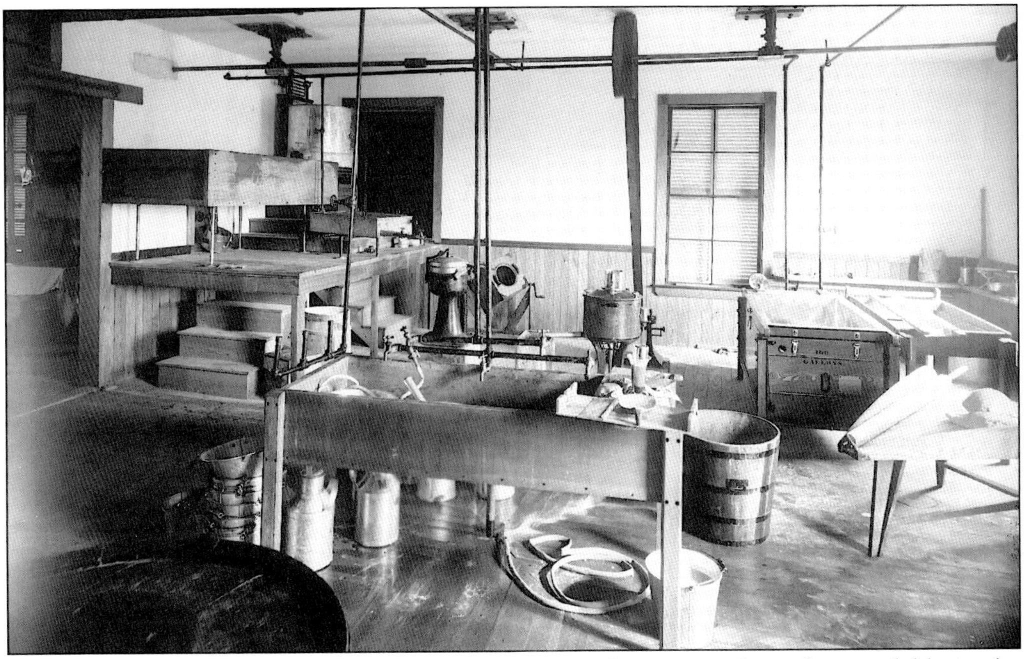

Inside the Dairy and Poultry Building, c. 1880. Instructional supplies available in the early days of Maine State College were sparse at best. The college was again dependent upon appropriations from the state legislature, which often questioned whether the school was needed and would endure. President Fernald stated at the opening of the school in 1868, that the physical inventory of instructional supplies consisted of "geography charts and a few pieces of physical apparatus." He estimated their total value at $141.65.

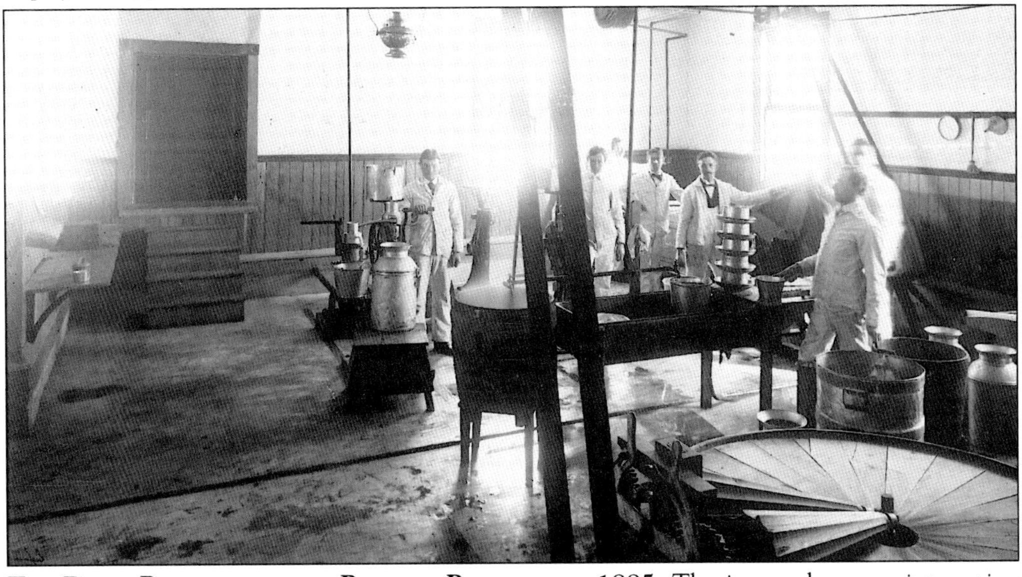

The Dairy Room inside the Poultry Building, c. 1885. The image shows an interesting view of students using churns and cream separators under the illumination of gas lanterns. Dairy products such as butter, cheese, and milk were sold off campus and to the dinning commons at the college. An early experiment charted the effects of milk consumption by students eating in the Oak Hall dining complex.

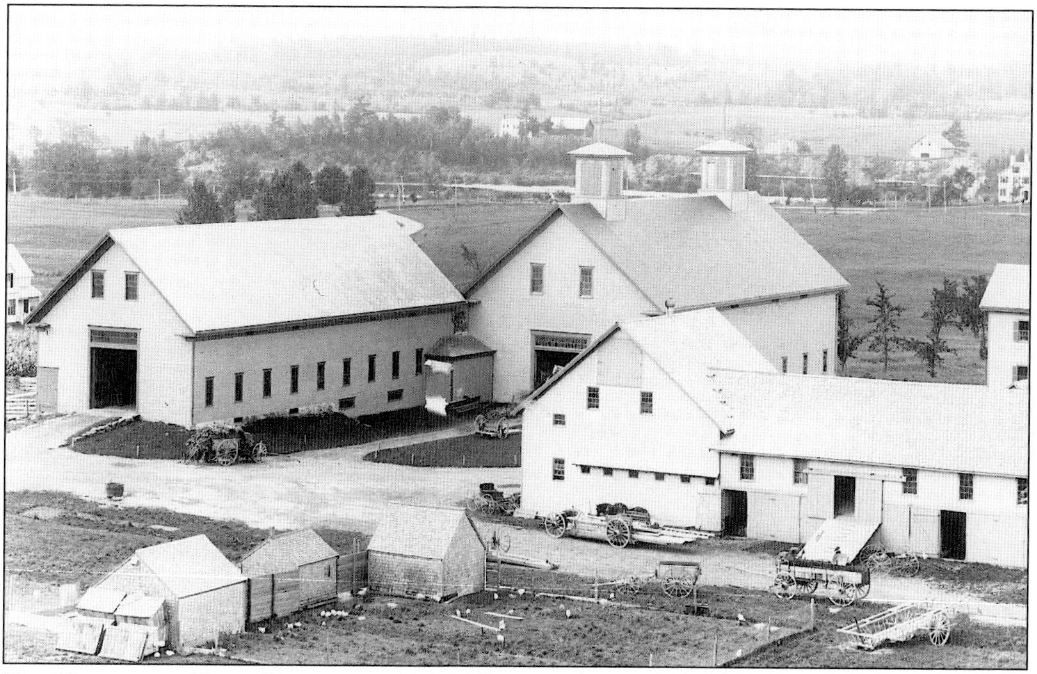

The University Farm Complex in 1906. The complex included hen houses, chicken coops, a greenhouse, several barns, and a livery stable. From its inception, a major thrust of Maine State College was to promote research in agriculture as necessitated by the Morrill Act. Its intent was also to educate and keep prospective Maine farmers in the state. Agricultural experimentation began on campus in 1867, a year before there was an operating university.

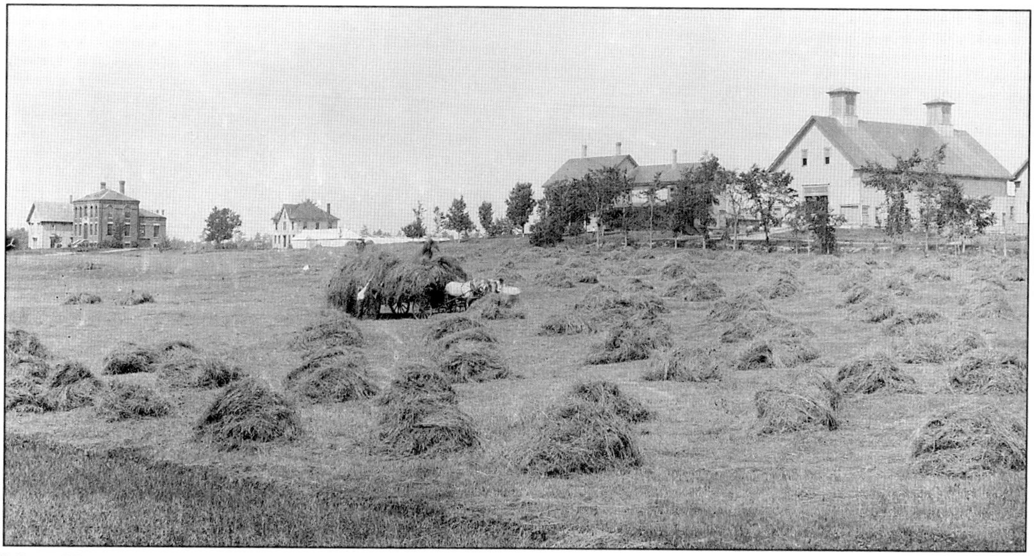

Not Exactly a Hayride: Students Labor on the Campus Farm, c. 1880. Maine State College became famous for its student labor system, which differentiated it from in-state counterparts Bowdoin and Colby. Initiated in 1868, the program was designed to cut the cost of education and develop a work ethic in students. Students received a grade for their efforts and were compensated about 9¢ an hour. The system was discarded after tuition was implemented in 1881.

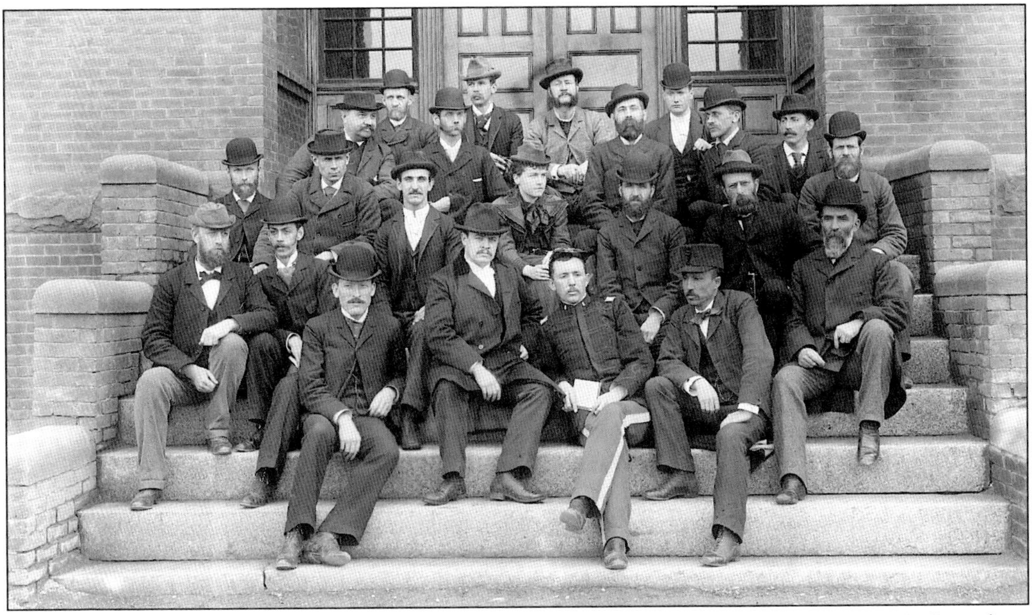

THE FACULTY OF MAINE STATE COLLEGE ON THE STEPS OF COBURN HALL IN 1895. President Harris is shown front and center. The photograph is significant in that four of the faculty members pictured have had campus buildings named in their honor: A.B. Aubert (seated top row, left), A.E. Rogers (back row, center), H.M. Estabrooke (back row, with the derby hat), and J.N. Hart (front row, left). Miss Harriet Converse Fernald, daughter of President Fernald and an early librarian at the school, is the young lady who is seated.

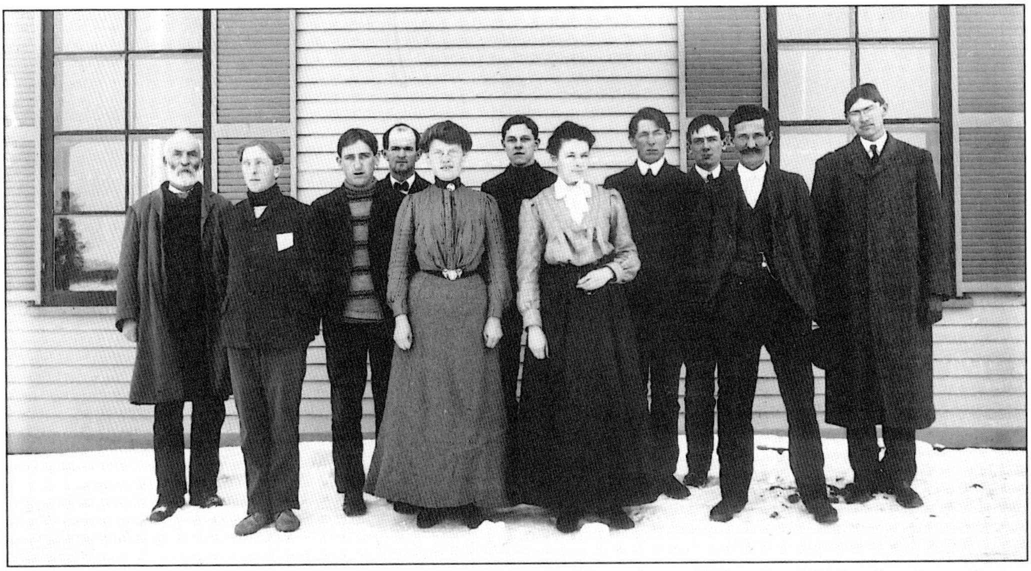

FACULTY MEMBERS, C. 1906. Note the appearance of female staff. In the 1880s, faculty salaries ran as high as $1,800, although new faculty started at around $600. In 1890, President Fernald's compensation was upped to $3,000. For most faculty, the job was year-round. Responsibilities included teaching, administration, and janitorial duties such as cleaning and putting classrooms in order.

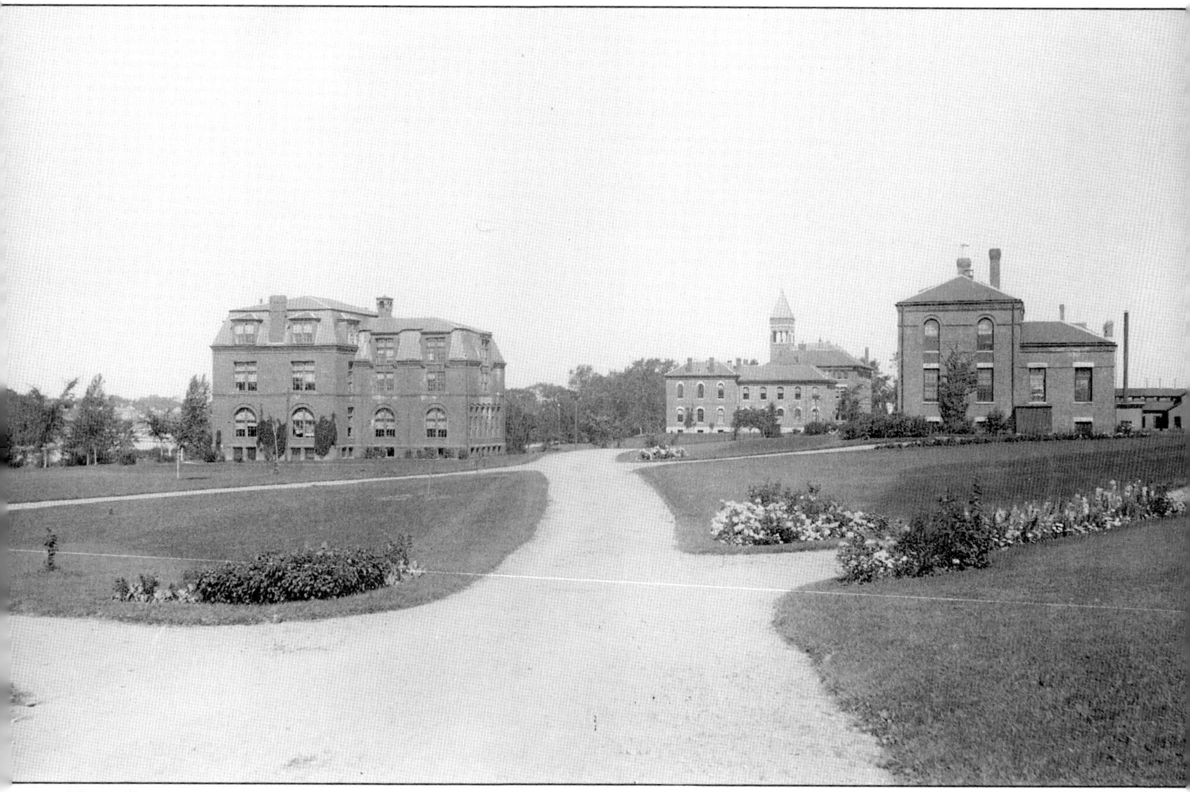

THE CROSSROADS OF THE CAMPUS, C. 1910. Shown here are Coburn Hall (to the left), Fernald Hall (to the right), Wingate Hall (with steeple), and the Experiment Station. Properly known as the Maine State College of Agriculture and Mechanic Arts, the school stood in the 1890s at the crossroads of either continuing in that vein or branching off to provide broader course offerings. Sen. Justin Morrill, whose father authored the initial Morrill Act, encouraged the expansion by stating, "I would hope that no farmer or mechanic would be so illiberal as to wish to have the monopoly of education in any of those Land Grant Colleges." After lengthy debate, the legislature voted to change the name of the school in 1897 to the University of Maine. The turn of the 20th century saw the emergence of studies in law, pharmacy, electrical engineering, and the College of Arts and Sciences.

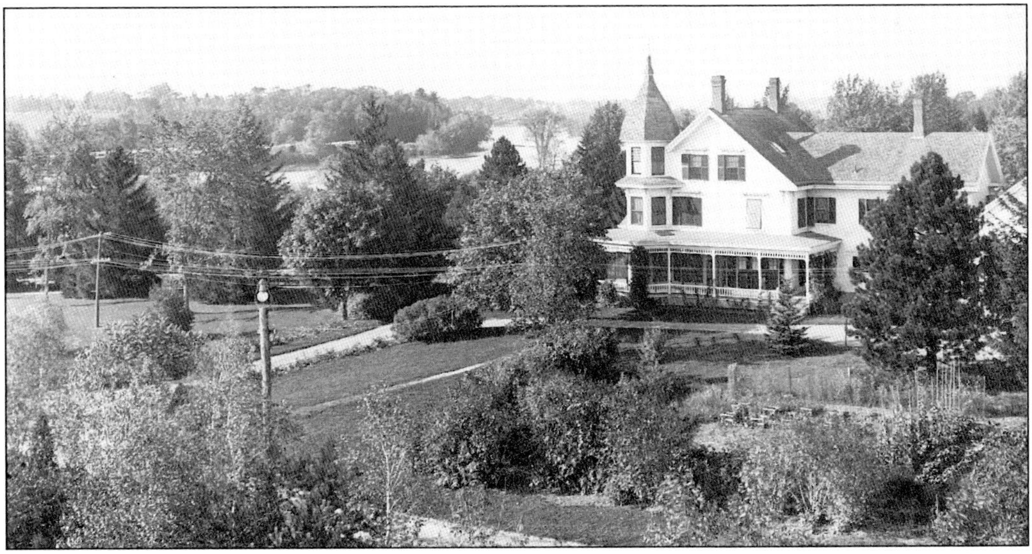

THE PRESIDENT'S HOUSE, C. 1895. The scene overlooks the Stillwater River and boasts considerable work being done by landscapers to beautify the campus. Built in 1872, the President's House has endured fire, renovation, and constant modification in its almost 160-year history. More importantly, its occupants have and continue to shape the course of the college. From the pioneering work of Merritt Caldwell Fernald to the period of great expansion and development under Arthur A. Hauck, the labors of university presidents have given them a prominent place in the history of the college. Eight presidents served the university from 1868 to 1940. They settled student dissension and battled the legislature for funding, while staying abreast of rapid changes in the knowledge and mores of their students. The image below shows the President's House before the 1893 fire and remodeling.

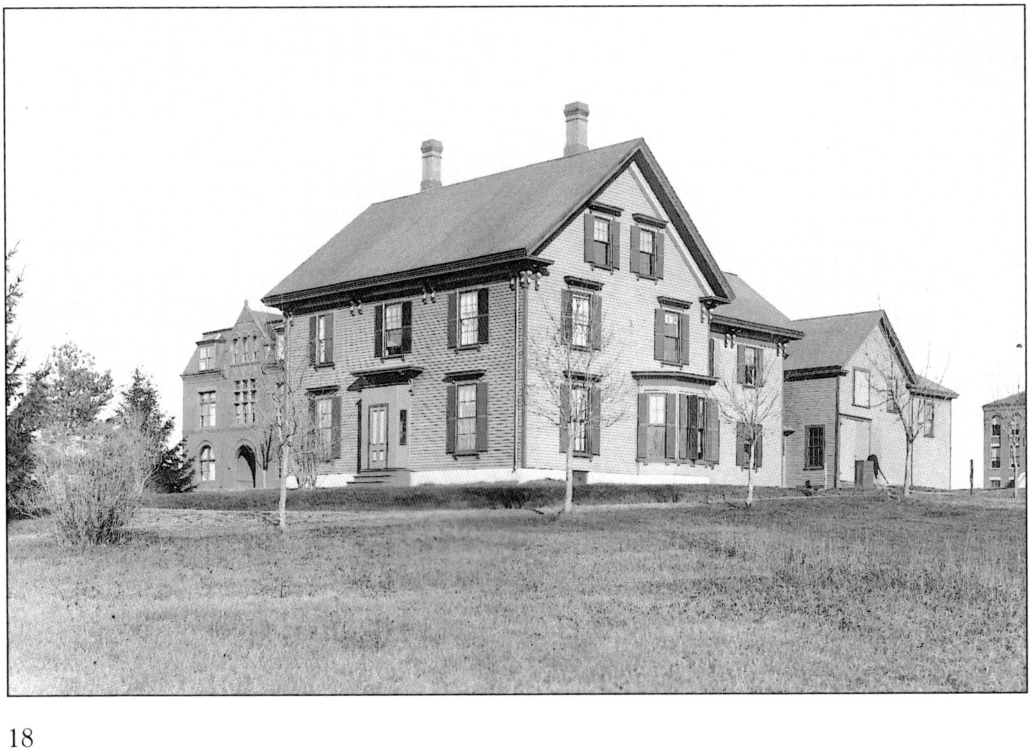

Merritt Caldwell Fernald, A.M., Ph.D. (1868–1871, 1879–1893). Dr. Fernald was the university's first acting president, first faculty member, and was president *pro-tempore* in 1902. Fernald wrote a history of the university that was published in 1916, shortly before his death. A Bowdoin College graduate, Fernald was a true pioneer who set and helped maintain the course of the college during its probationary years. Fernald wrote of those years: "The three years from 1868 to 1871, constituted one of the trying and critical periods in the history of the institution. At their close, questions of title and permanency were now happily questions of the past." Shown below is Chemical Hall as it appeared in the 1880s. The building was renamed Fernald Hall in 1896 in honor of President Fernald.

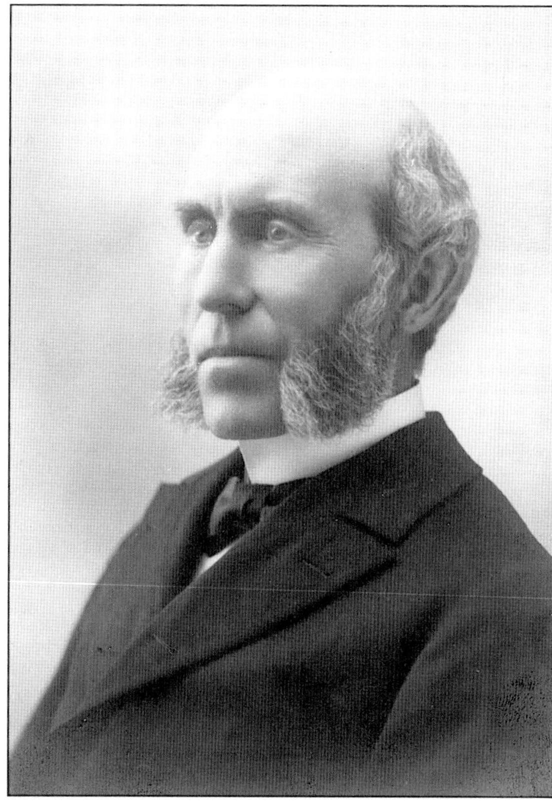

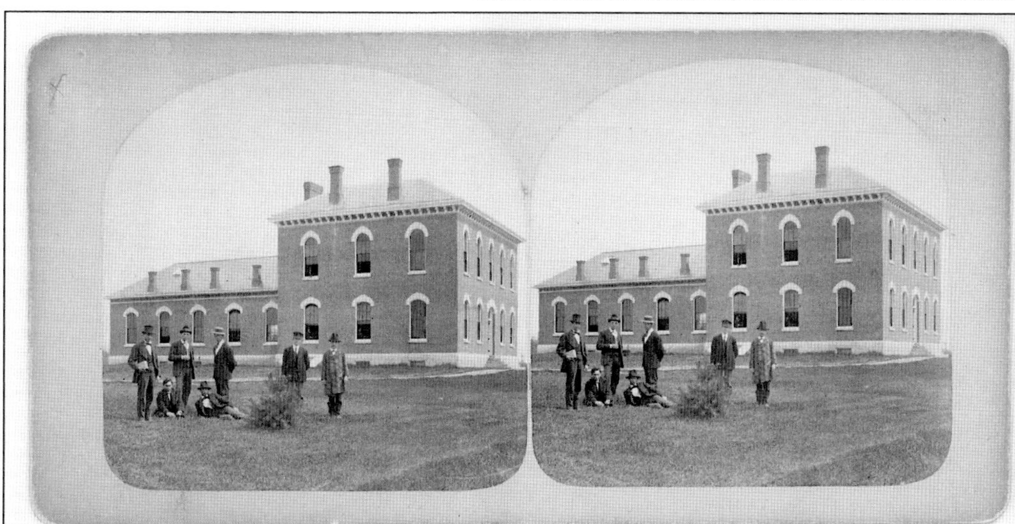

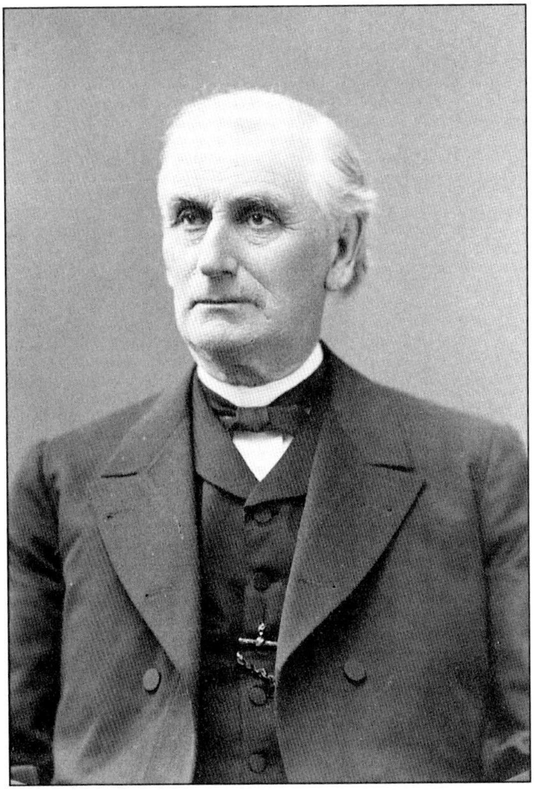

REVEREND CHARLES FREDERICK ALLEN, A.M., D.D. (1871–1879). The college's first president, Allen was appointed after Gov. Joshua Chamberlain refused the position. His inauguration was the first major public ceremony on the campus. A Methodist minister of repute, Allen brought a stamp of Christian virtue to the college. The 1912 *Prism* wrote of Allen: "Broader than his denomination, greater than any sect, and a representative of the highest material interests and best good of the entire state of Maine." Allen left the university to re-enter the ministry, where he served until his death in 1899. Among his accomplishments were the integration of both classical and scientific studies and the acceptance of female students to the college.

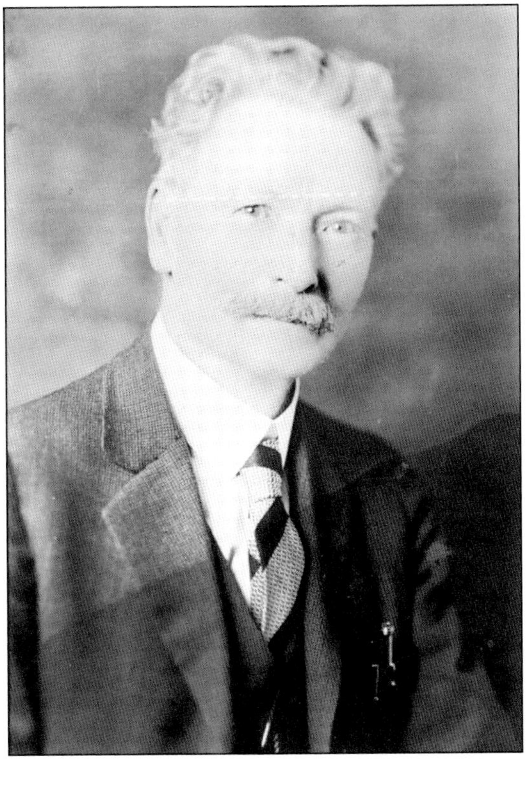

GEORGE EMORY FELLOWS, PH.D., LH.D. (1902–1910). The Fellows administration was characterized by a large increase in building construction on campus. Holmes Hall was erected during this time and housed the Experiment Station. Fellows oversaw the construction of Lord Hall, Winslow Hall, and the Hannibal Hamlin Dormitory. In 1905, Fellows received a $50,000 grant from Andrew Carnegie to build a library. In 1903, due to a small pox epidemic in Bangor and Old Town, he had an infirmary established. Much of Fraternity Row was also built during his tenure.

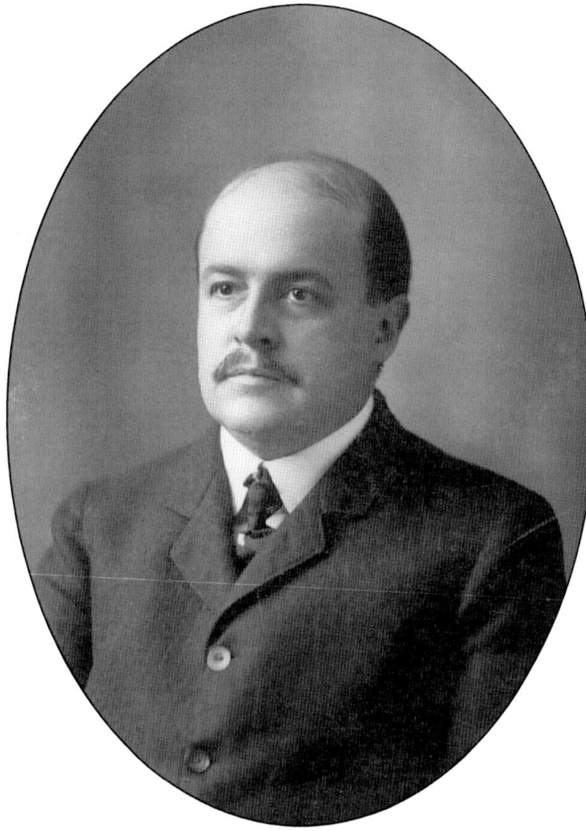

Abram Winegardner Harris, Sc.D., LL.D. (1893–1901). Harris succeeded President Fernald after his second term in 1893. Harris was educated in German universities and brought to the university a synthesis of European and American ideals in education and culture. He was the first president to propose a statewide mill tax that would increase with the population and wealth of the state. He believed that the tax would provide enough certain funding to perpetuate the university. A state mill tax was not adopted until 1929, during the Boardman administration.

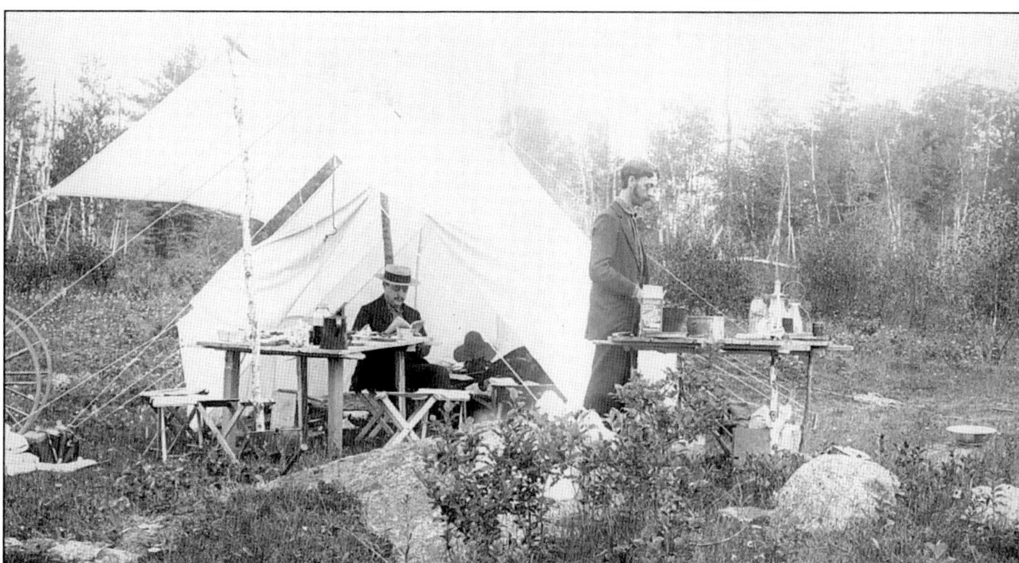

Hands-on Presidency: Harris Participates in a Field Day Exercise in 1895. One of President Harris's legacies to the university was the establishment of the Experiment Station in Holmes Hall. The station gained and shared agricultural information with other land grant colleges around the country.

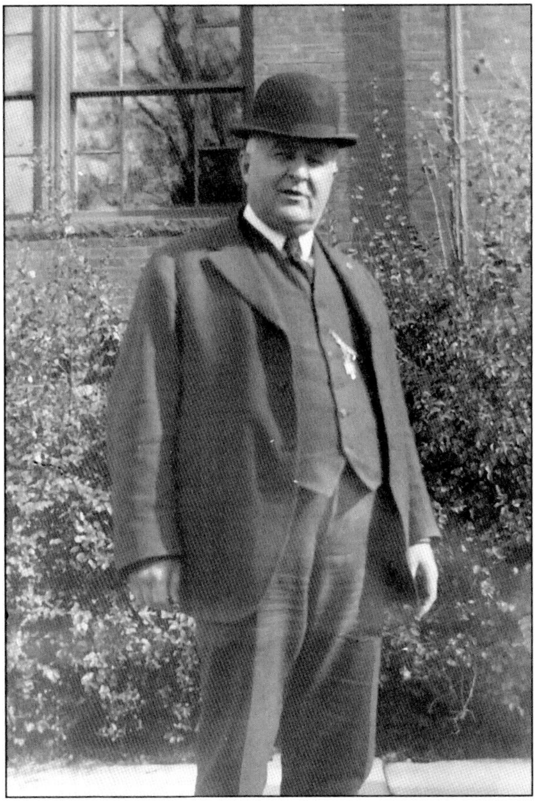

President Aley Poses outside Alumni Hall, c. 1915. Among the milestones achieved during the Aley administration was an enrollment of 1,000 students, a dream of President Fernald. Aley's term marked the transition from what Feranald called the pioneering period to the development period, creating an assurance that the university was no longer an experiment but was here to stay. Aley oversaw the building of Aubert Hall (touted as being one of the finest and best equipped laboratories in New England) and Ballentine Hall, which was to accommodate the growing population of female students.

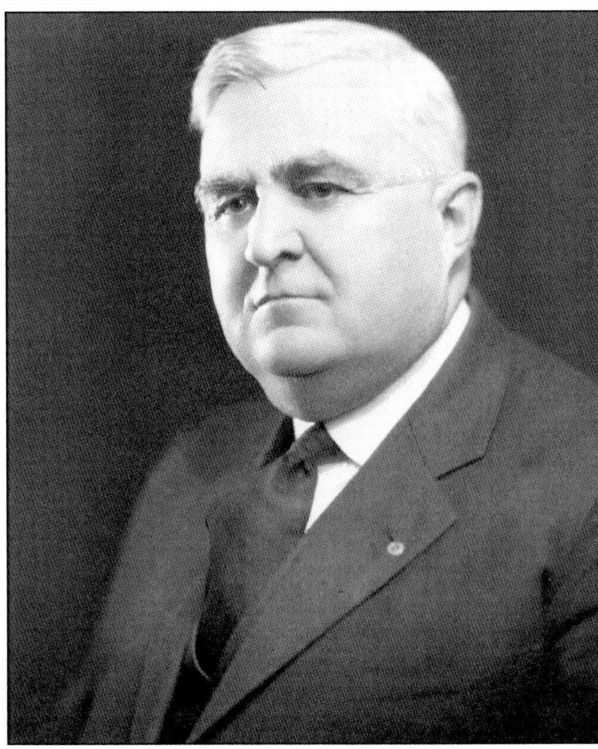

Robert Judson Aley, Ph.D., LL.D. (1910–1921). Aley is best remembered for his strong leadership at a crucial juncture in the university's history as the country entered into a world war. He served as an official with the League to Enforce the Peace, a predecessor to the League of Nations, which was founded after the war.

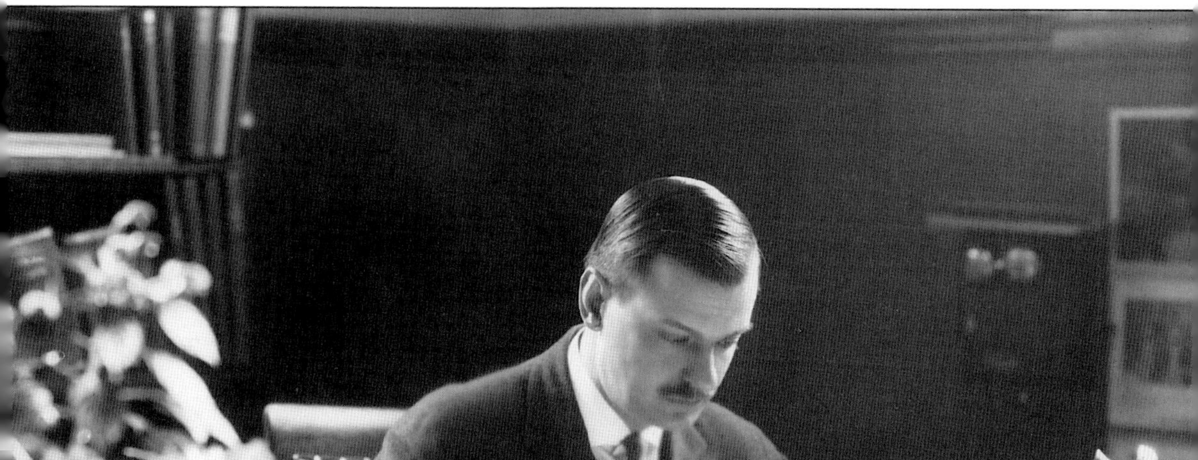

CLARENCE COOK LITTLE, PH.D. (1922–1925). Little is seen here working at his desk *c.* 1924. A distinguished geneticist, Little had a short and sometimes frustrating tenure at the university before resigning to go to Michigan State University in 1926. His negotiations with Gov. Baxter and the Maine Legislature over a mill tax to support the college failed but were revived and finally ratified in 1929. Little believed that a college education must challenge the body as well as the mind. He opened the campaign for the building of the Memorial Gymnasium and Armory and was an advocate for women's athletics. Intercollegiate sports at U. Maine enjoyed a renaissance during his administration.

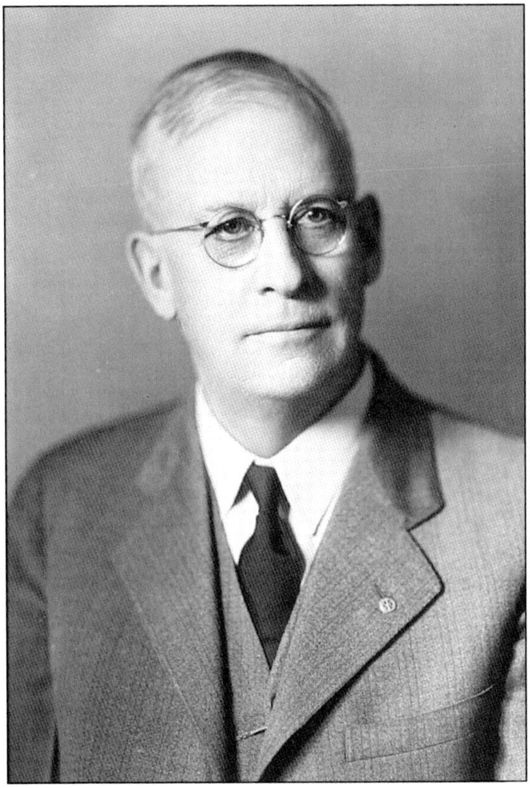

HAROLD SHERBURNE BOARDMAN (1926–1934). President Boardman worked his way from being a U. Maine student (class of 1895), to professor, to college dean, before serving as the school's seventh president. Boardman worked congenially with the Maine Legislature and Gov. Tudor Gardiner to ratify a mill tax in 1929 that helped place the school on secure financial footing. The establishment of the mill tax also helped free university presidents from the scourge of politics in Augusta.

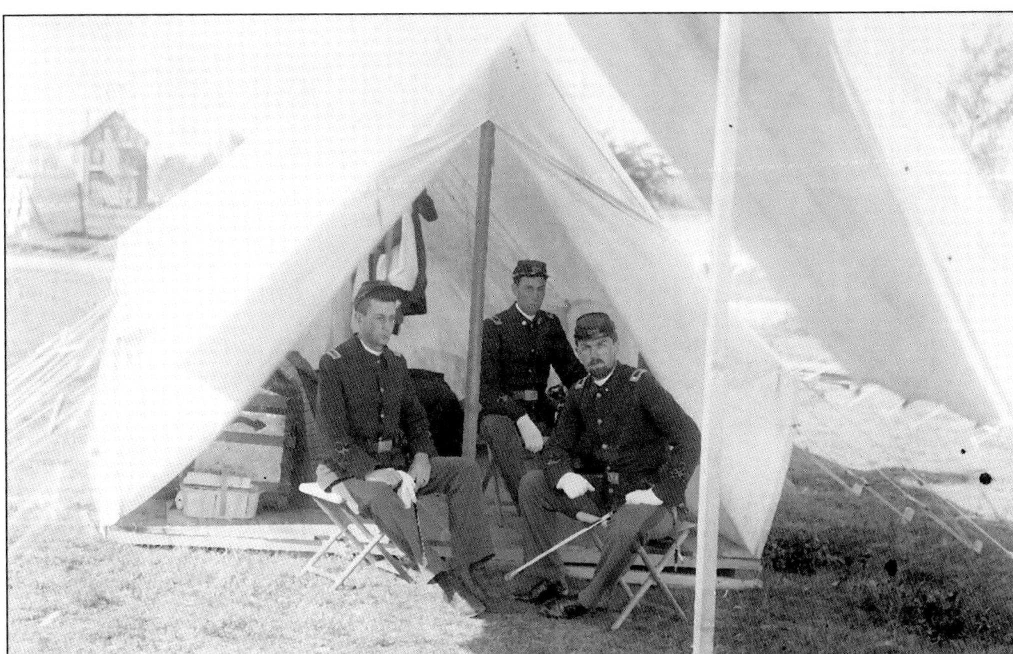

PRESIDENT BOARDMAN (FRONT LEFT) SEEN AS A MEMBER OF THE COBURN CADETS AT A CAMP-OUT EXERCISE IN OCTOBER OF 1894. He is flanked by Earl Merrill (center), and W.W. Chase.

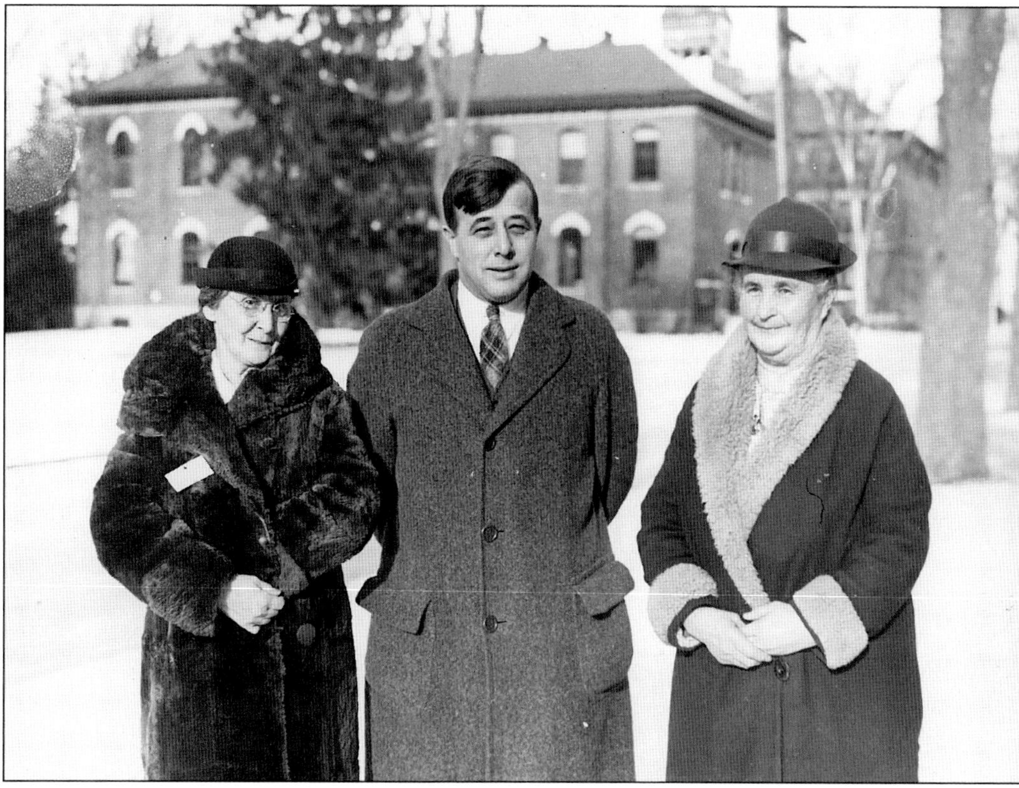

Arthur Andrew Hauck (1934–1958). The longevity of the Hauck administration saw it through Depression years, World War II, the Korean Conflict, and numerous changes on campus. Hauck came to the university via Columbia University with a field of specialty in international relations. His administration was characterized by respectful relationships between students, faculty, and administration. He brought the National Youth Administration to the college to help students secure fellowships, scholarships, and loans. NYA funds were used in 1937 to help build the University Cabins, which provided affordable housing for needy students.

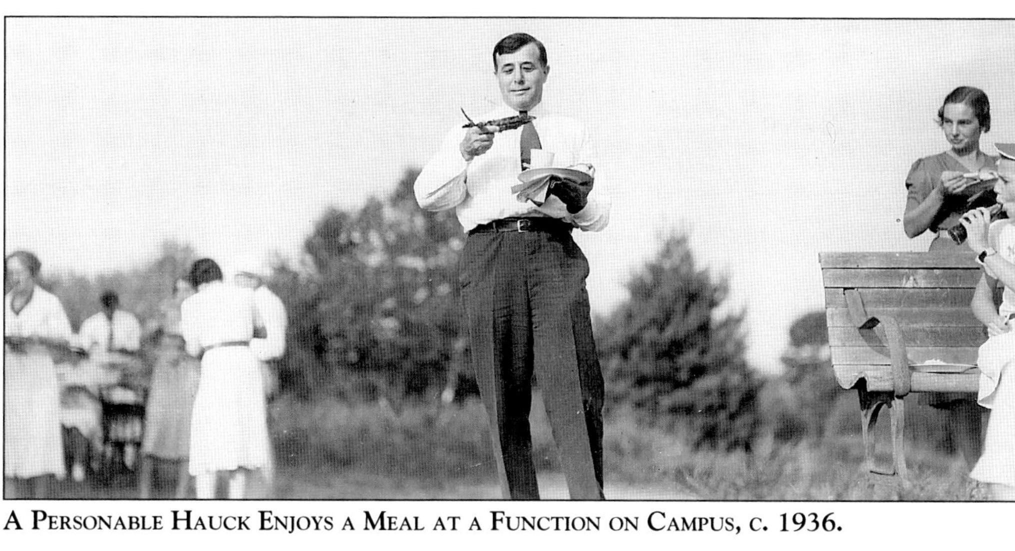

A Personable Hauck Enjoys a Meal at a Function on Campus, c. 1936.

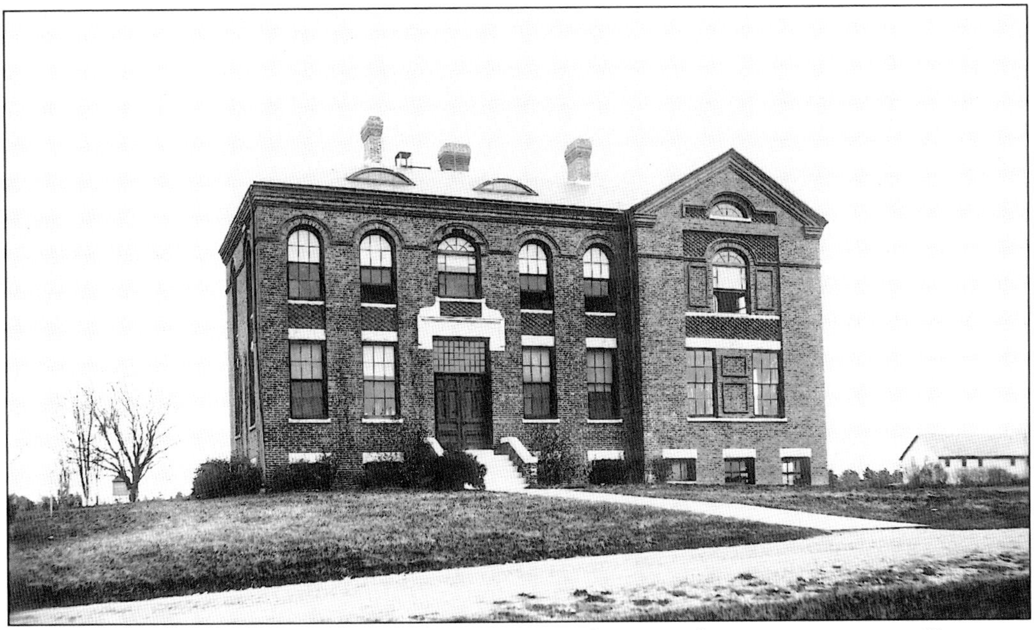

A FRONT VIEW OF THE HOLMES HALL EXPERIMENT STATION SHORTLY AFTER THE BUILDING WAS COMPLETED IN 1888. In 1885, an agricultural experiment station was first established at the university and held in the college barn. In some ways it functioned independently of the college and was used to test fertilizers, seeds, and foods. Agricultural experiment stations were in theory and effect forerunners of the Food and Drug Administration.

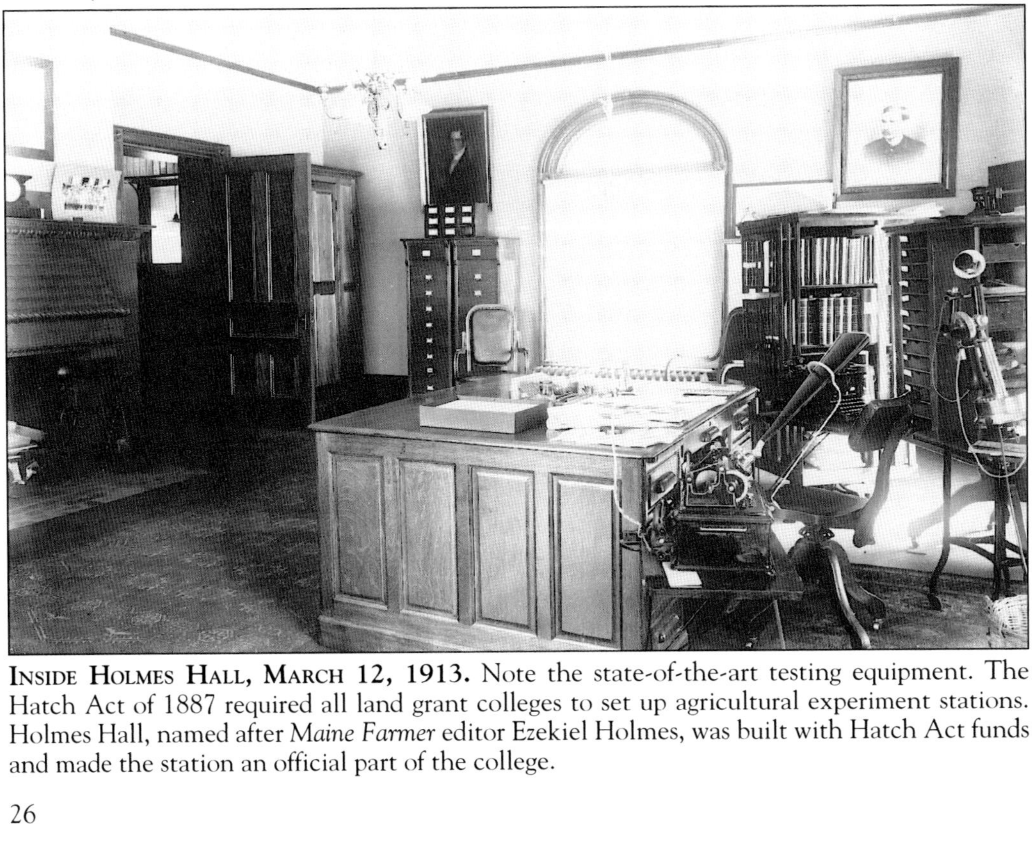

INSIDE HOLMES HALL, MARCH 12, 1913. Note the state-of-the-art testing equipment. The Hatch Act of 1887 required all land grant colleges to set up agricultural experiment stations. Holmes Hall, named after *Maine Farmer* editor Ezekiel Holmes, was built with Hatch Act funds and made the station an official part of the college.

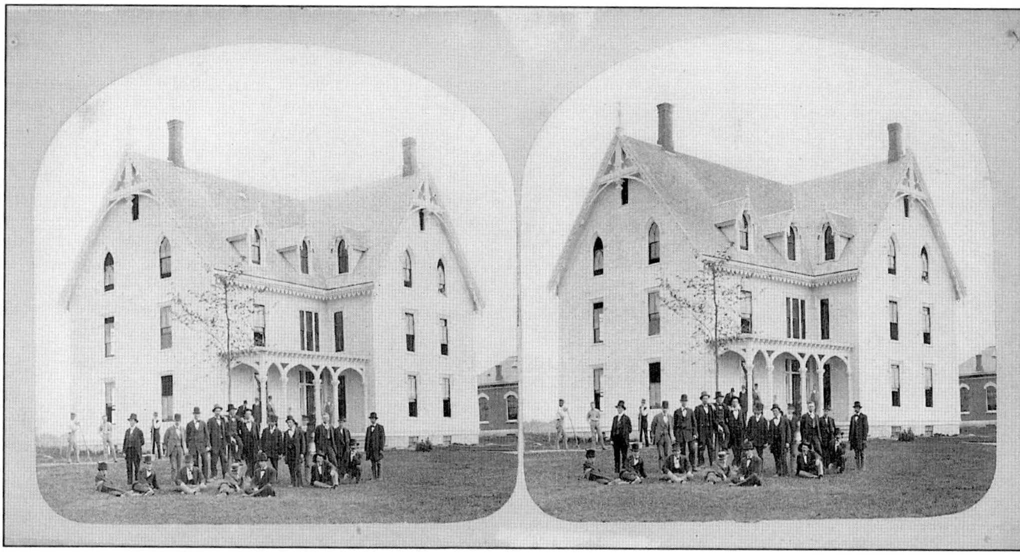

Students outside of White Hall, with Fernald Hall in the Background. Completed in 1868, White Hall was the first building on campus erected for college purposes. It provided dormitory space, reading rooms, and classroom space. Early presidents Fernald and Allen had their offices on the second floor of the building.

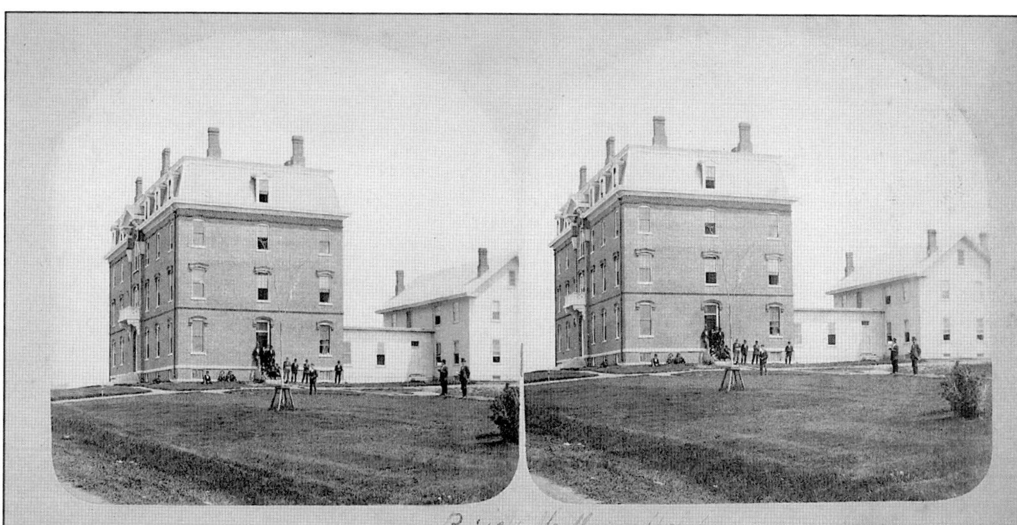

A View of Oak Hall and Commons, c. 1885. The building was originally known as Brick Hall and was constructed in 1871 from bricks manufactured by students. Other residential opportunities for male students included fraternity houses, the University Inn in Orono, and area boardinghouses. The earliest complaints about dorm life concerned food service, which nearly created a riot in 1885. Students circulated a petition about the quality of food, boycotted meals, and walked to Orono to dine in protest.

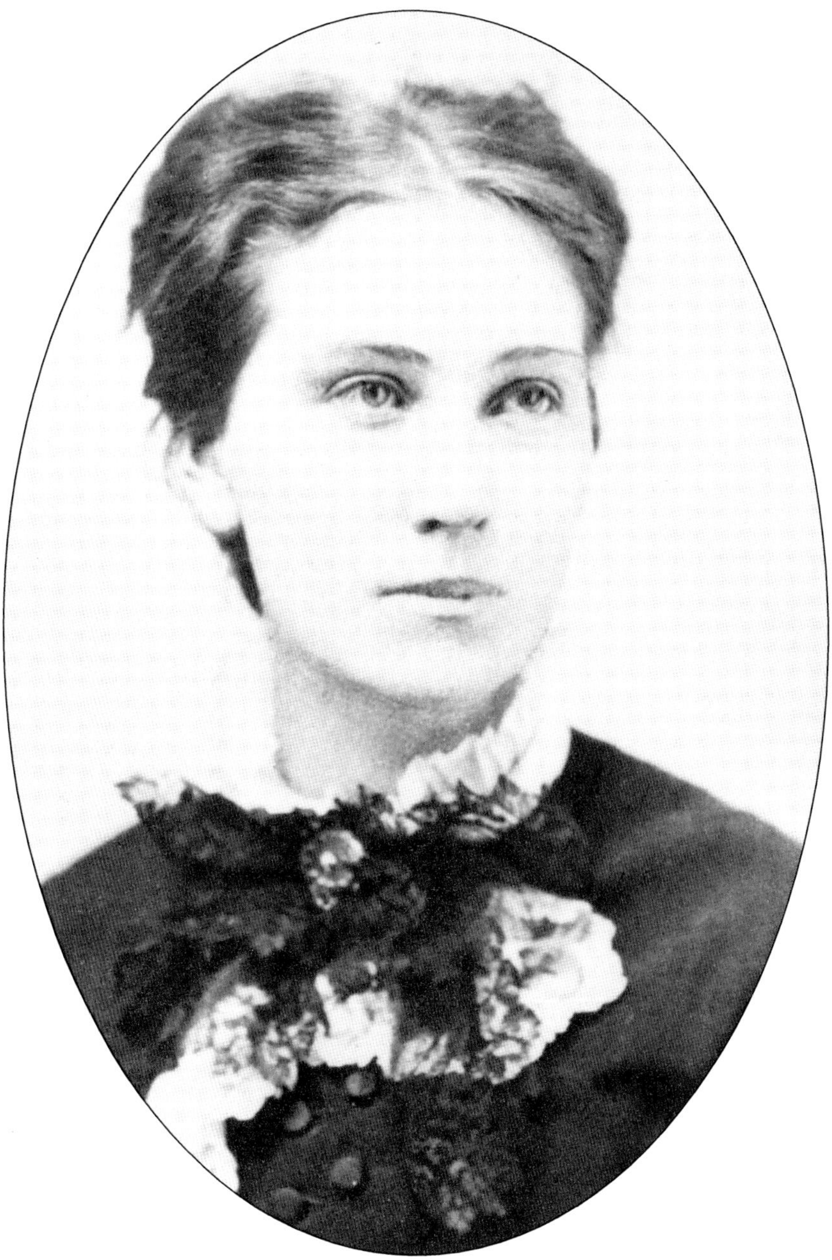

LOUISE HAMMOND RAMSDELL, THE FIRST WOMAN STUDENT AT MAINE STATE COLLEGE, AS SHE LOOKED IN 1874. In February of 1872, a law was passed by the Maine Legislature allowing the admission of women students to the college. Louise Ramsdell of Atkinson, Maine, was admitted to the college and given junior standing. She lived on campus with President Fernald and his family and graduated at the commencement of 1874. President Fernald's reply to the ongoing debate to make the university more accessible to women was this: "Equally with men they have shared these privileges and under the law equally with men they will continue to share whatever educational facilities and advantages the University of Maine can offer." The 1912 *Prism* satirically defined a co-ed as "The first step in the development of a suffragette."

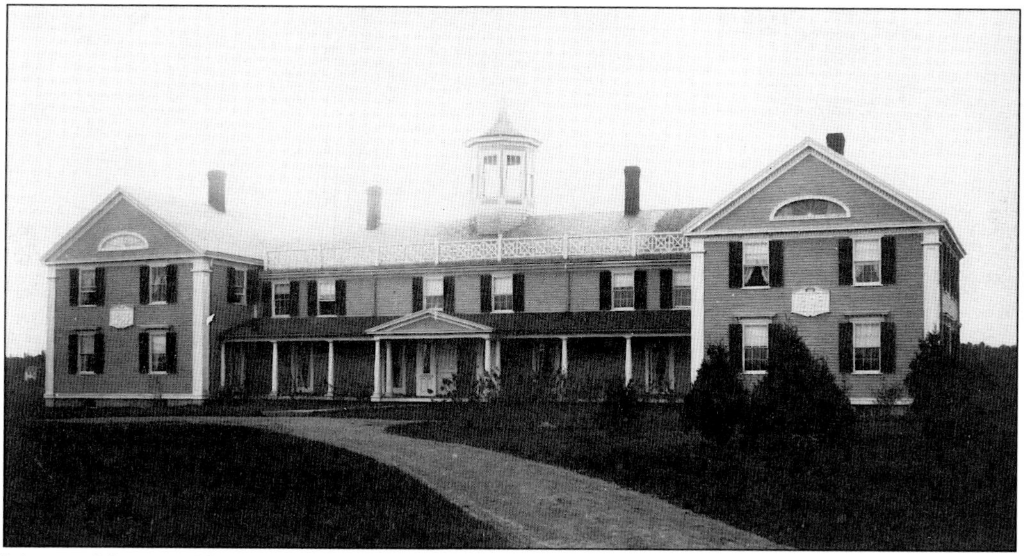

Mount Vernon House after Renovations in 1898. Formerly the White Farm House, the building was renovated to provide dormitory space for women students. For the first 20 years, young women could attend the college only if they could board with families living on campus or in homes within walking distance of the college. In 1914, Ballentine Hall was built to further accommodate female students.

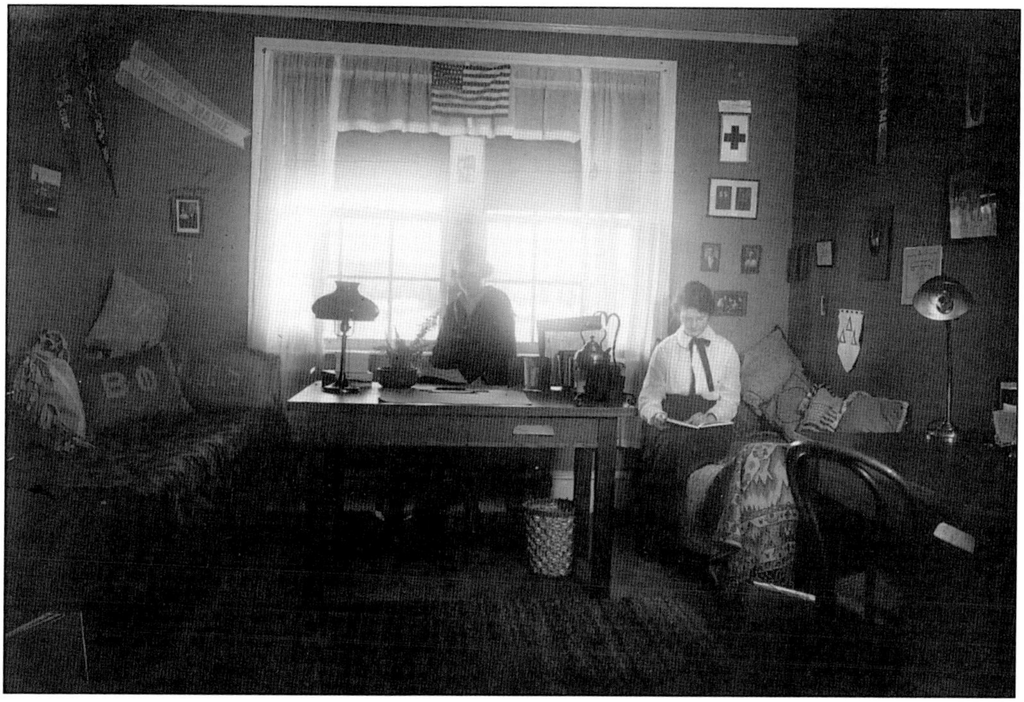

Inside a Dorm Room at Mount Vernon, c. 1900. The view provides an interesting look at dorm life and student tastes. Upon its remodeling in 1898, the Mount Vernon House contained a parlor for socializing with male students, a dining room, a kitchen, and 16 study or dorm rooms accommodating two students each. A single bathroom was used to accommodate upwards of 35 female residents.

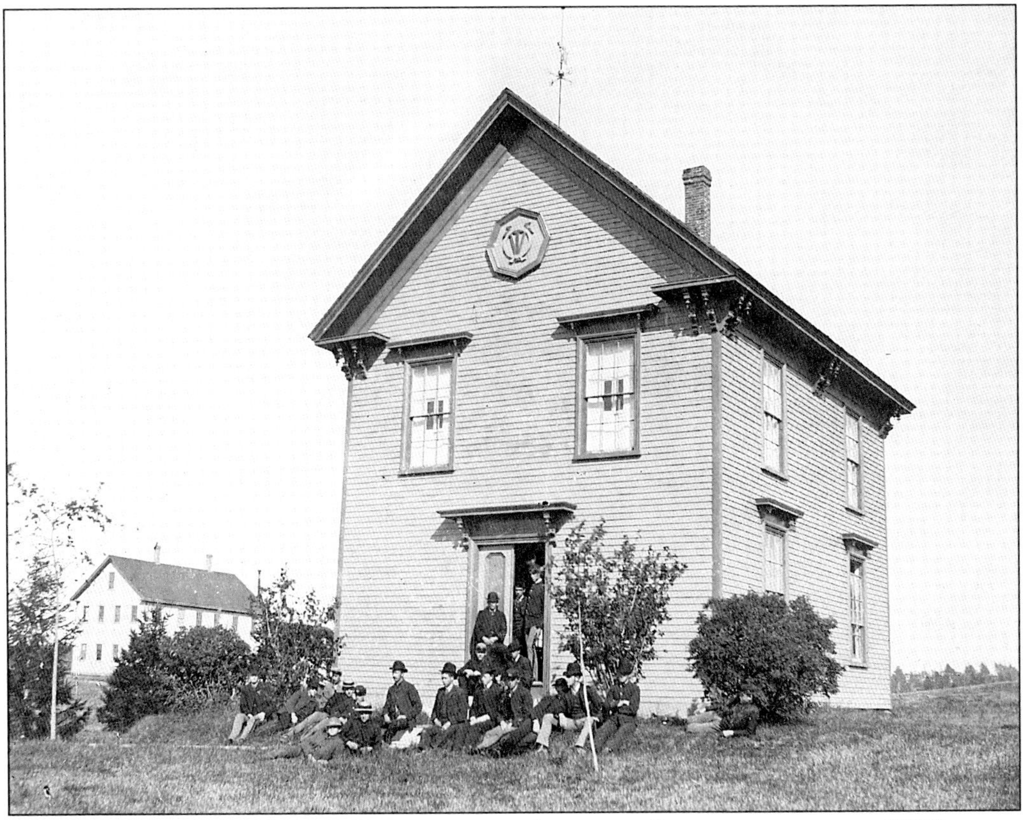

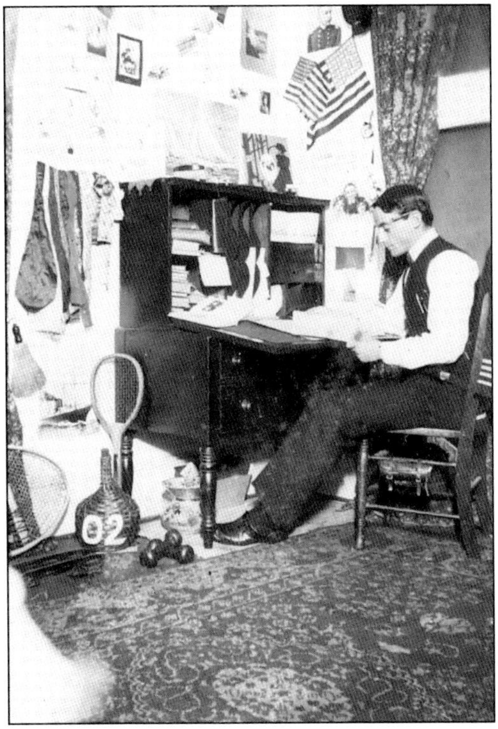

STUDENTS GATHER OUTSIDE THE QTV FRATERNITY HOUSE, C. 1890. National Greek Letter Fraternities were at first reluctant to grant chapters to the upstart land grant colleges. The QTV fraternity, founded at Massachusetts Agricultural College in 1869, opened its second chapter at Maine State College in 1873. The QTV house was first located on the site of Coburn Hall and was later relocated to College Avenue, thus beginning Fraternity Row.

INSIDE ALPHEUS CROSBY'S ROOM AT PHI GAMMA DELTA IN 1902. The legislature passed an act in 1903 guaranteeing loans for the building of fraternity houses that allowed several fraternities to build houses on College Avenue and other parts of campus. In 1916, President Fernald said, "The university authorities have never found the fraternities to be a problem at Maine that they had been at some institutes. They have proved helpful in promoting the welfare of their members morally, and intellectually."

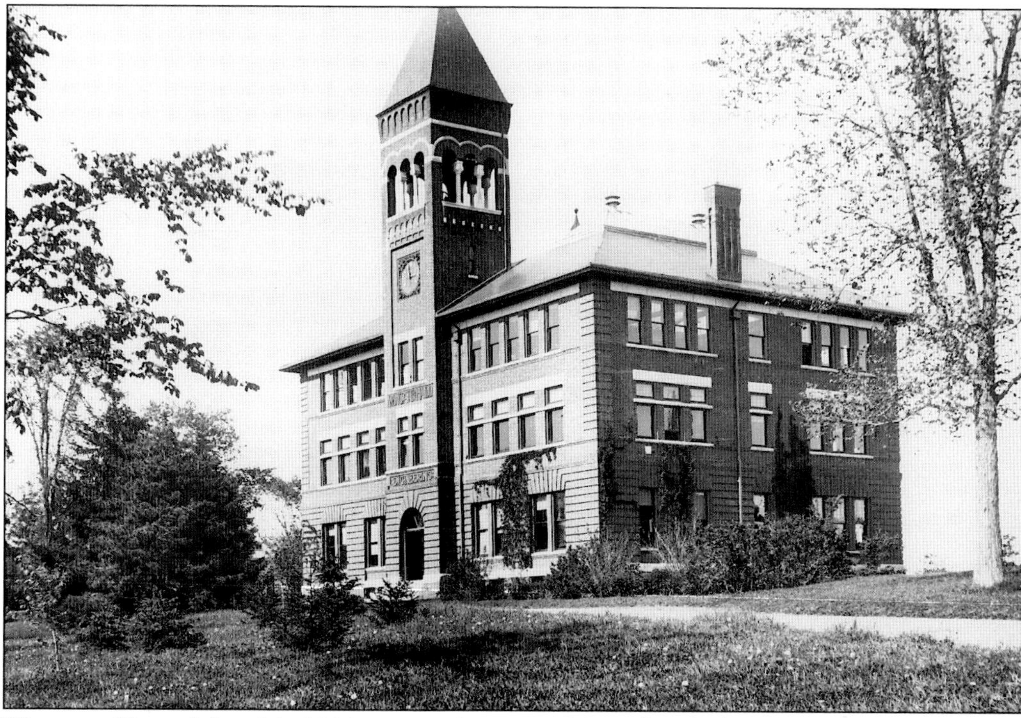

Wingate Hall, May 14, 1902, about 3:00 p.m. Note the clock and tower that stood until destroyed by fire in 1946. A summer school officially opened at the university in 1902. The summer session of 1902 consisted of 13 students. Tuition was $5 for Maine residents and $10 for out-of-state students.

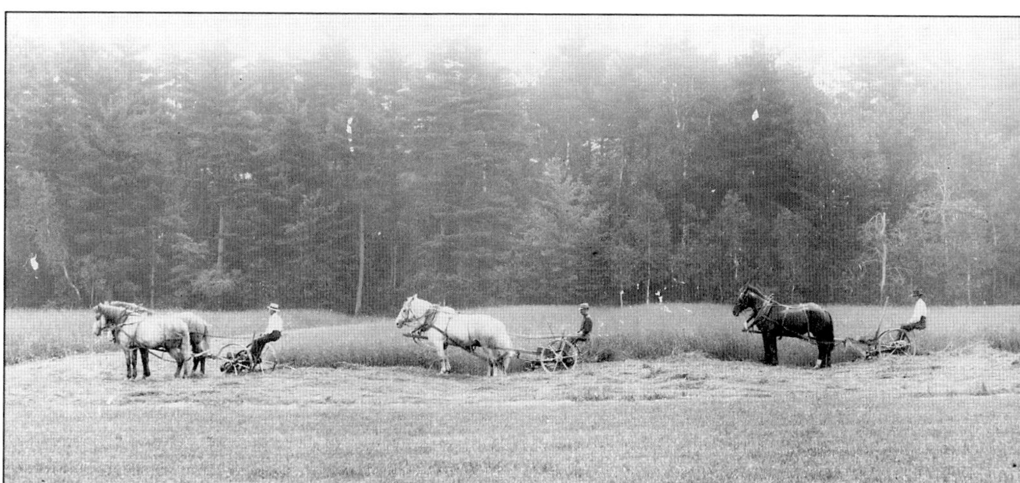

Students Mowing in University Hayfields, c. 1880. On one occasion, student labor, which continued into the summer term, proved tragic. On July 19, 1870, John Jackson lost his life attempting to cool off in the Stillwater River after a full day of haying on the college farm. Upon entering the river, Jackson was attacked by a cramp and drowned before he could be brought to shore.

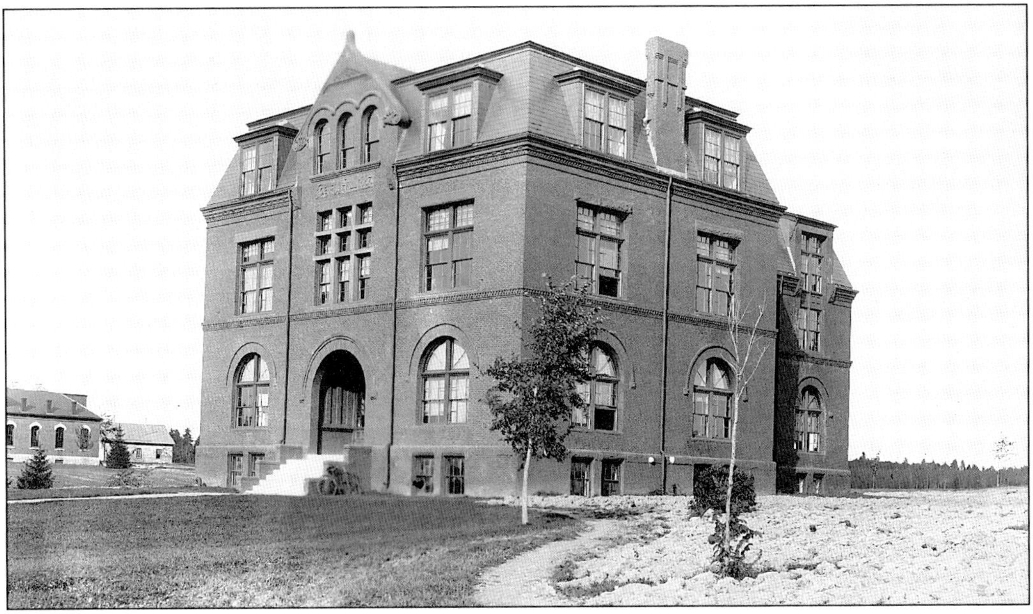

Coburn Hall, Shortly after Construction in 1888. It was built in honor of Abner Coburn, one of the original trustees of Maine State College and the former governor of Maine. Coburn used his considerable influence—and pocketbook—to help establish the college. There was a move in the early years to set the school on an independent financial basis and change the name of the school to Coburn College.

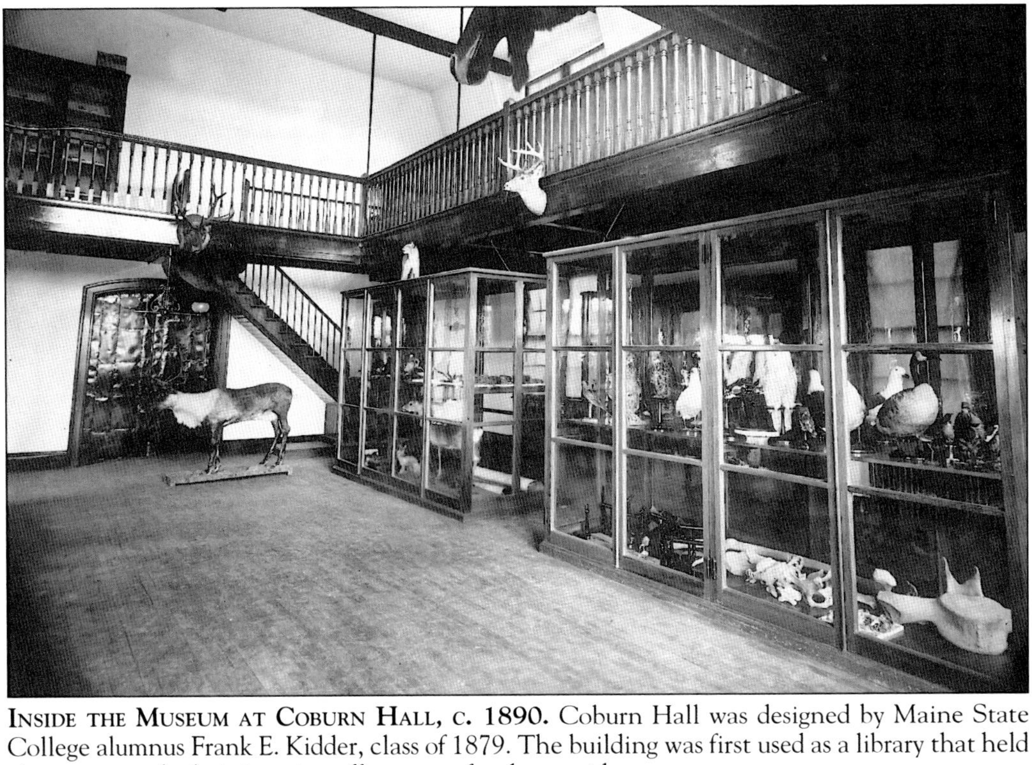

Inside the Museum at Coburn Hall, c. 1890. Coburn Hall was designed by Maine State College alumnus Frank E. Kidder, class of 1879. The building was first used as a library that held classrooms and administrative office space for the president.

Caroline Colvin, c. 1915. Colvin began her long tenure of service to the university in 1902 as a history instructor. Her career spanned 30 years and she earned the distinction of being one of the first women in the country to be named head of a major university department. She also became one of the country's first female Ph.Ds.

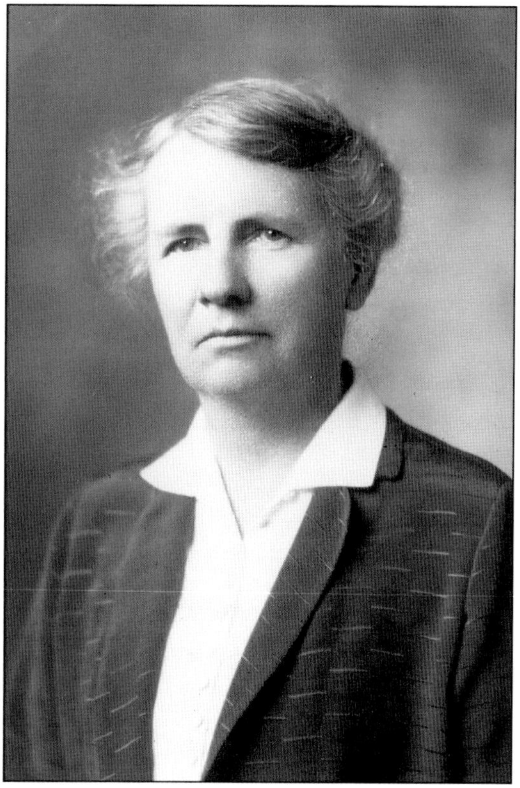

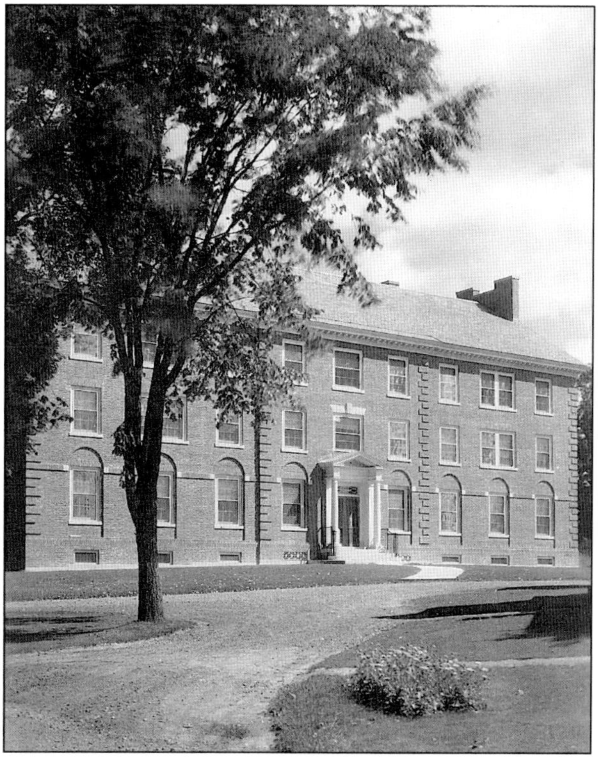

A View of Colvin Hall, c. 1935. Colvin championed many women's causes at Maine. She helped establish a service sorority called All Maine Women in 1925, and established the first chapter of the American Association of University Women in the state. Colvin Hall was built and appropriately named in her honor.

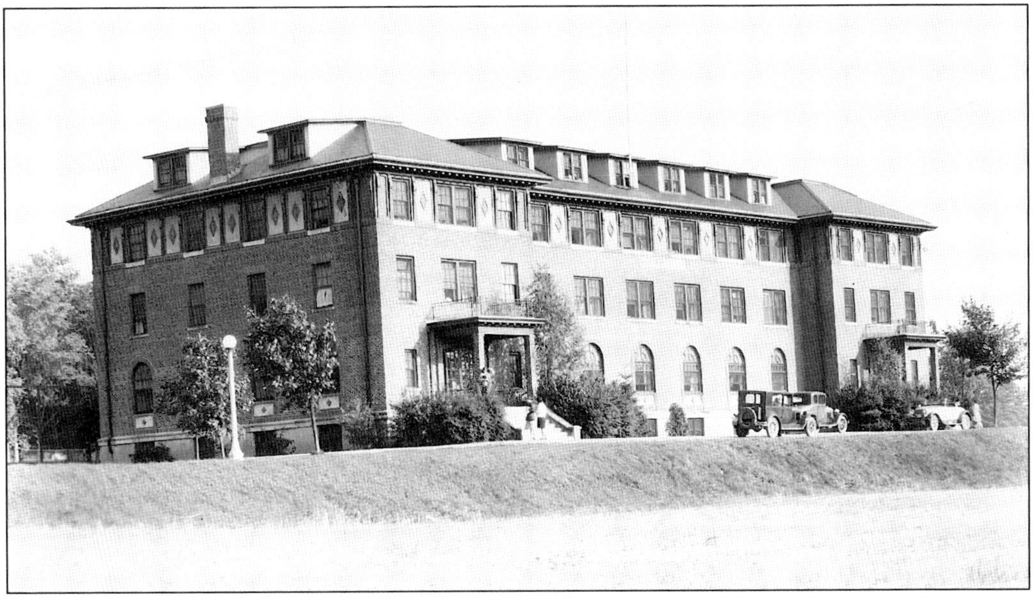

Balentine Hall in the 1920s. The dorm was built in honor of Elizabeth Abbott Balentine, who served the university in many capacities during her long tenure at the school. She first served as secretary to the president before becoming college treasurer and finally as registrar in 1912. She was eulogized by acknowledging that she could call every student by his or her first name from the mid-1880s until her death in 1913.

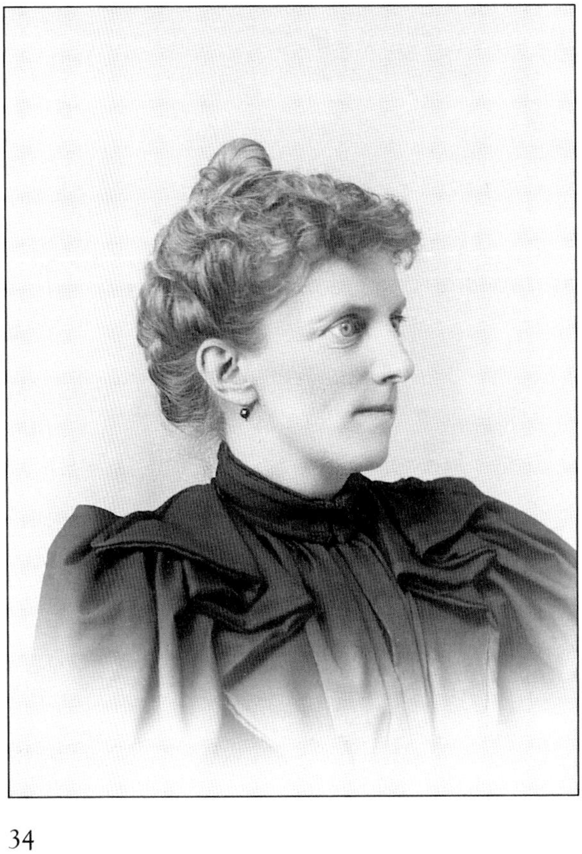

Elizabeth Abbott Balentine, c. 1890. Balentine was the niece of President Allen and the wife of Walter Balentine, one of the college's first professors.

Two

STUDENT LIFE

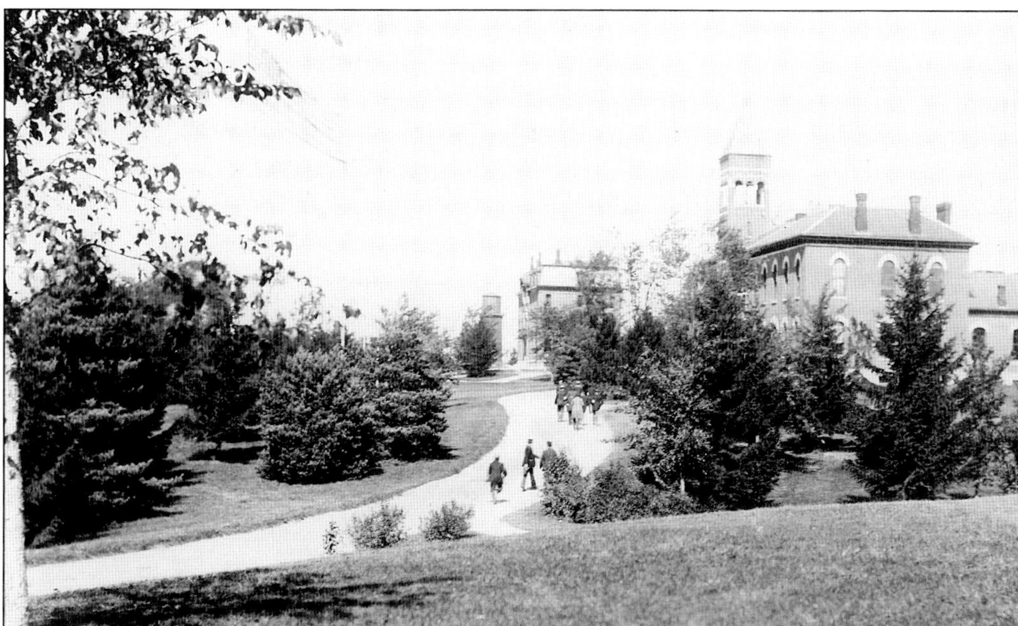

LATE FOR CLASS? A student runs to catch the pack on their way to class, c. 1905. In the background, from left to right, are the stand pipe, Oak Hall, Wingate Hall, and Fernald Hall. Although tuition was not charged to students entering the college, an admissions test was administered to screen prospective students. It required proficiency in math, geography, English grammar, history of the United States, and algebra. Students had to be at least 15 years of age, and "A satisfactory testimonial of good moral character and industrious habits" was to be "rigidly exacted." Academic offerings for students entering the first class at Maine State College in 1868, which was divided into three terms, included rhetoric, book keeping, history, physical geography, and horticulture. In 1876, a two-semester system was established that remains to the present. Classes ran about one hour and ended before noon to allow for a full afternoon of student labor.

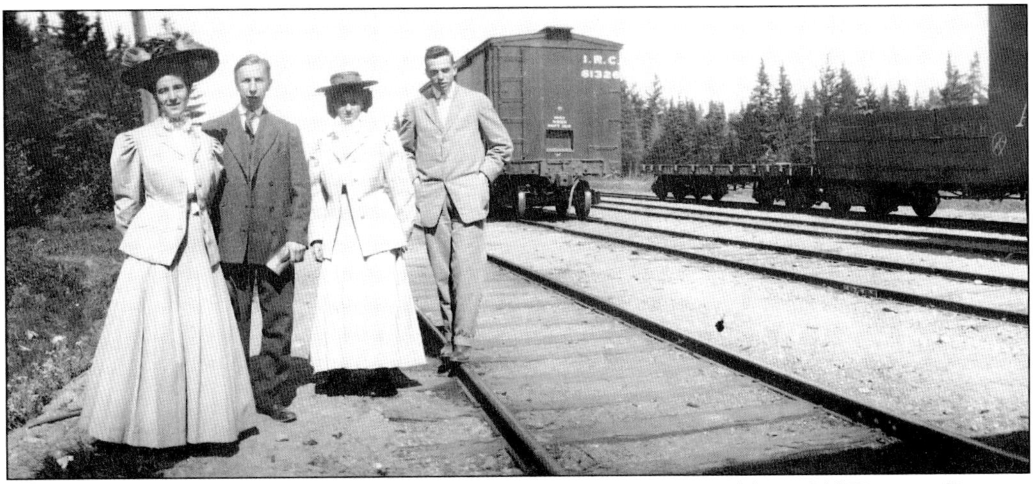

Students outside a Railway Depot in 1908. This depot was possibly in Old Town or Bangor, where students waited to be shuttled via carriage or trolley to campus. The photograph is dated Monday, September 14, 1908, and bears the comment "back to civilization."

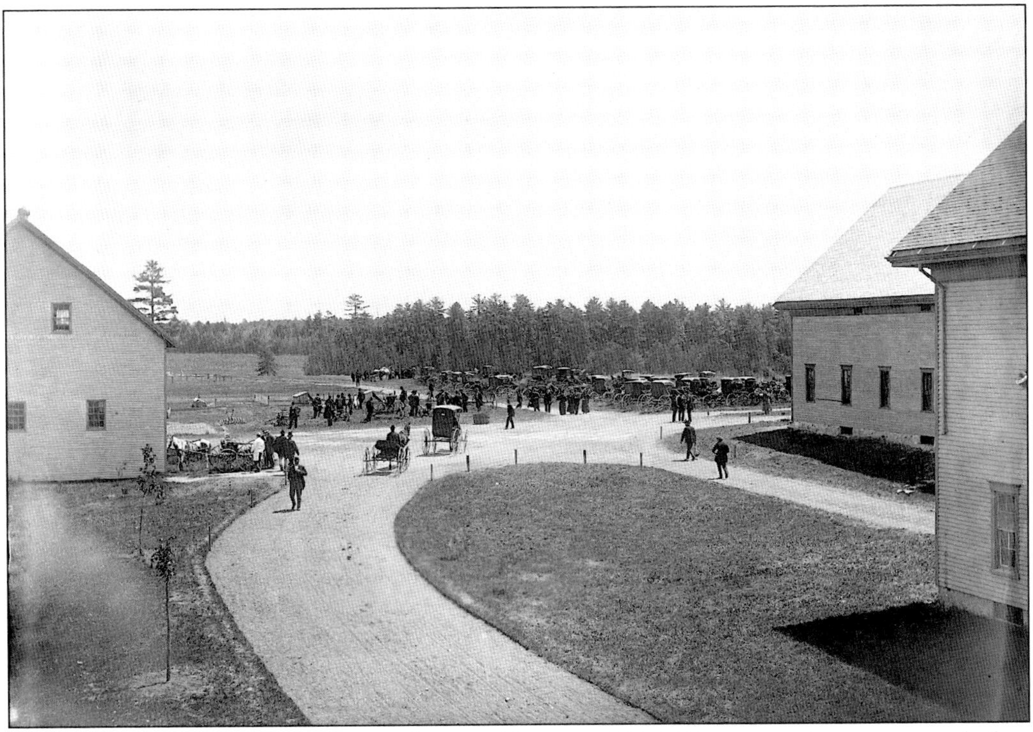

A Buggy Parking Lot outside the College Farm, c. 1890. Transportation to campus before the 1890s was primarily limited to railway. Around campus, horse-drawn carriages, bicycles, and an occasional rider on horseback could be seen. Footpaths and boardwalks lined the campus for travel from building to building. The automobile did not make an impact on campus until the 1920s and was mostly limited to faculty and administration.

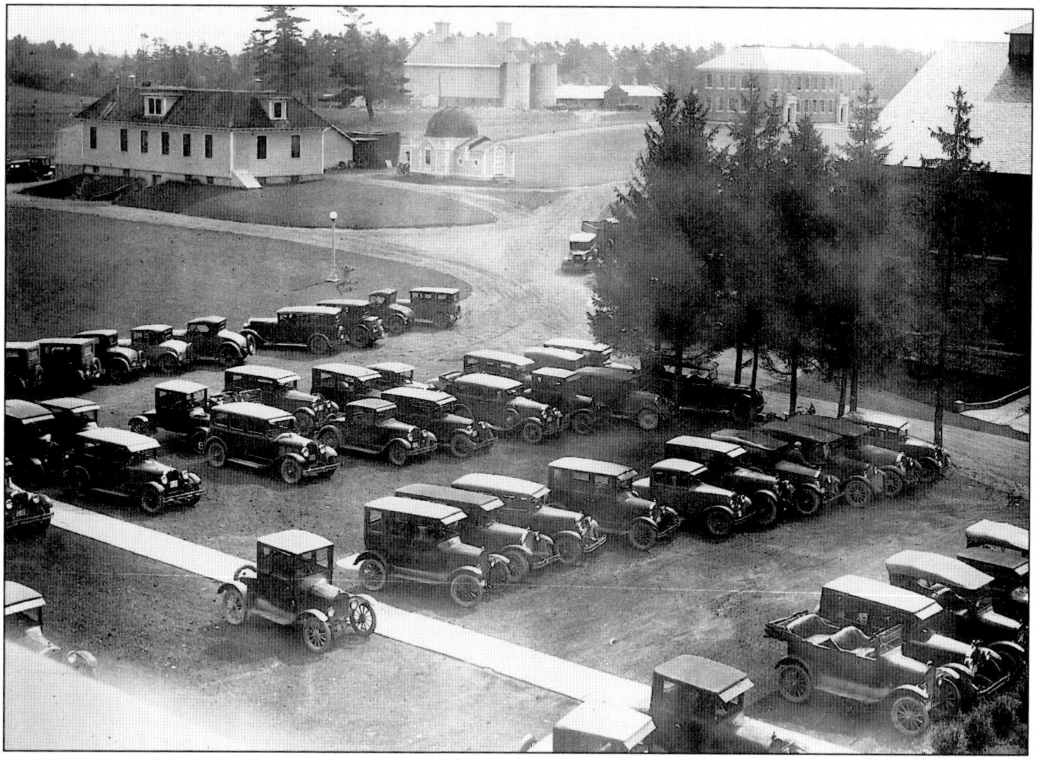

Opening of Classes, September 1928. This image is believed to be the buggy parking lot at a later date, and the cars probably belonged to professors and administrators. Parking appears to have been a problem from the earliest times.

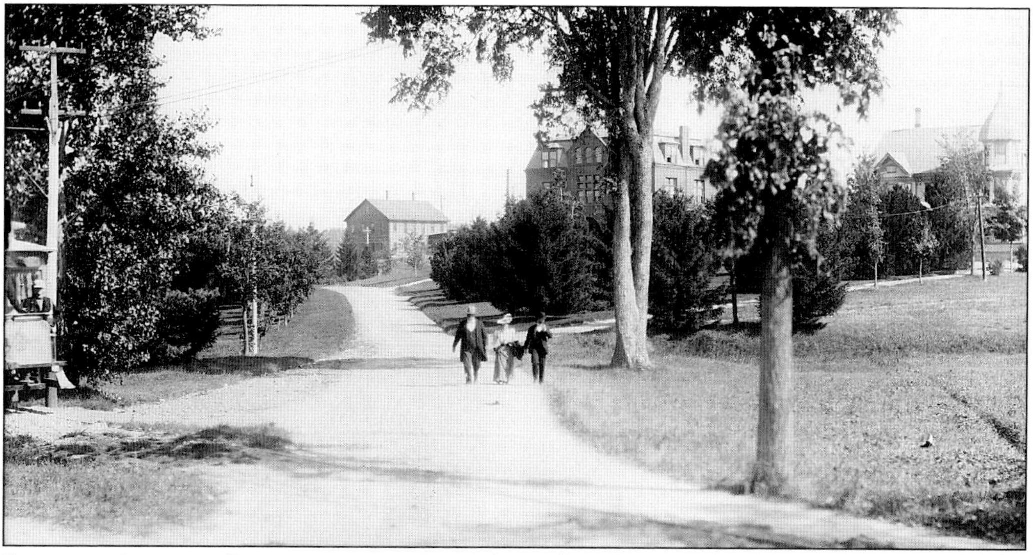

Students Leaving Campus, c. 1895. Note the trolley in the bottom left of the photograph. In 1895, an electric rail or trolley opened and was a boon to students commuting to the university as well as those seeking social and cultural pursuits in Bangor. Students could attend sporting events at the Bangor YMCA, drama at the Bangor Opera House, and silent picture shows in Old Town.

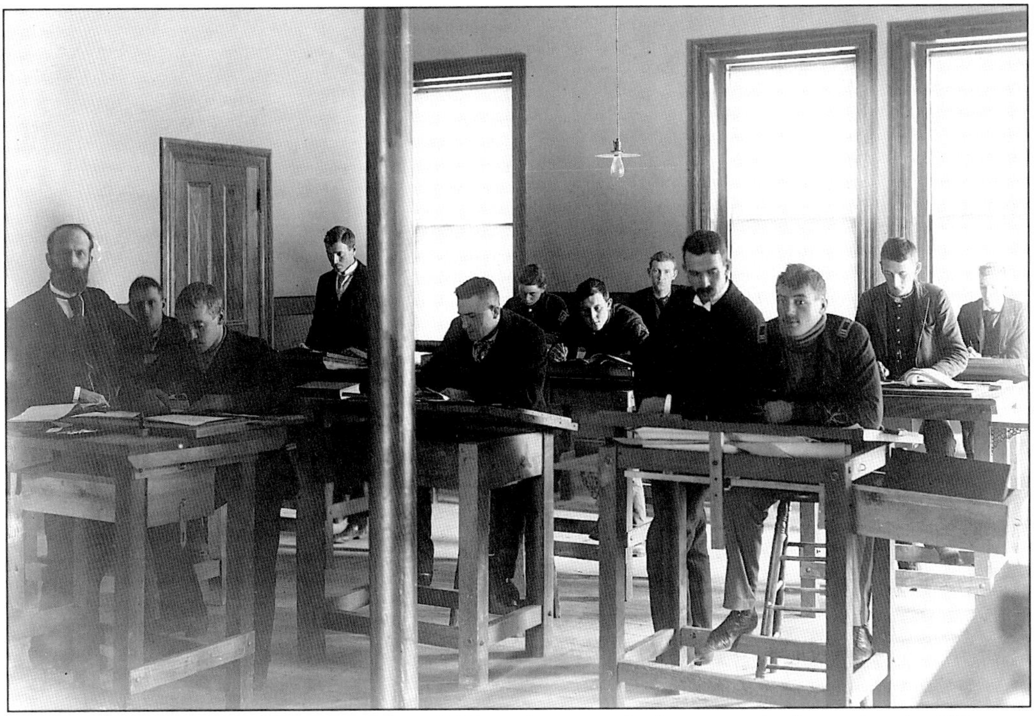

"YOU CAN'T HIDE THOSE LYING EYES." This photograph depicts a drafting class in Wingate Hall in 1890. The gentleman at the front table appears to be looking at the work of another student. An admitted, and unfortunate, aspect of college life has been cheating. A serious cheating scandal occurred on campus in 1907, and a committee was appointed to investigate. A discipline board was later established to "deal with dishonesty, morality, and other like offenses" among students.

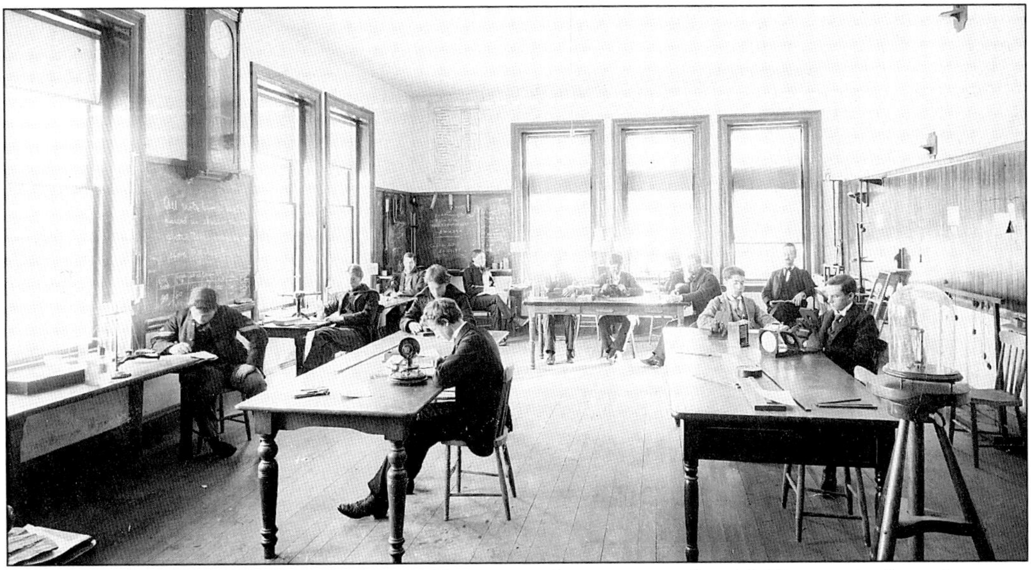

A CLASS IN WINGATE HALL, 1890. Classroom decorum in the 1890s required students to remove hats and coats, allowed no visiting between tables, and forbade loud talking or whistling. Students found in violation were fined, given demerits, or forfeited lab privileges.

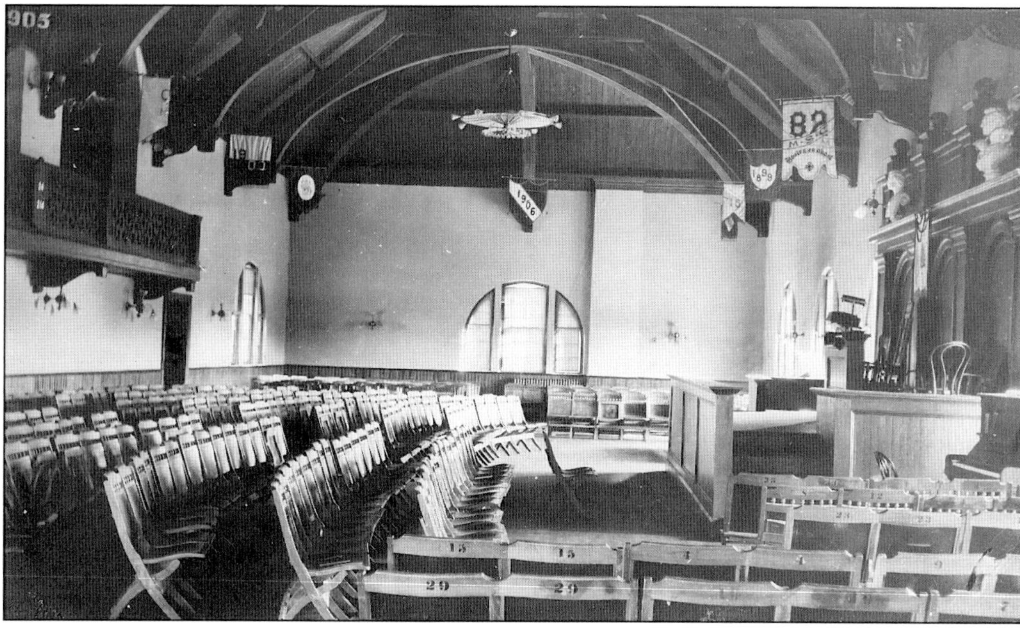

GETTING READY FOR CHAPEL SERVICE IN ALUMNI HALL, C. 1905. Attendance at chapel service for faculty and students had been compulsory since the opening of the university in 1868. Chapel was encouraged by Presidents Fernald and Allen, both devout Christians, who believed that a complete education must account for the spiritual as well as the intellectual. By the 1890s, chapel expanded to include declamations and oratory exercises. After WW I, chapel was compulsory but met only twice a week. It disappeared as a part of academic life in the 1920s but retained a presence in groups such as the Maine Christian Association and the YMCA. The photograph below depicts a chapel service in Coburn Hall, *c.* 1890. Chapel was first held in Fernald Hall and services were sometimes conducted by area ministers as well as Presidents Fernald and Allen.

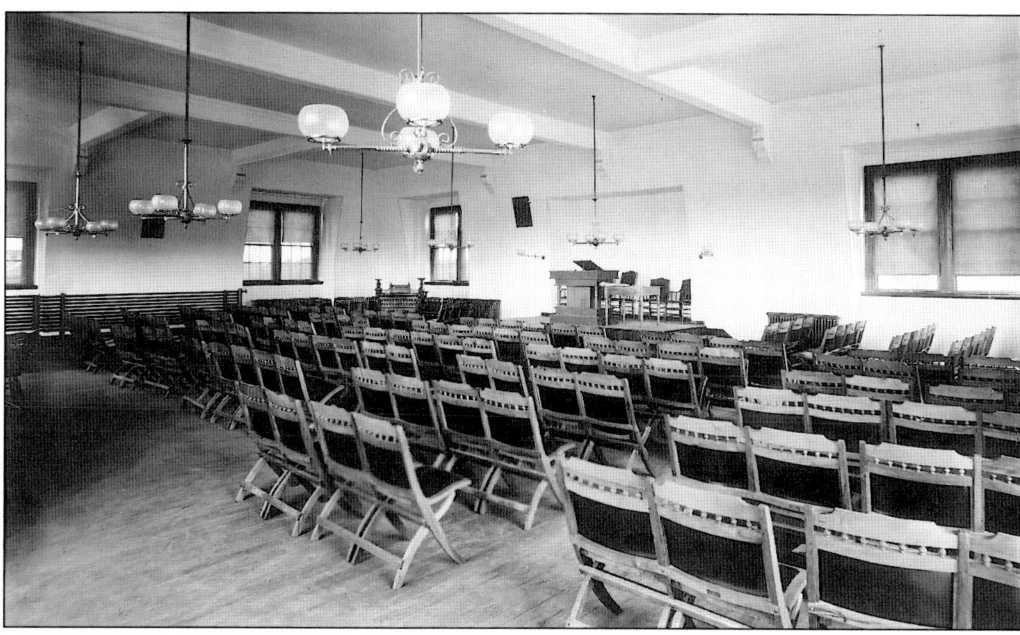

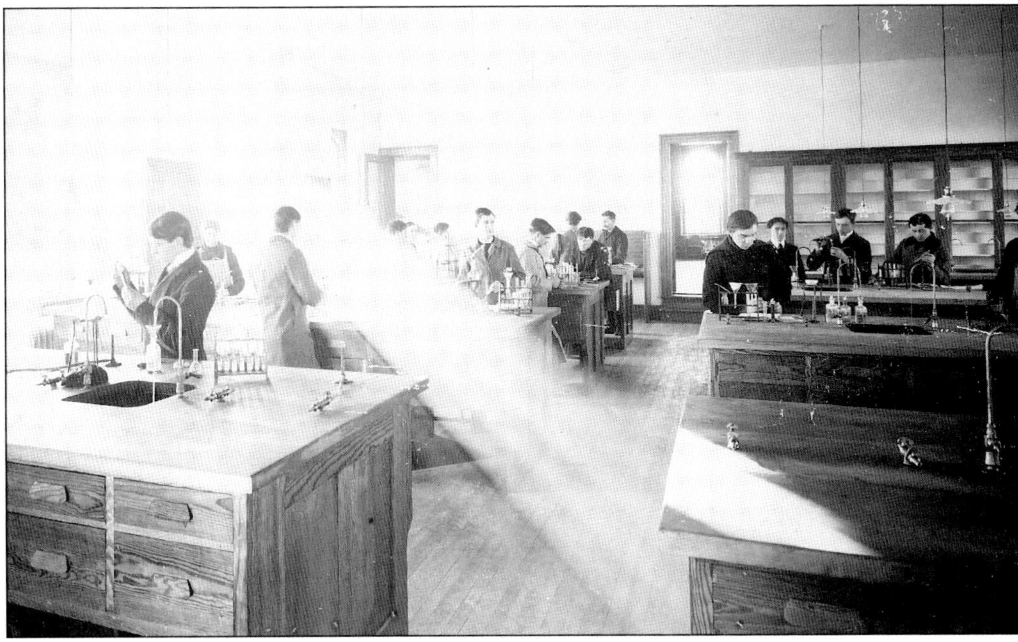

Students Participating in Physics Lab at Fernald Hall, c. 1890. Although there were no tuition charges during the university's first 13 years, students did incur some expenses. In the 1880s, board was $30, room was $5, and a fuel charge of 73¢ was levied per semester. The average price of a four-year degree program during this period was under $1,000.

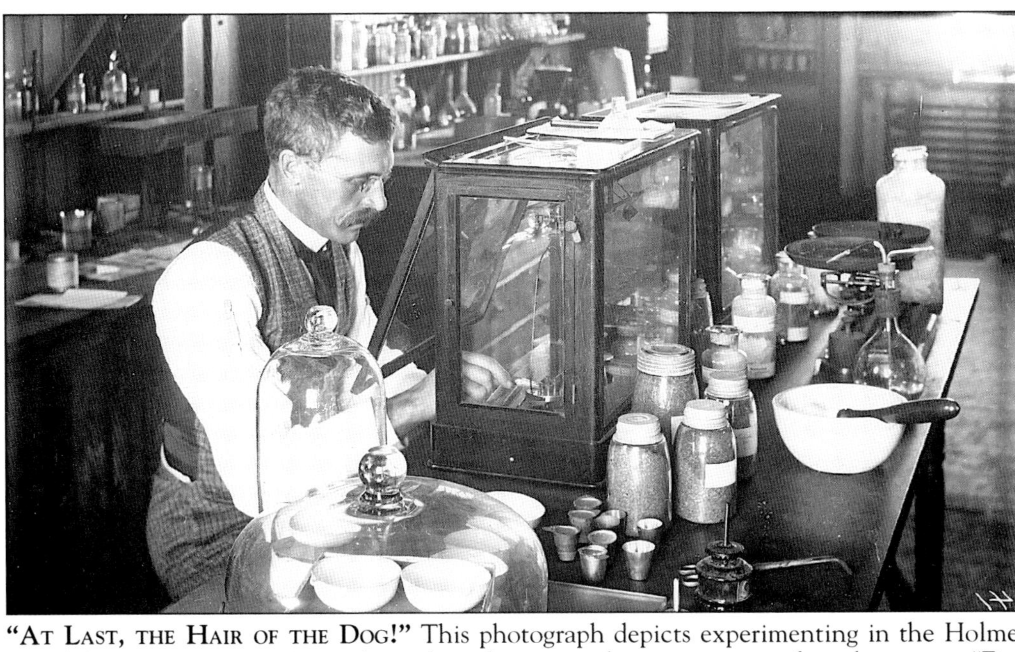

"At Last, the Hair of the Dog!" This photograph depicts experimenting in the Holmes Hall laboratory, c. 1900. An early student diary records a prescription for a hangover: "Five grams of sulphate of iron, one peppermint, eleven drachmas of water, and one drachma of spirits of nutmeg to be taken twice daily."

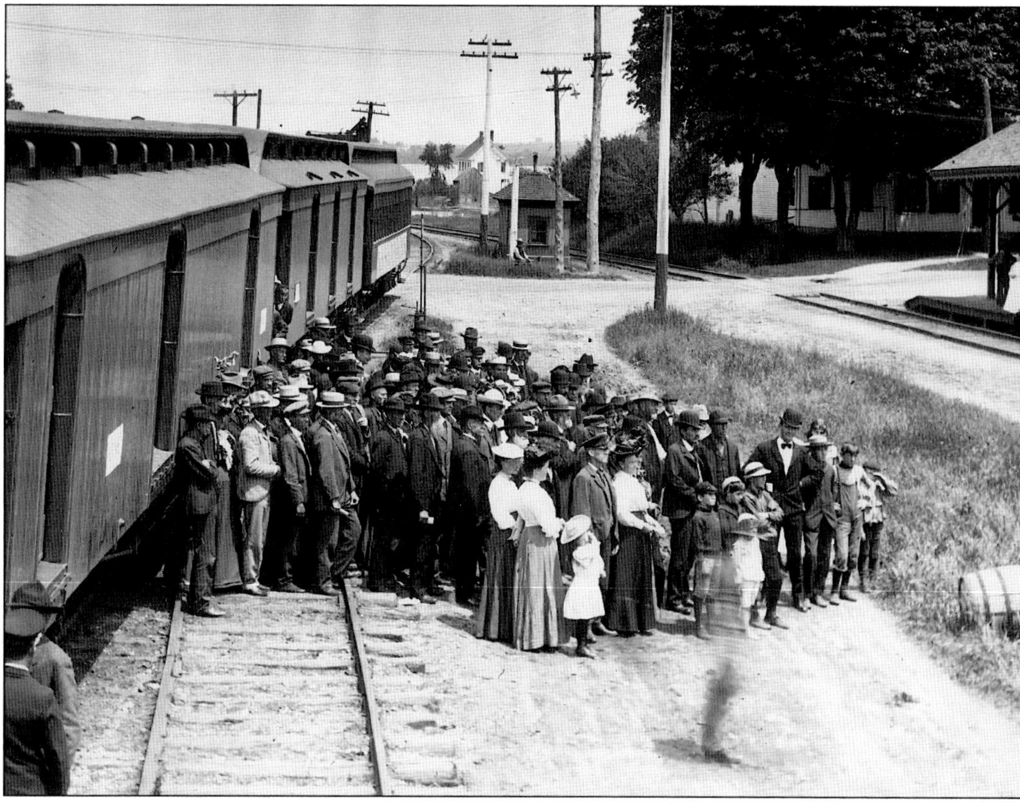

A University Gathering outside the Railway Depot. This image is most likely of the Farming Special Train and dates around 1905. The state department of agriculture united with forestry and agriculture students and faculty to travel the state on the Bangor and Aroostook Railroad. It was estimated that between 60,000 to 70,000 people annually witnessed the exhibitions, lectures, and experiments conducted on the five-week excursions. The photograph below was taken inside the Farming Special Train, *c.* 1910. Note display cases and images of university buildings on the walls.

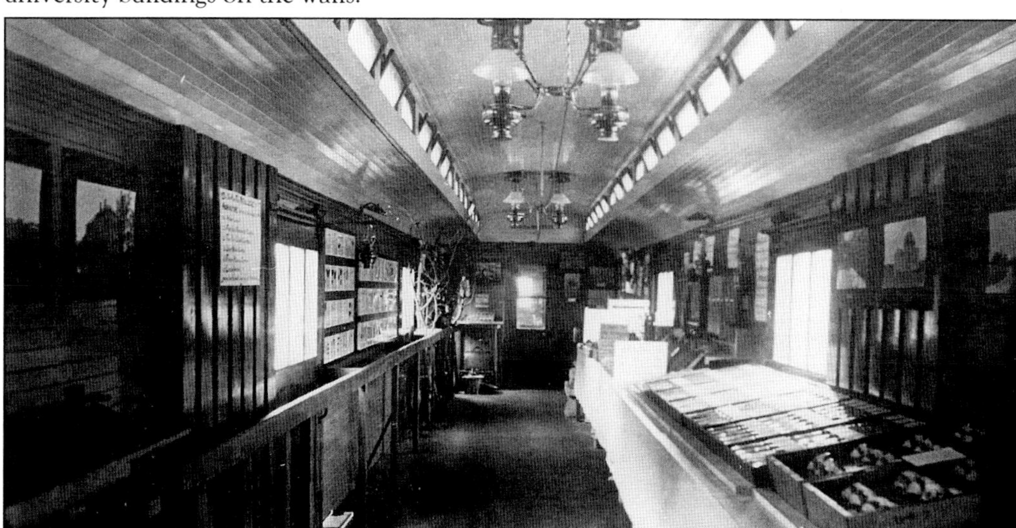

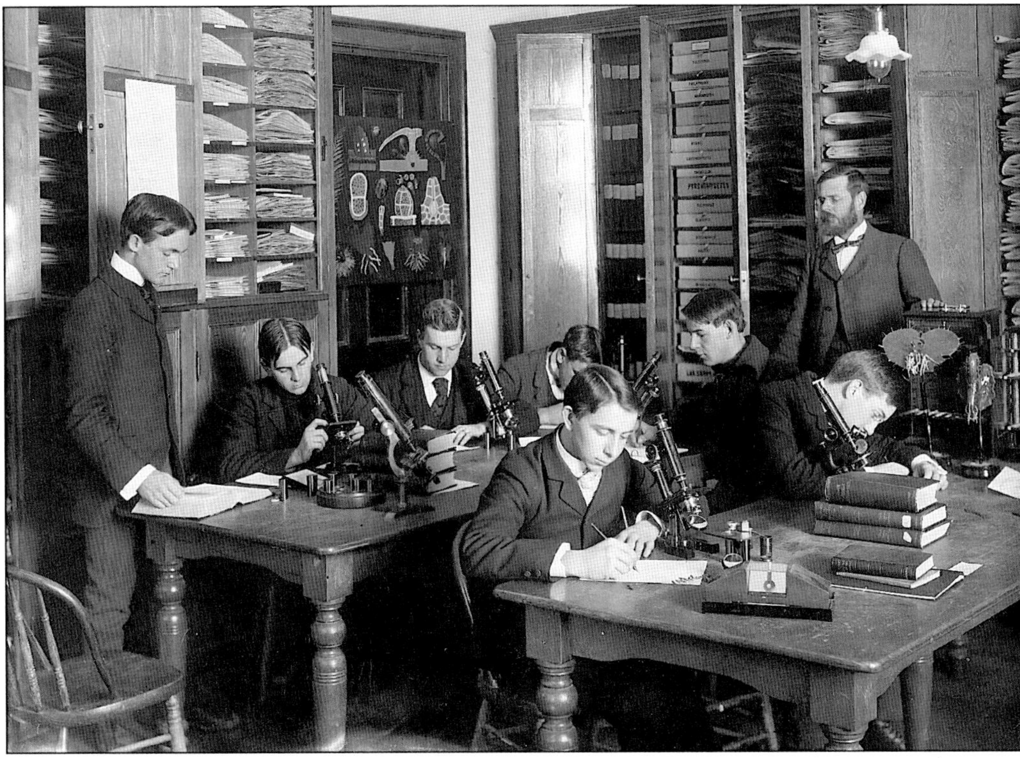

STUDENTS LOOKING THROUGH MICROSCOPES IN BOTANY LAB IN 1898. This image shows no female students, but the class of 1910 would supply one of the university's finest. Edith Patch became one the first women in the country to teach science at the university level. She also gained national notoriety for publishing her findings and writing children's books.

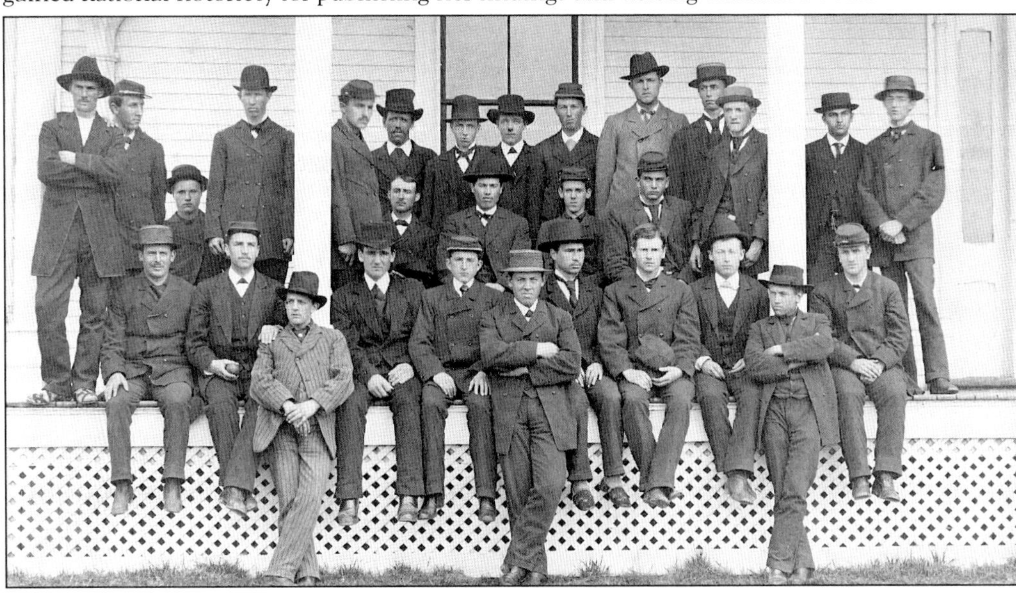

STUDENTS OUTSIDE WHITE HALL, C. 1885. Students and faculty appear together in this unidentified photograph. One suggestion is that it is of a student engineering group, as students often fraternized in groups of their academic study.

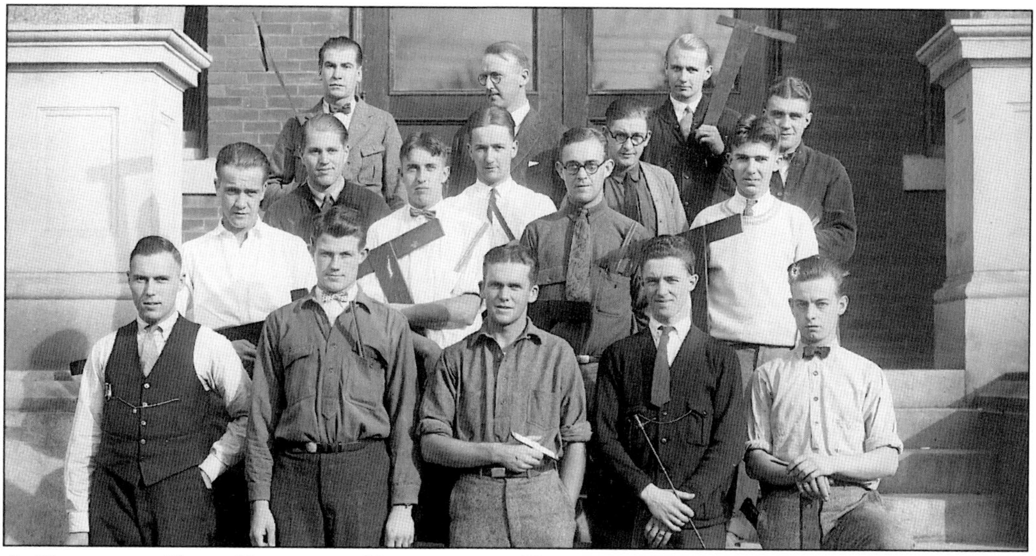

A Group of Civil Engineers Posing with Drafting Instruments in Hand, c. 1920. A study in civil engineering was the first engineering course offered at the university. It was soon followed by a course in mechanical engineering that was listed in the 1873 catalog. Early contributions from U. Maine engineers included testing materials used in making early Maine roads. Charles A. Morse, class of 1879, went on to become one of America's most distinguished engineers and was called a pioneer in railway construction. Francis Crowe, class of 1905, is said to have built more dams than any man in history and was the architect of the Boulder Dam. Percival H. Mosher, class of 1902, was engineer for Boston's Sumner Tunnel as well as the tunnels under the Mystic and Saugus Rivers. In the photo below, mechanical engineers pose with the tools of the trade, *c.* 1915.

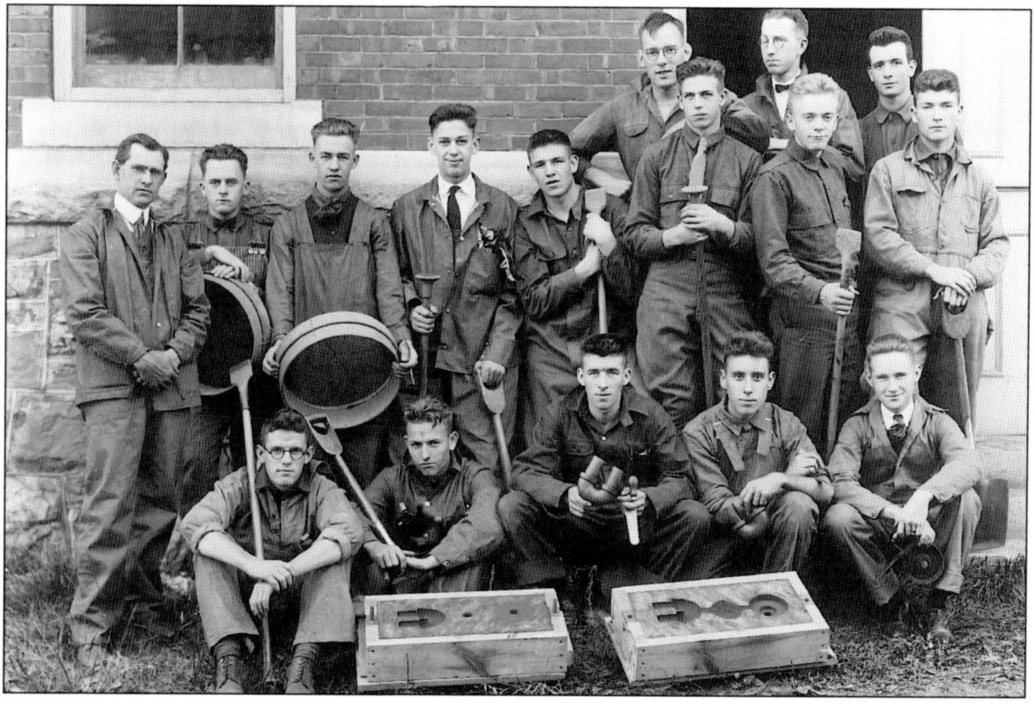

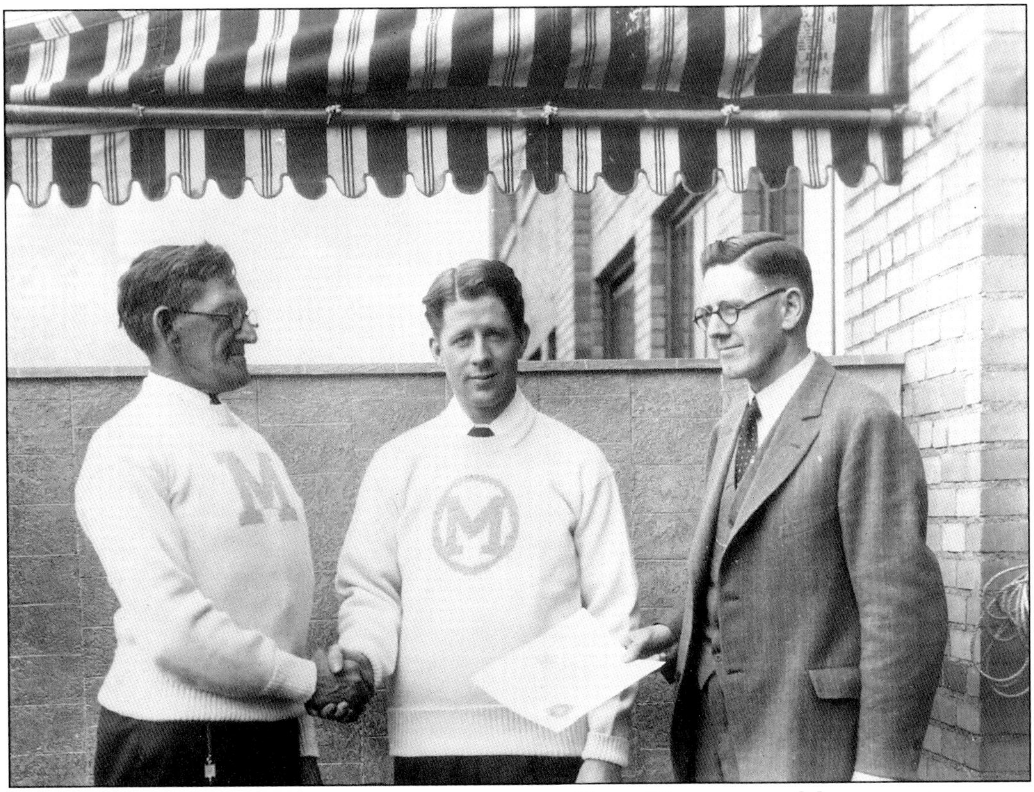

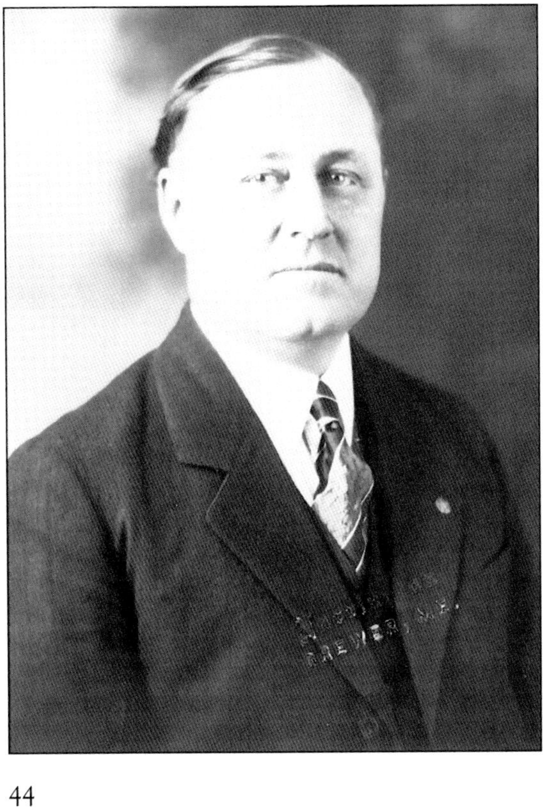

RUDY VALLEY WITH MEMBERS OF THE M CLUB AFTER RECEIVING AN HONORARY SWEATER IN 1931. Valley (center) was responsible for many firsts in the entertainment industry. He was the first to use a megaphone, special lighting effects, and to have his band carry a public address system. He was a pioneer in the early days of radio and was chosen as a host for the Fleischman Radio Hour. His hit recording of the U. Maine Stein song in the 1930s has sold 600,000 copies.

BALLARD FREEZE KEITH, RHODES SCHOLAR. The Old Town native earned the distinction of becoming the first U. Maine student to achieve the status of Rhodes Scholar. A gifted athlete, Keith was chosen over classmate Harold Ellis; athletic ability was counted as highly as scholarship as criteria for the award.

CONTEMPLATING A PRANK? Students are shown here outside Winslow Hall, c. 1910. Despite high standards for student behavior set forth by Presidents Fernald and Allen, students were not always agreeable to the strict moral code. Pranks were common on campus as skeletons were placed on the gable in Coburn Hall and on the roof of Winslow Hall. Students chained the wheels of professors' buggies, stole from the college orchard, raided hen houses, and captured turkeys to be used in unauthorized celebrations.

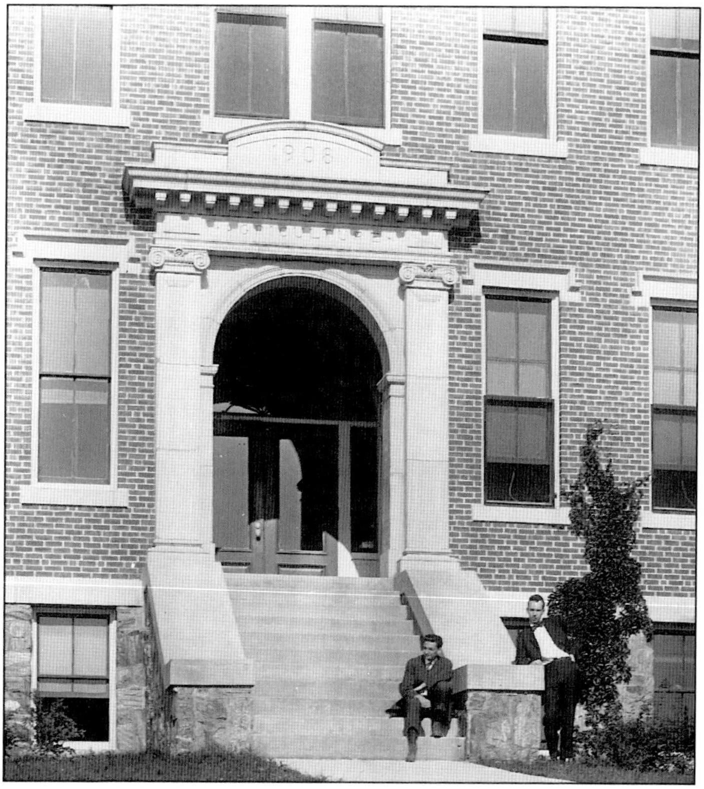

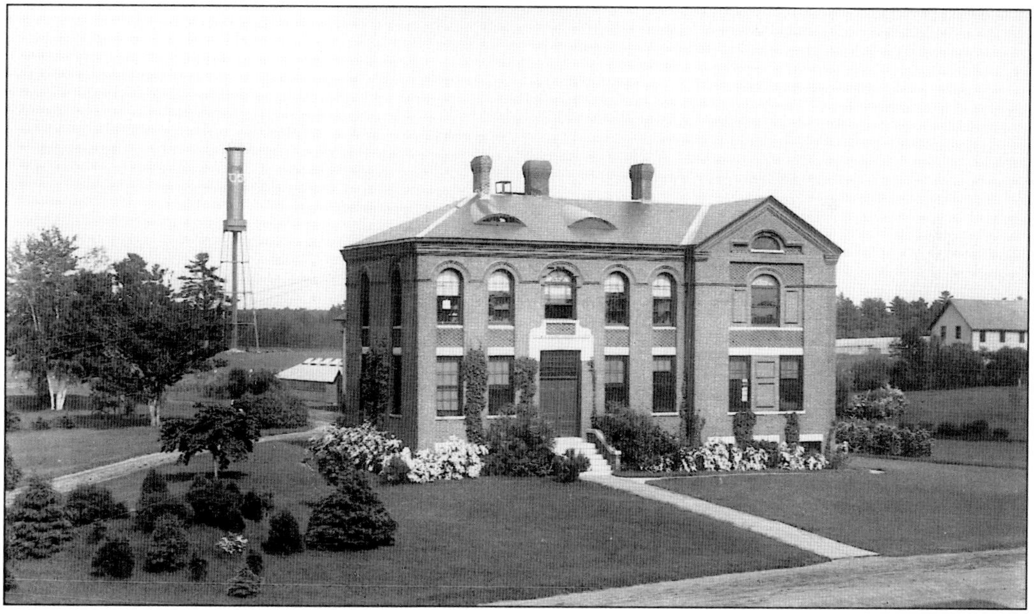

THE VIEW IN FRONT OF HOLMES HALL, SPRING OF 1906. In the background is the stand pipe that was used for fire protection and also by students to mark class supremacy. This long-standing tradition, still seen at many high schools, ended in 1911. The 1912 *Prism* provided the following commentary: ". . .abolished the petty struggle for class supremacy on the stand pipe when (the class of 1911) painted over its own numerals and replaced them with a big 'M'."

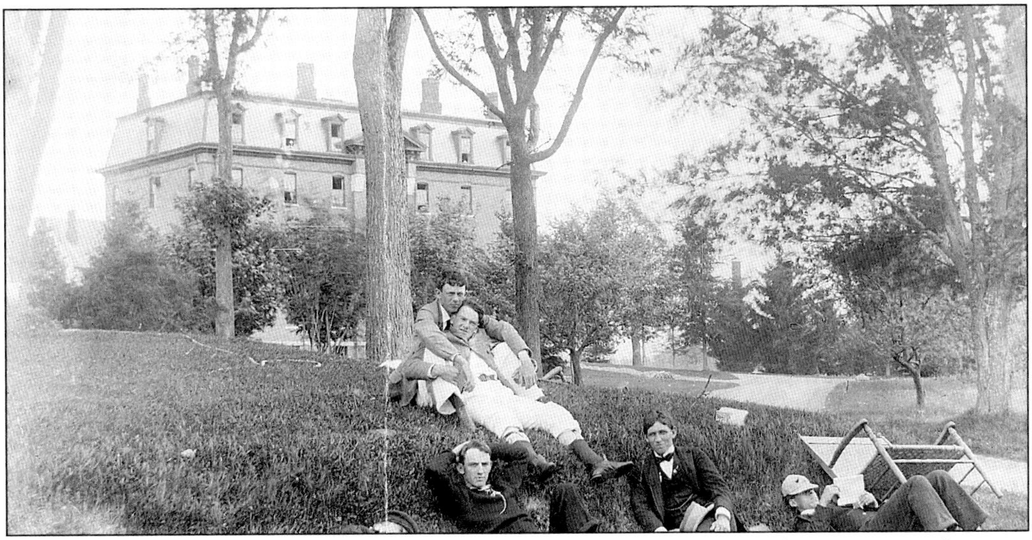

Students Horsing around in front of Oak Hall, c. 1890. Horseplay among students on campus was not always innocent fun. Hazing, or harassment, of incoming students began as early as 1869 and often escalated into serious incidents. In 1896, after the expulsion of several students, a non-hazing pledge had to be signed by every student at the university. Hazing included paddling, dunking in the Stillwater River, parading around campus in night clothes, and other supposed rights of initiation into manhood.

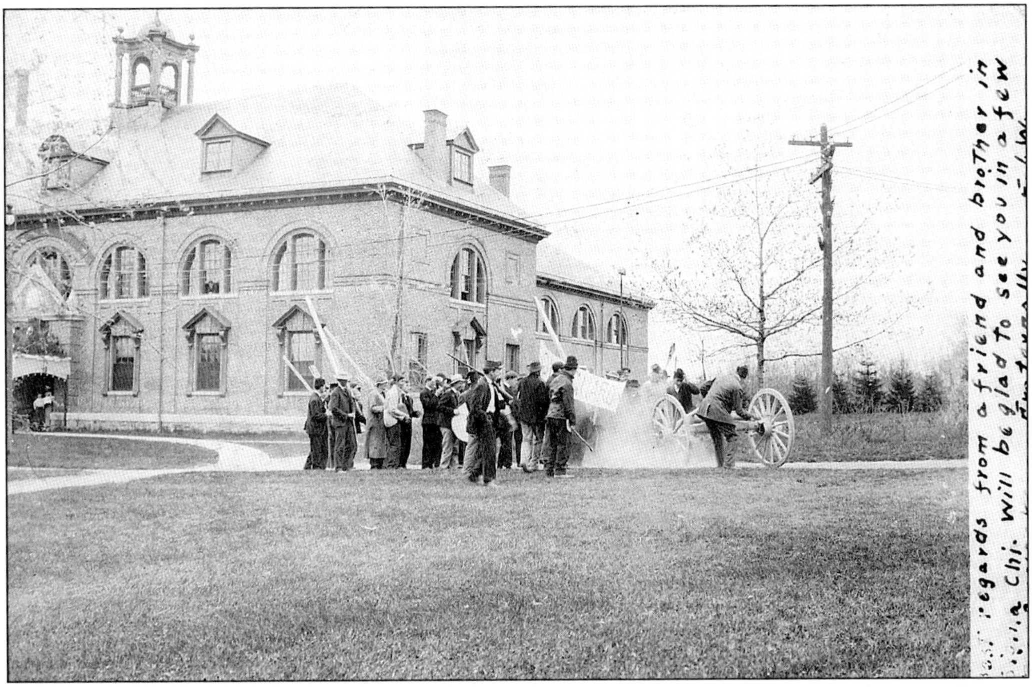

A Postcard Sent between Fraternity Brothers at Sigma Chi in 1906. It depicts a hazing incident involving the class of 1906, a student group that openly practiced hazing. Hazing, and other incidents causing tension between students and administration, came to a head in the fall of 1909. A student riot broke out with strikes and protest, culminating in a student march of solidarity around Alumni Field.

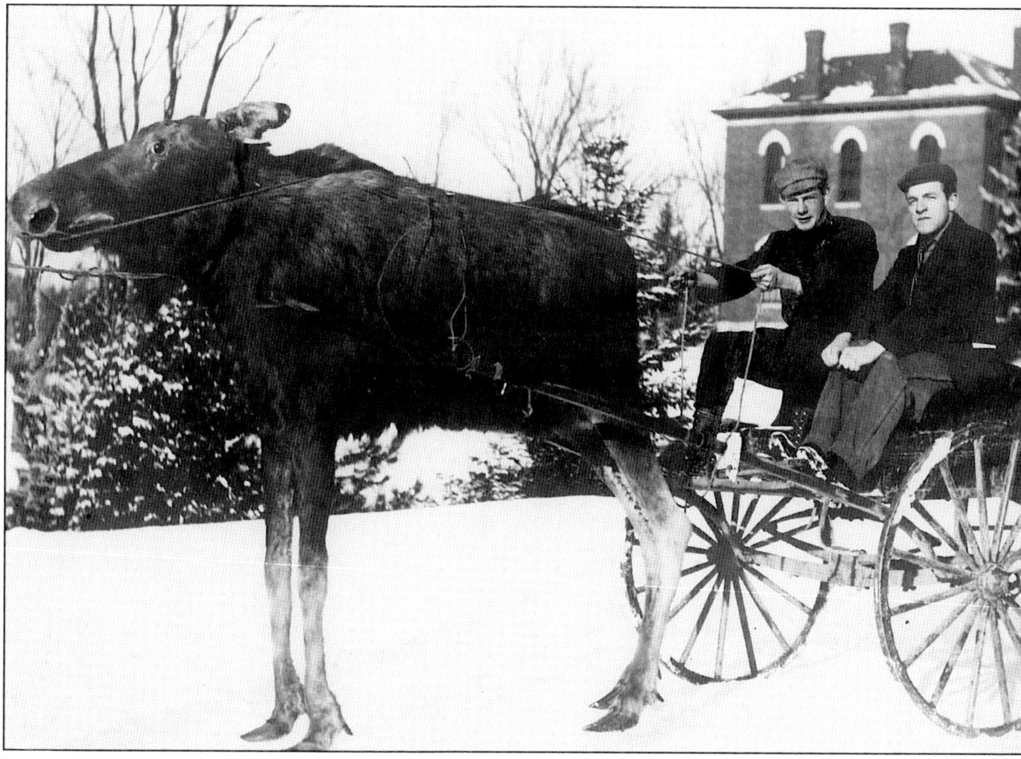

Moose on the Loose outside Fernald Hall, c.1905. Students involved in the prank were caught by this incriminating photo. The "borrowed" moose was likely "on loan" from the museum in Coburn Hall.

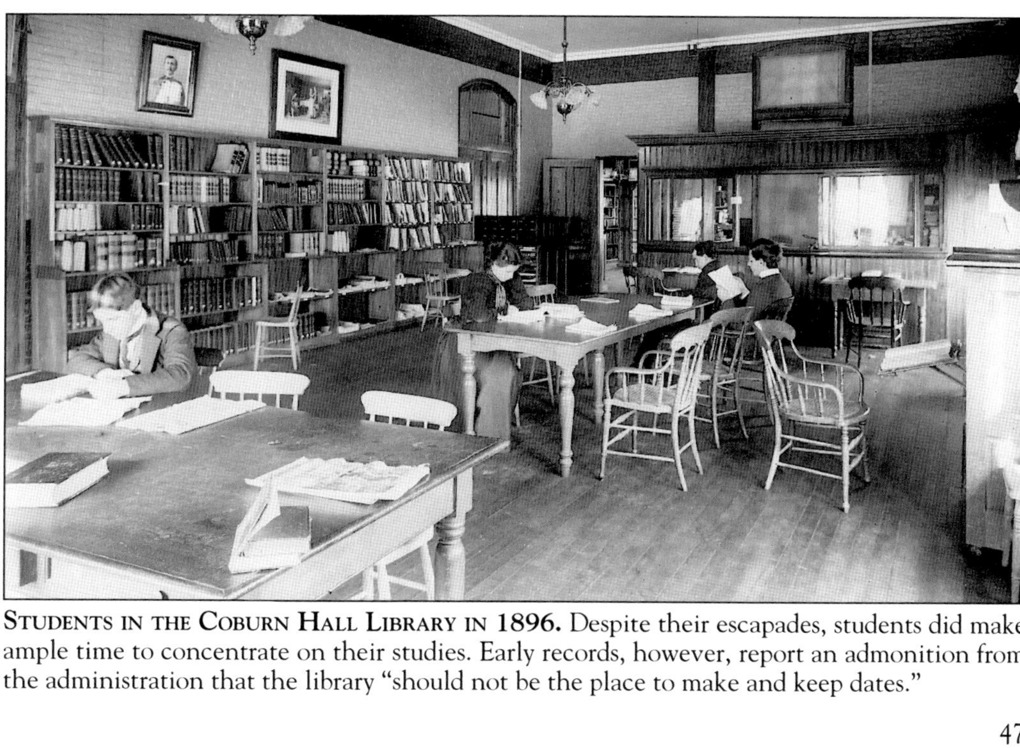

Students in the Coburn Hall Library in 1896. Despite their escapades, students did make ample time to concentrate on their studies. Early records, however, report an admonition from the administration that the library "should not be the place to make and keep dates."

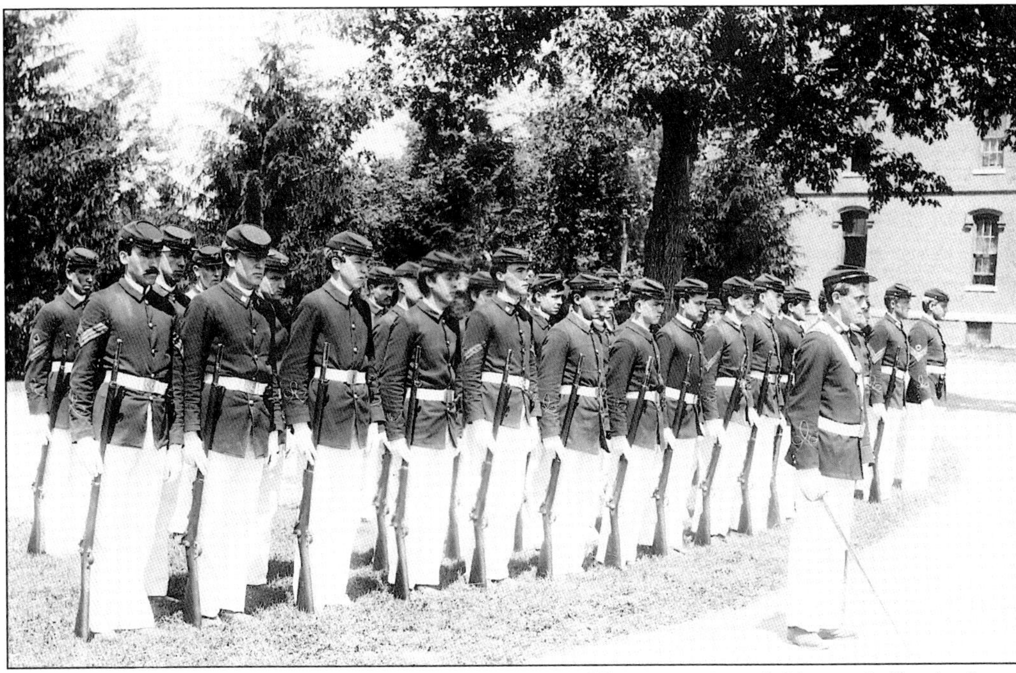

COBURN CADETS PREPARE FOR DRILL BESIDE FERNALD HALL, C. 1910. Military drill, which was a requirement of the Morrill Act, has been practiced by U. Maine students since the inception of the college. For the first 25 years, military instruction was run like any other course at the college. Instruction was first led by Civil War veterans and later by war department officers sent to train the cadets.

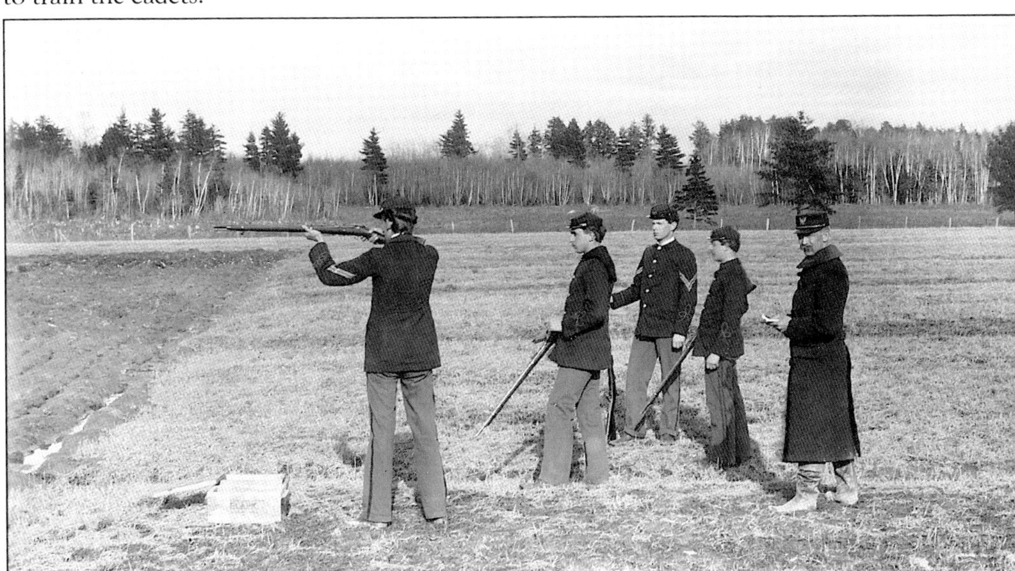

CADETS FIRING AT A TARGET, C. 1890. The Coburn Cadets were named in honor of former Maine governor and Maine State College benefactor Abner Coburn. The uniforms worn by the cadets were replicas of those worn by cadets at West Point. Cadets trained for four days a week for three hours and were issued firearms. They were predecessors of the ROTC groups seen on campus today.

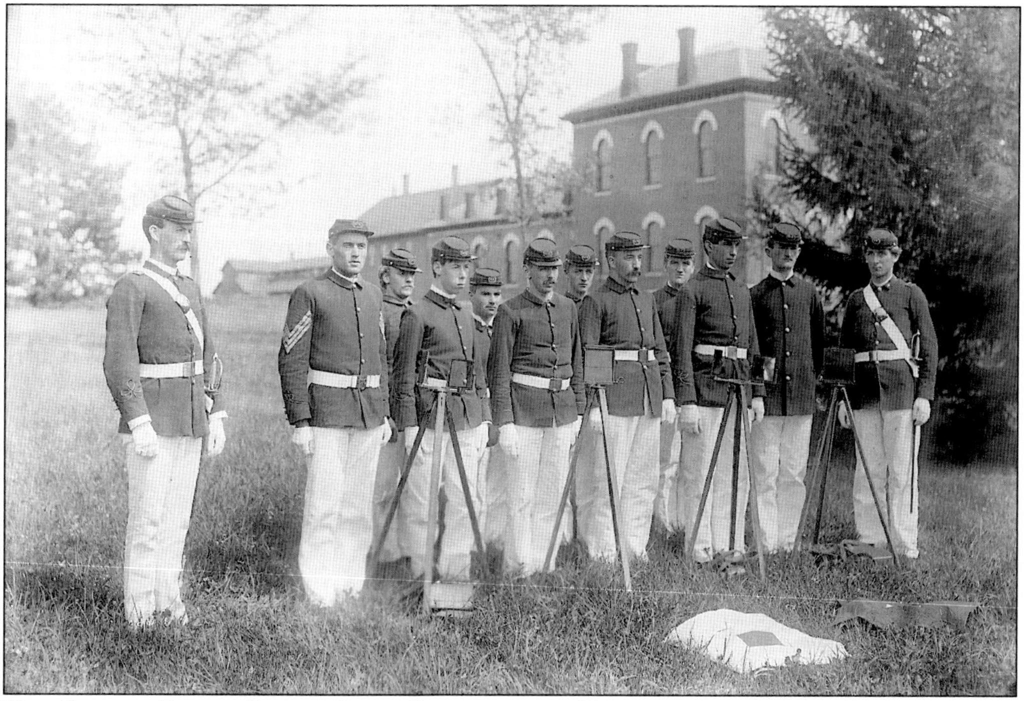

The Coburn Cadets Signal Corps Preparing for Drill beside Fernald Hall in June of 1895. When the battleship *Maine* sank in Havana Harbor in 1898, patriotism to participate in the "Cuban War" ran high among students. Sixty-six university students enlisted for battle, and four never returned, dying of typhoid fever. The taste of war led to disillusionment with drill until sentiment ran high again as America entered WW I.

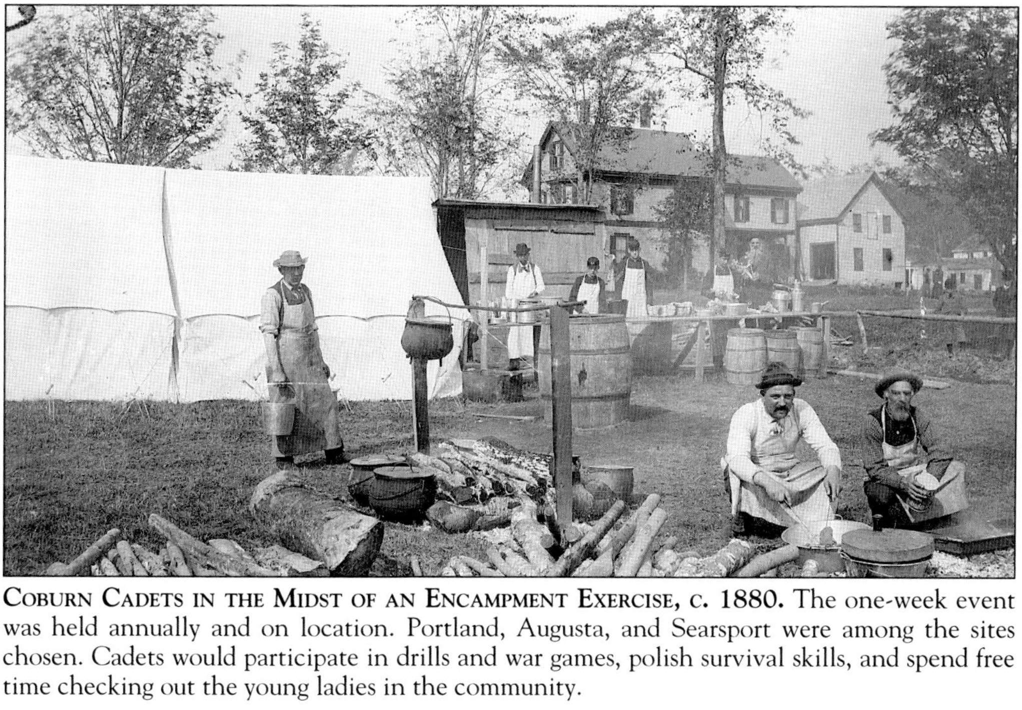

Coburn Cadets in the Midst of an Encampment Exercise, c. 1880. The one-week event was held annually and on location. Portland, Augusta, and Searsport were among the sites chosen. Cadets would participate in drills and war games, polish survival skills, and spend free time checking out the young ladies in the community.

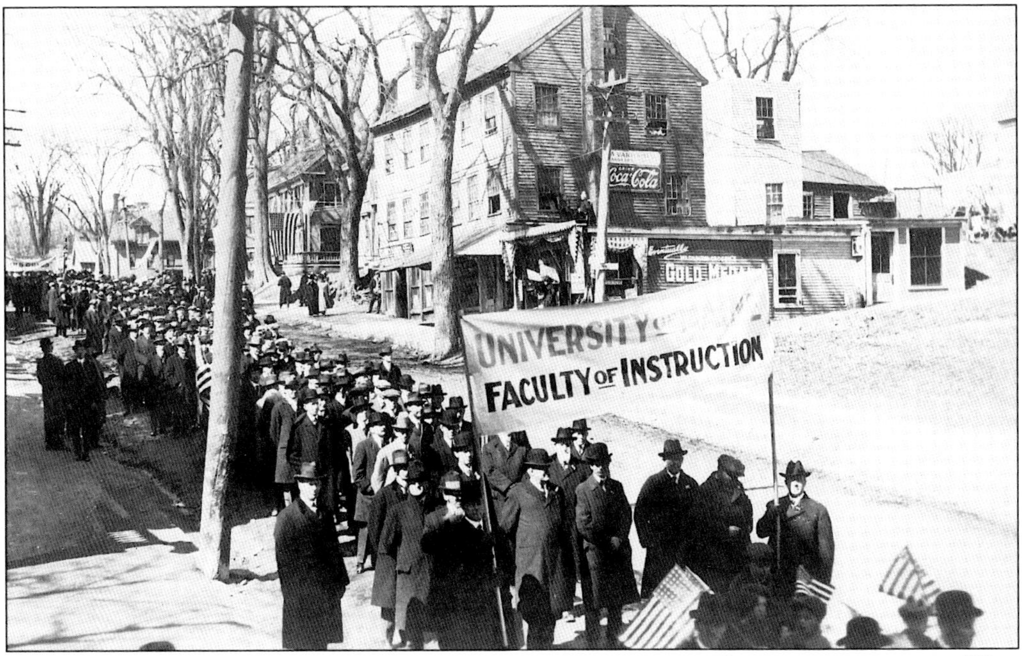

RESPONSE TO PRESIDENT WILSON'S PLEA FOR THE UNIVERSITY TO GET INVOLVED IN THE WAR EFFORT. President Aley exhorted students to conserve, construct, economize, and buy Liberty Bonds. The *Maine Campus* called for the reinstatement of military drill saying: "We owe it to the nation, the state and the university, and to ourselves to put our best effort to work." This image likely dates from February of 1916.

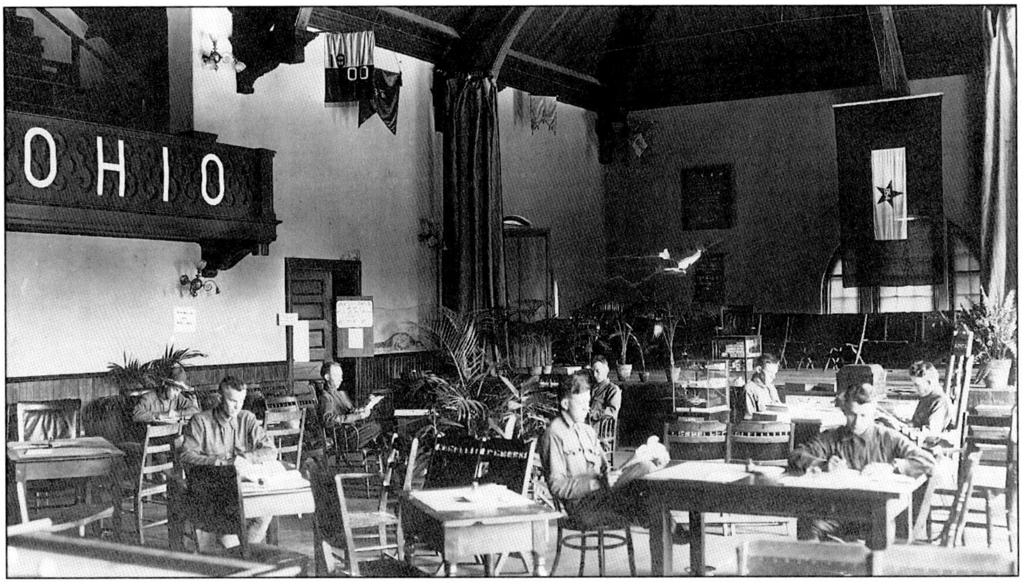

THE STUDENT ARMY TRAINING CORPS IN ALUMNI HALL IN 1917. During the WW I years, the college resembled more of a military barracks than a state university. Most aspects of college life, including curriculum, were dictated by Washington. Fraternities shut down and male students came under the discipline of army officers. Courses in German language and culture were eliminated and a popular song circulated on campus titled "Canning the Kaiser."

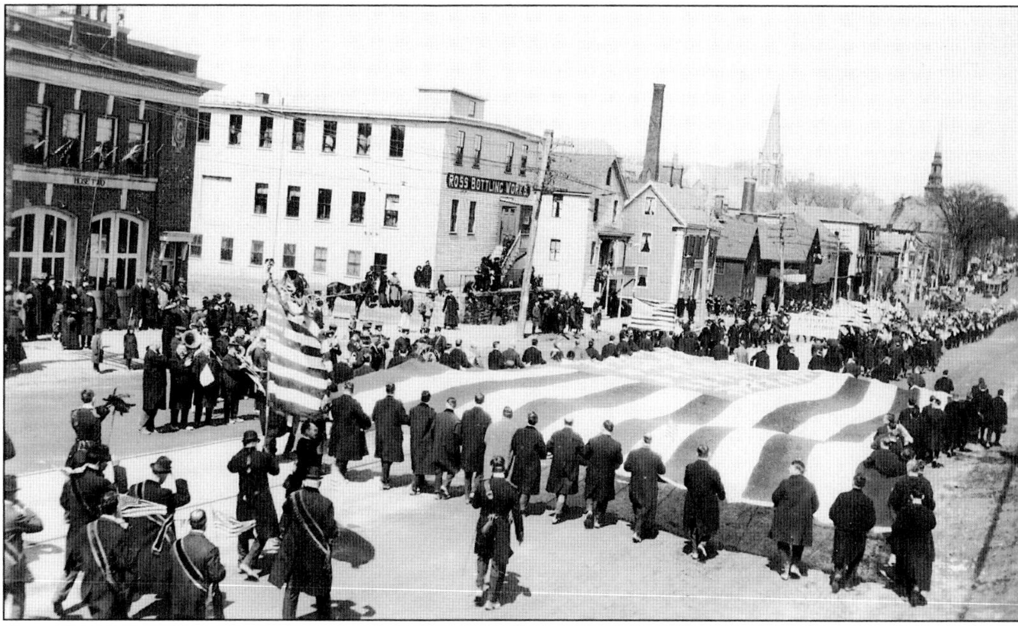

STUDENTS AND FACULTY PARADING ON BANGOR STREET TO CELEBRATE THE ANNOUNCED END OF THE WAR, NOVEMBER 11, 1918. The event was followed by wild celebrations on campus and a return to normalcy.

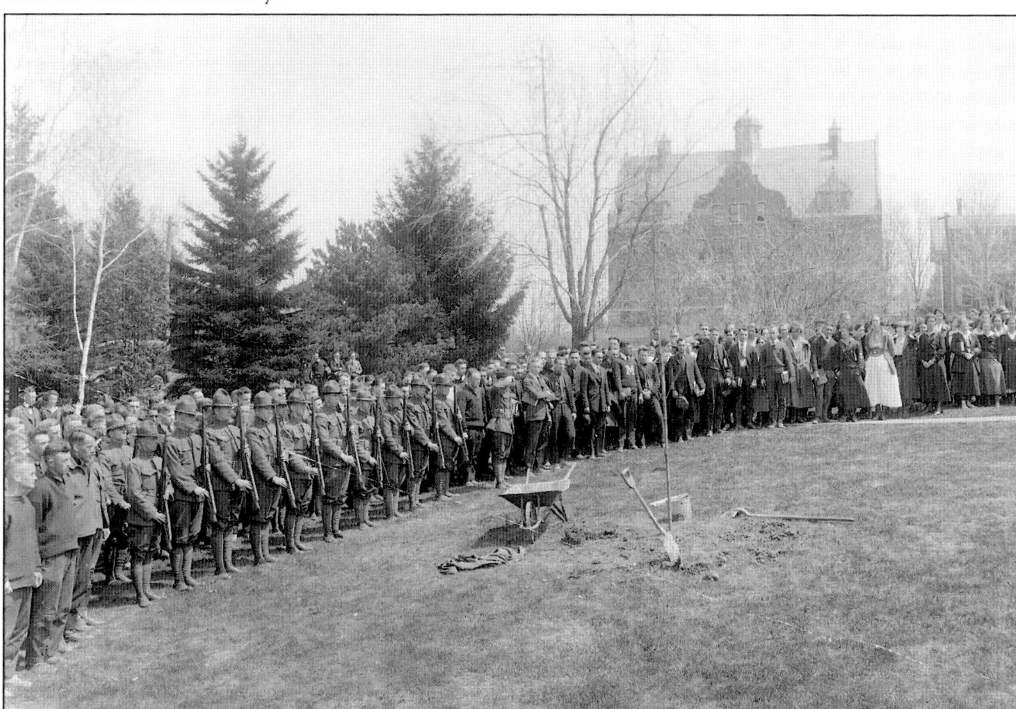

A TREE-PLANTING CEREMONY IN FRONT OF WINSLOW HALL, C. 1920. The occasion for the ceremony was most likely an Armistice Day event presided over by President Aley, celebrating the end of "The War to end all Wars."

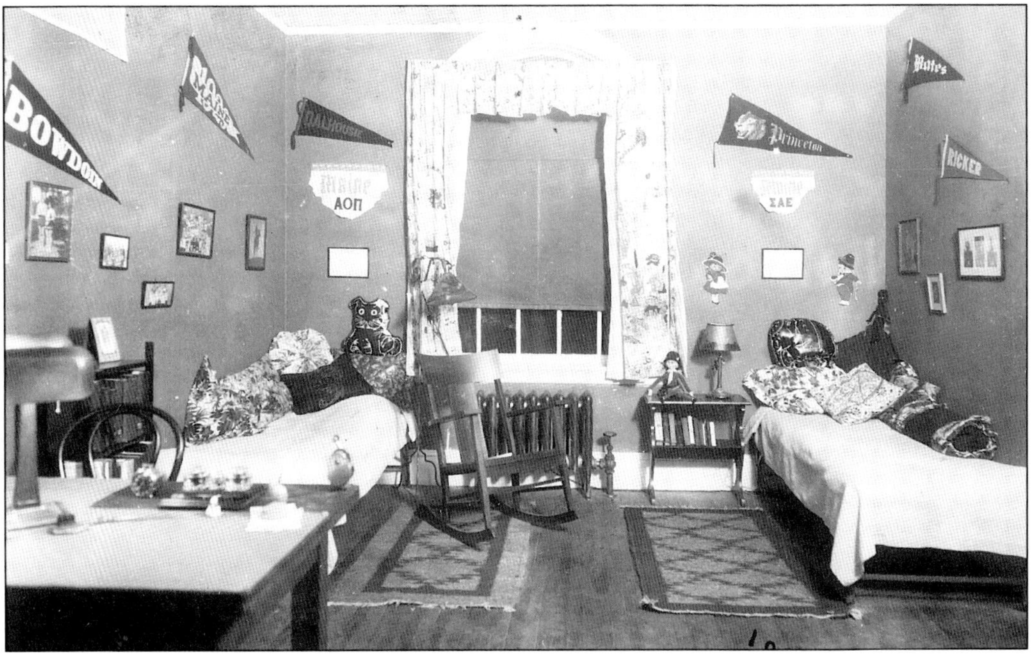

NOTHING TO HIDE. This photograph offers a look inside 104 Balentine Hall in 1916. In the mid-1880s, weekly inspections of dorm rooms were mandatory and became a point of contention between students and faculty. In 1892, Lt. Edgar Howe was given the responsibility, and students disdained his insistence on strict compliance. Students broke out in protest, stole guns from the armory, captured Howe, and locked him in a basement for 36 hours.

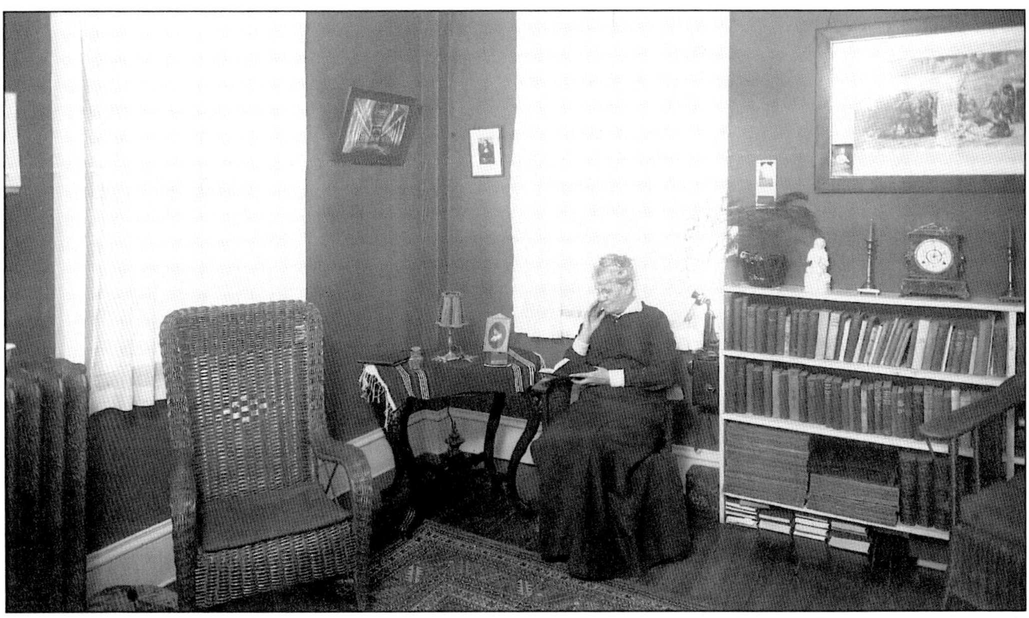

KATE "MA" ESTABROOKE, WAITING FOR A PHONE CALL INSIDE MOUNT VERNON, IN 1916. Estabrooke served for many years as a housemother and was the wife of early university professor Horace Estabrooke. In 1940, Estabrooke Hall was opened and named in her honor.

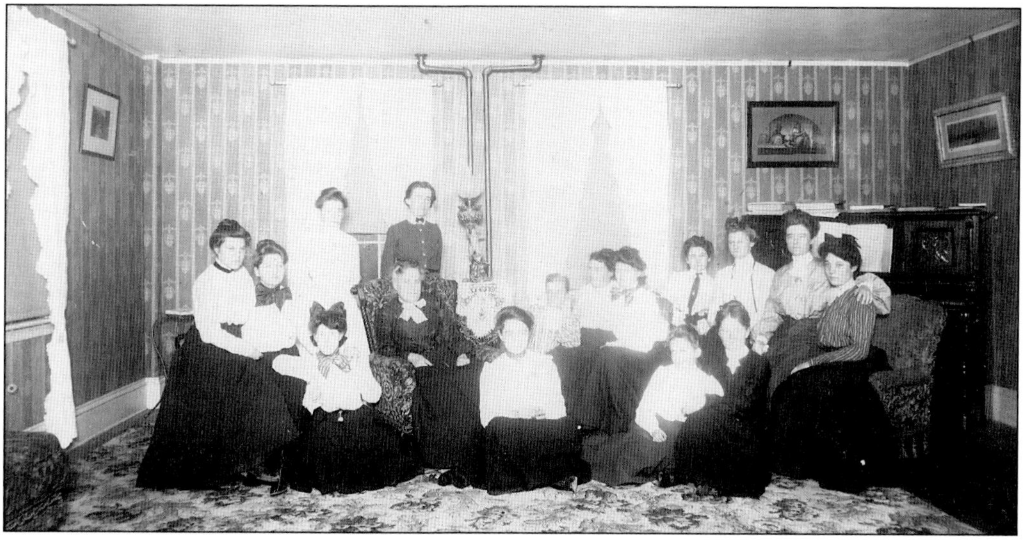

INSIDE THE PARLOR OF MOUNT VERNON IN 1906. Per order of President Fellows, this is as far as male students could proceed. Ironically, after Balentine Hall was opened in 1914, Mount Vernon served as a residence for bachelor faculty. The building was destroyed by fire in 1933 and was never rebuilt.

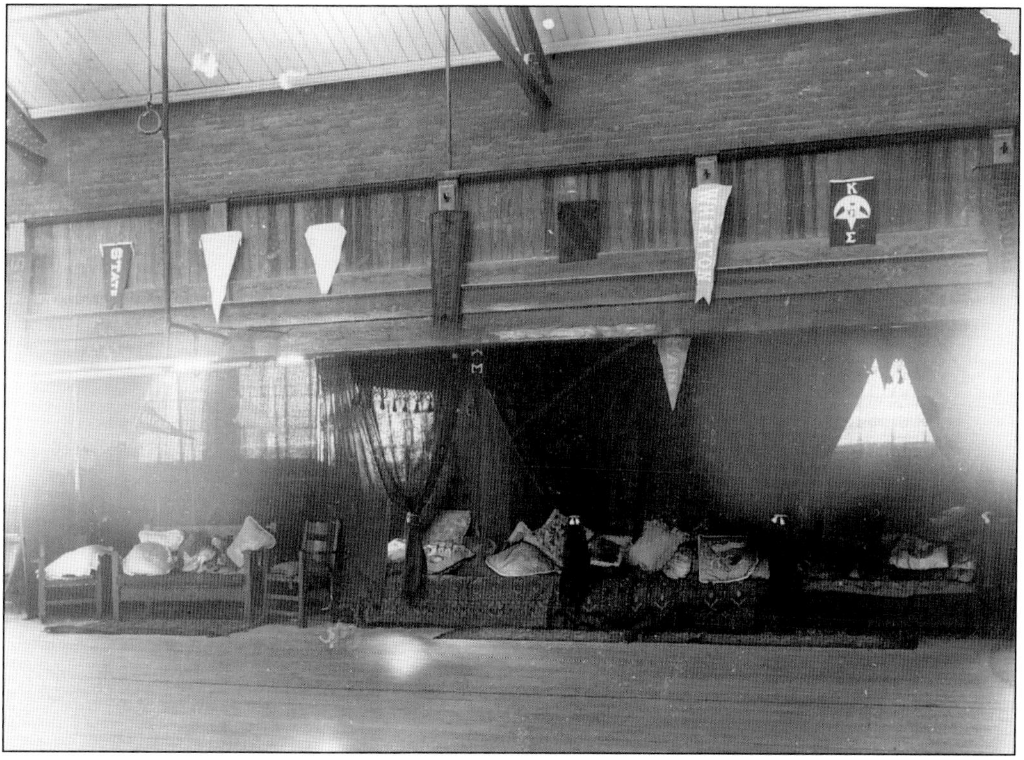

GETTING READY FOR A DANCE INSIDE ALUMNI HALL IN 1905. The new gymnasium, built in 1901, quickly became a headquarters for student affairs and social events. Pictured here are the controversial cots and "cozy corners" whose use became a point of contention between students, faculty, and parents.

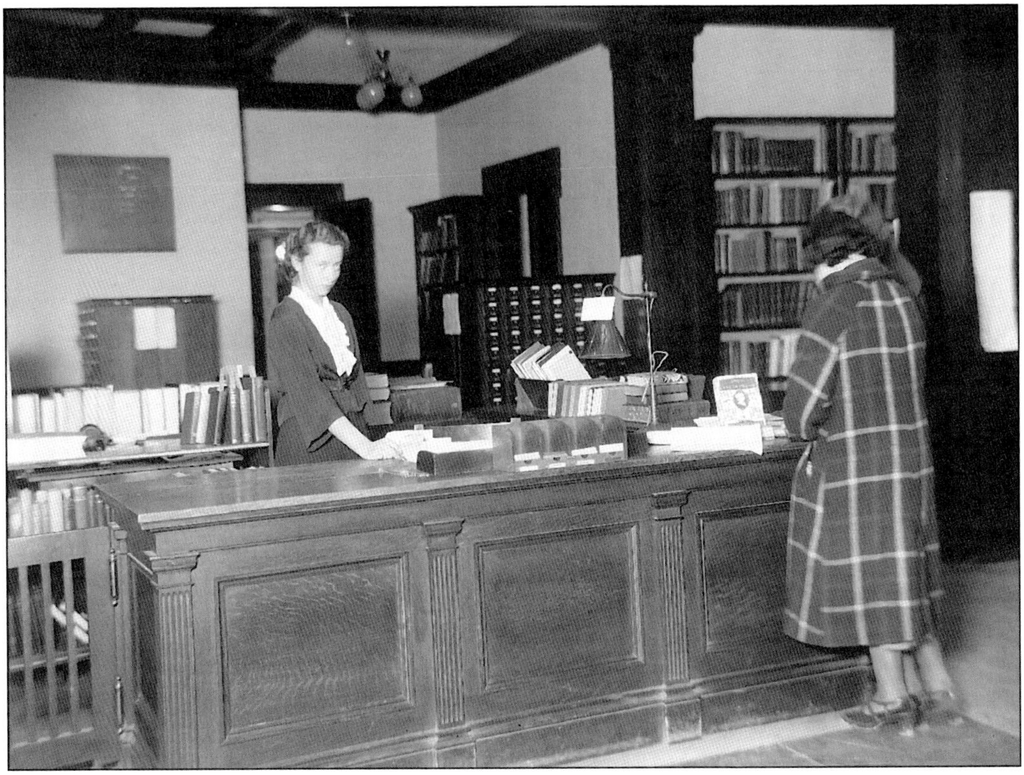

May I Help You? This photograph depicts a librarian helping students in the library at Carnegie Hall. It took 25 students less than three days to move the library from Coburn Hall to its new quarters at Carnegie Hall during Thanksgiving break in 1906.

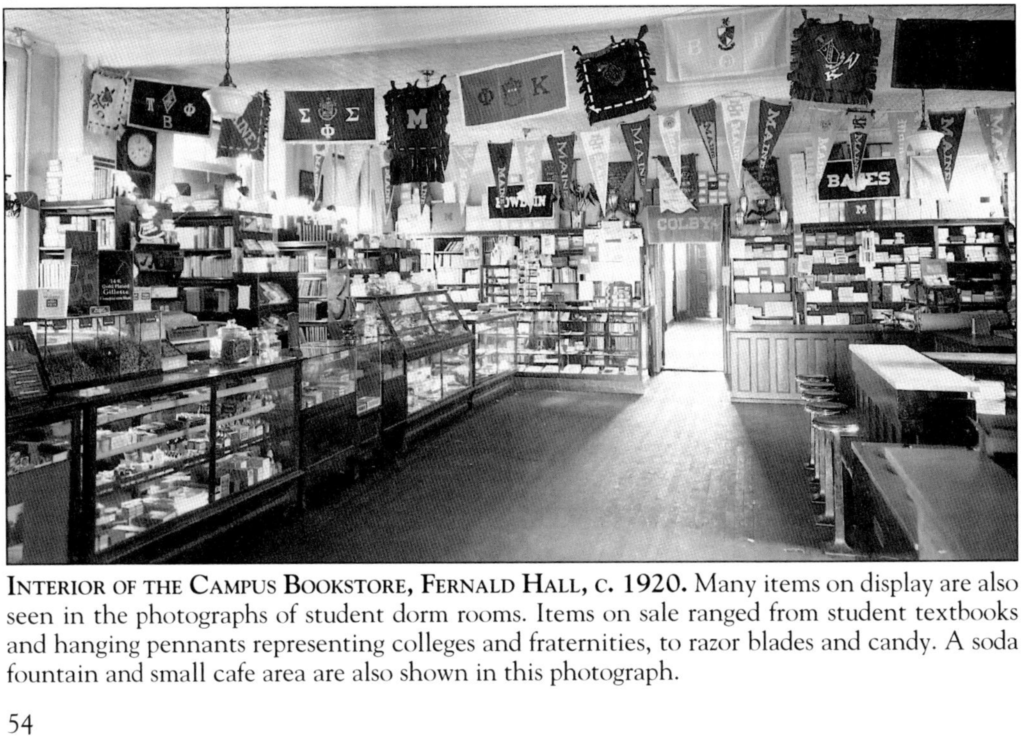

Interior of the Campus Bookstore, Fernald Hall, c. 1920. Many items on display are also seen in the photographs of student dorm rooms. Items on sale ranged from student textbooks and hanging pennants representing colleges and fraternities, to razor blades and candy. A soda fountain and small cafe area are also shown in this photograph.

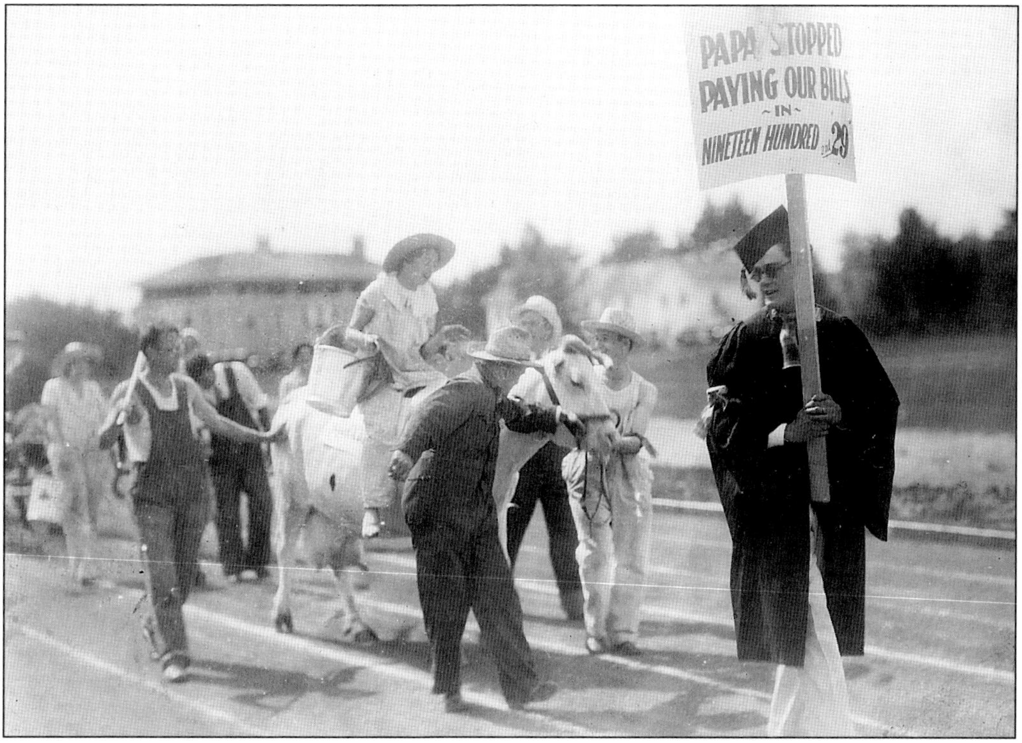

An Early Request for Student Aid? While mill tax funding helped the university carry on during the difficult Depression years, students still had the expense of paying for books, tuition, and other necessities. They may have welcomed the labor-for-tuition program enjoyed by their predecessors.

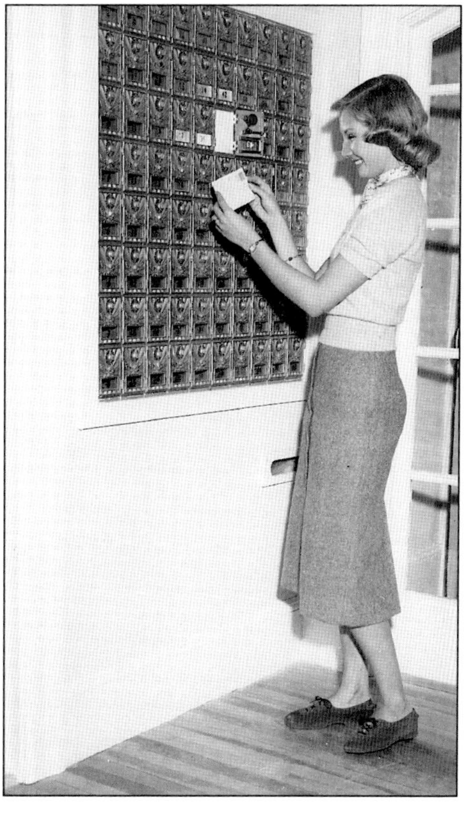

"Sure Hope Its Money!" A co-ed receives mail in the lobby of Balentine Hall, *c.* 1925. A note from home or a significant other has always brightened the day of university students. Students worked as the first mail carriers on campus as part of the labor program.

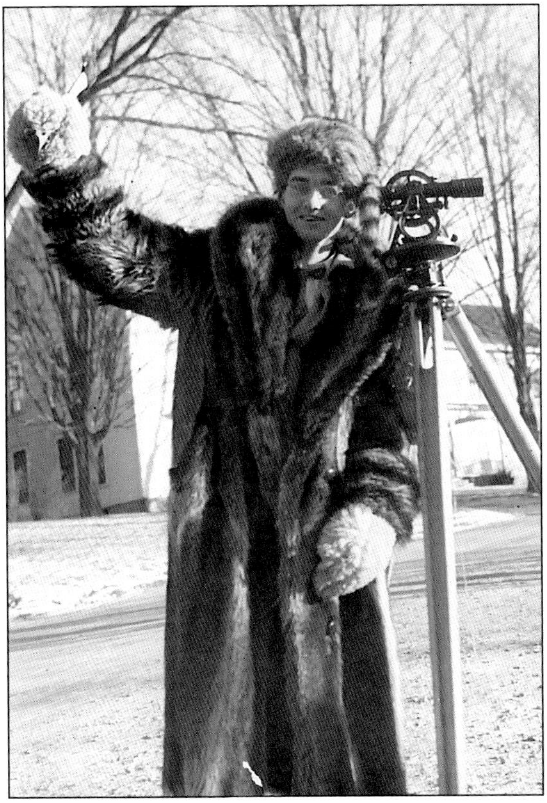

A Student Surveyor Wearing a Raccoon Coat and Hat During a Winter Surveying Project, c. 1930. Raccoon coats were in vogue on campus in the 1920s and 1930s and also proved to be great insulation from the cold Maine winters. President Fernald kept a meteorological journal from 1868 to 1893, in which he noted heavier snowfall but somewhat milder temperatures than those in recent years.

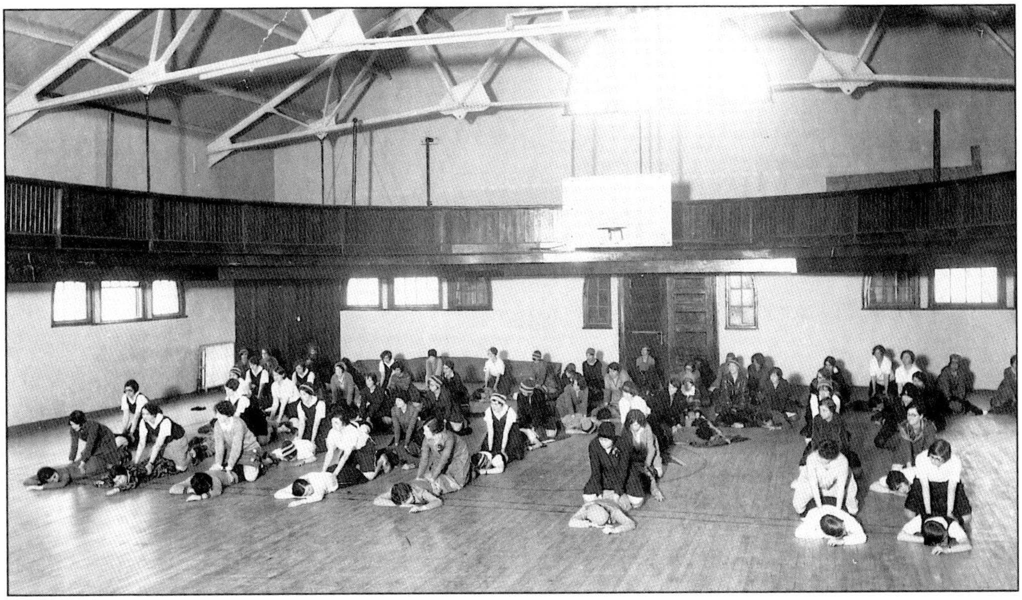

Students Participating in Extra Curricular Activities, Alumni Hall, 1928. This photograph shows university women receiving instruction in the prone pressure method of artificial respiration. By the early 1900s, students could participate in a wide range of activities including a press club, boat club, photo club, bicycle club, prohibition club, and various athletic clubs.

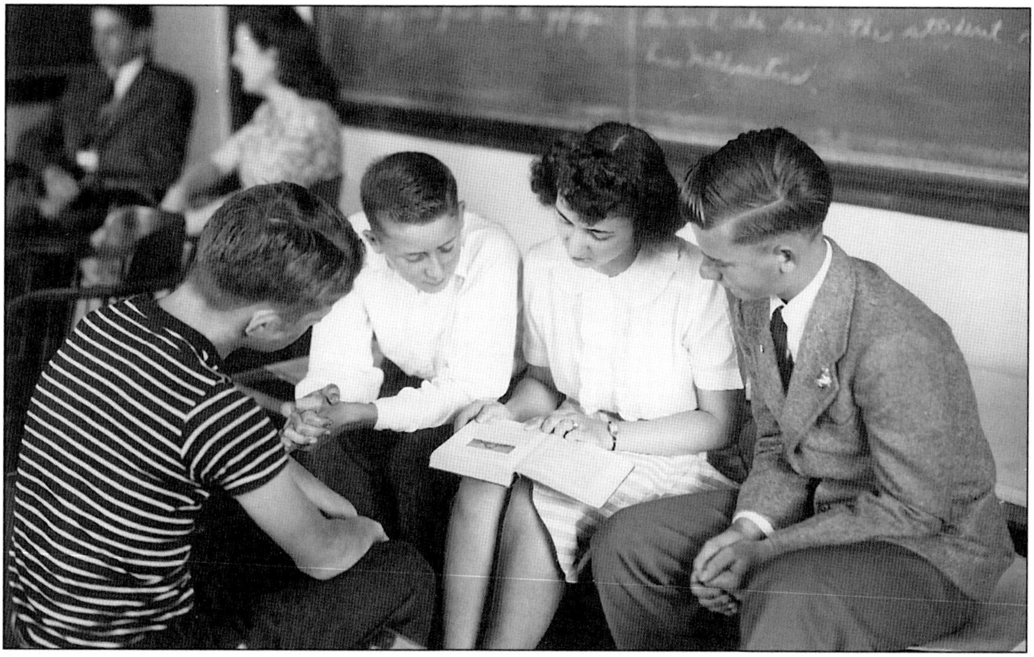

STUDENTS GATHERING INSIDE A CLASSROOM, C. 1929. The diversity of dress suggests no formal dress code.

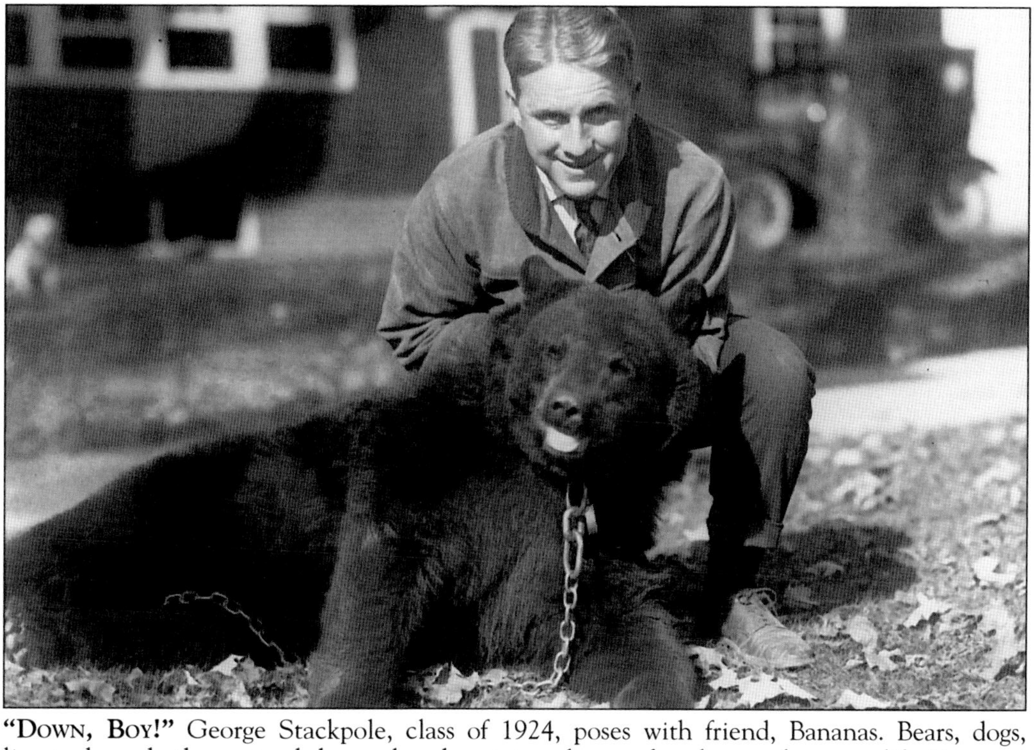

"DOWN, BOY!" George Stackpole, class of 1924, poses with friend, Bananas. Bears, dogs, livestock, and other animals have played an integral part of student and campus life. Bananas, the adopted sports mascot, was frequently chained to a tree on the commons to fraternize with students passing by.

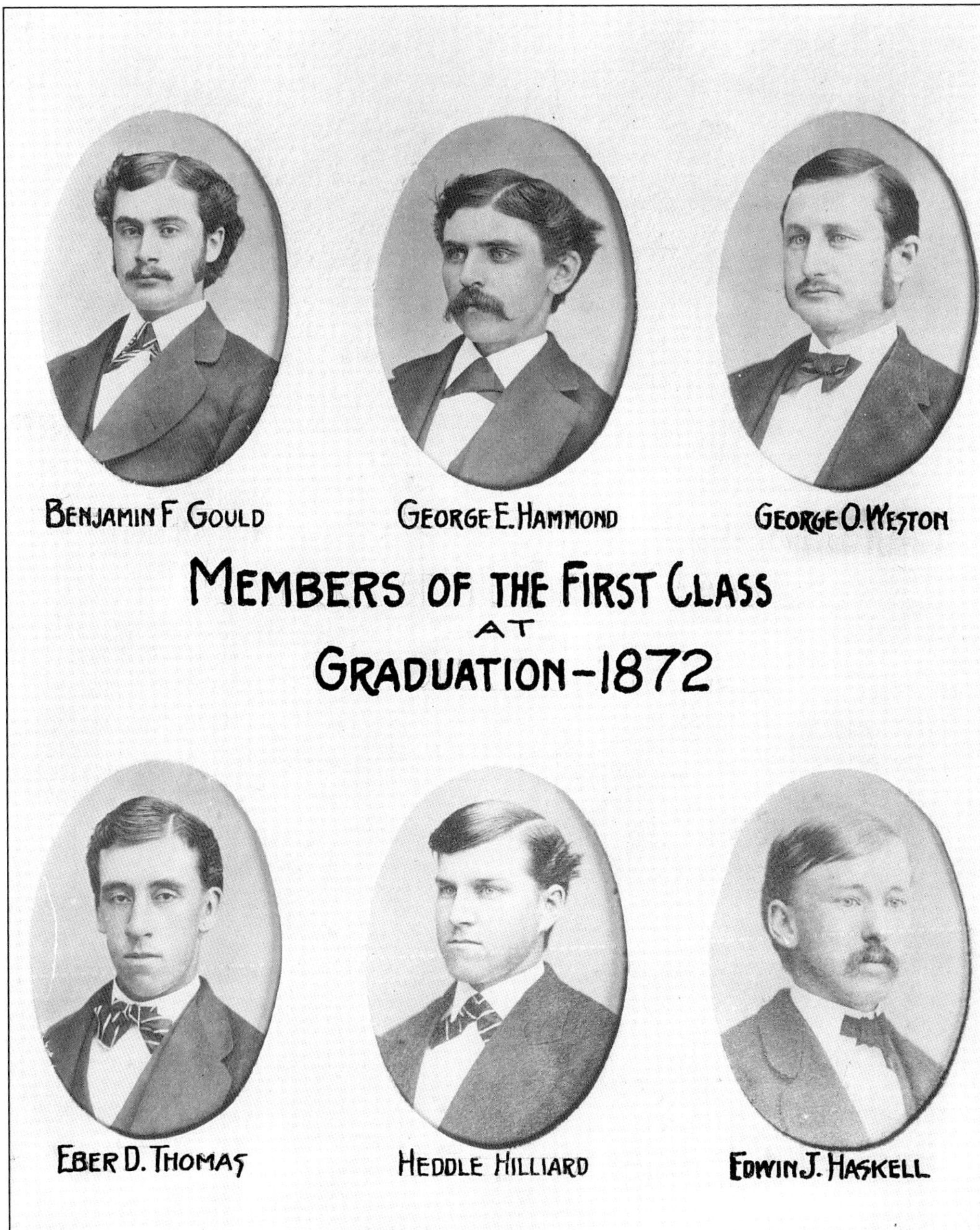

MEMBERS OF THE FIRST GRADUATING CLASS AT MAINE STATE COLLEGE. Of an original class of 12, only six finished their term as four members graduated with degrees in civil engineering, one in agriculture, and one in an elective course. Edwin Haskell recalled being one of the first five collegians to spend a night on campus. They boarded on the second floor of White Hall, borrowed a candle from the farmhouse, and took turns reading from a daily paper.

Three

Campus Views

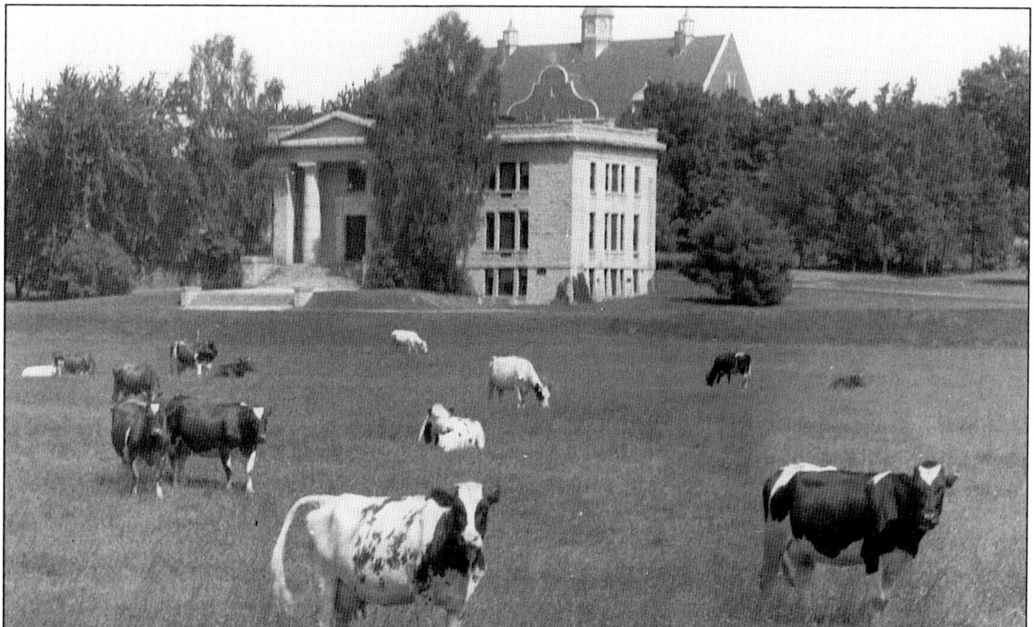

The College Herd outside Carnegie Hall in 1939, with the Winslow Hall Agricultural Building in the Background. This scene typifies the many transitions that took place as the college emerged from the limited scope of the Maine State College to a full-fledged university. The college underwent great changes both physically as well as ideologically during its first 70 years. The campus emerged from a modest start of 3 buildings in 1868, to 9 by 1881, to 33 by 1916, and by 1940 there were almost 50 buildings in use. Fire, subsequent renovation, and the emergence of Fraternity Row also left their mark on the campus landscape. Monuments to the past, like Fernald Hall, stand to this day. Coburn and Holmes Halls also stand as a remembrance to the developing days of Maine State College. Winslow Hall remains as a poignant reminder of the founders' earliest goals to promote agricultural interests at the college.

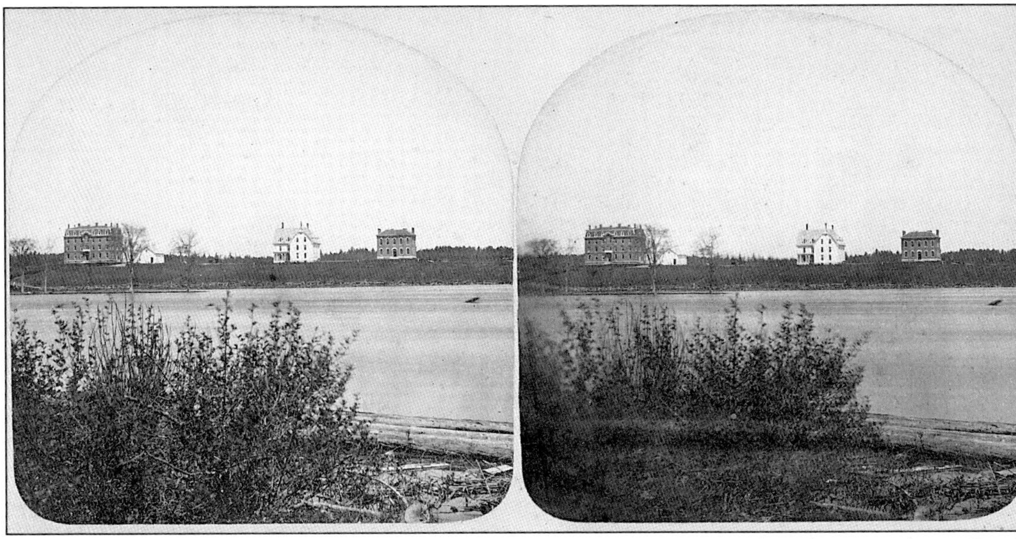

One of the Earliest Images of the Campus, c. 1873. Shown in this photograph are Brick Hall and barn (far left), White Hall (middle), and Chemical Hall (far right).

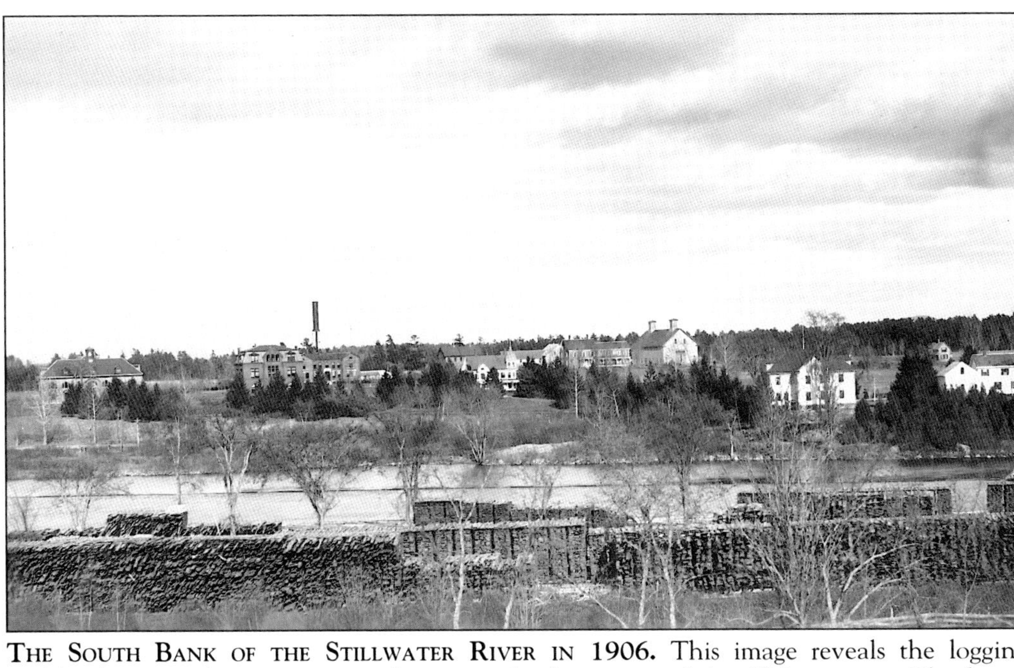

The South Bank of the Stillwater River in 1906. This image reveals the logging and lumbering industry active in Orono in the later part of the 19th century. The broad view of the campus shows Alumni Hall (far left), Coburn Hall, the President's House, and the college farms.

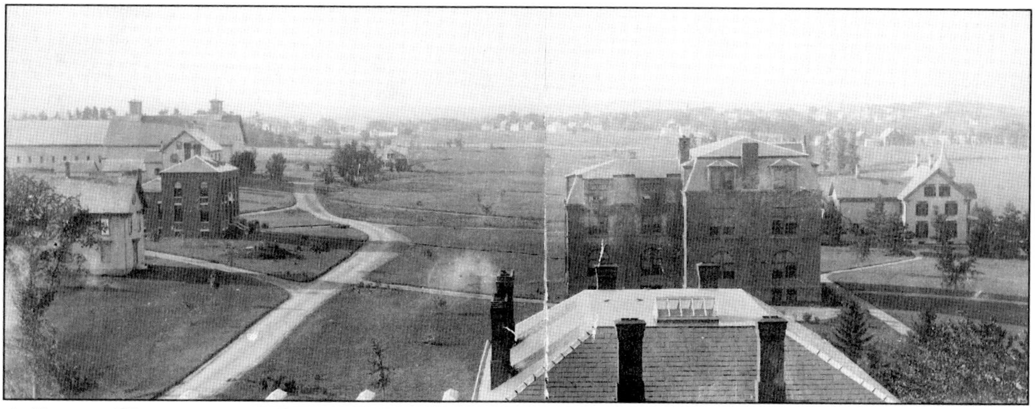

A Broad View of the Campus, Probably Taken from the Roof of Oak Hall, c. 1890. Shown in this photograph (far left) are the QTV fraternity house, Holmes Hall, and College Farms. Coburn Hall and the President's House can be seen on the right.

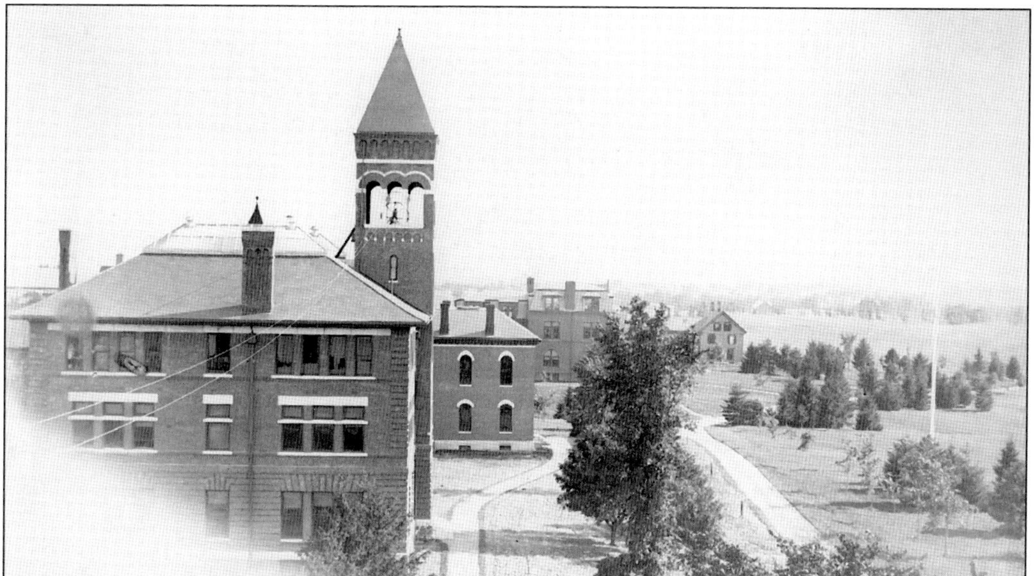

Wingate Hall, c. 1895. Wingate Hall was built in 1892, in honor of Judge William P. Wingate, president of the board of trustees and benefactor of the college. It was built on the site where White Hall stood before it was destroyed by fire in 1890. The tower and belfry atop Wingate endured until they were destroyed by fire in 1946.

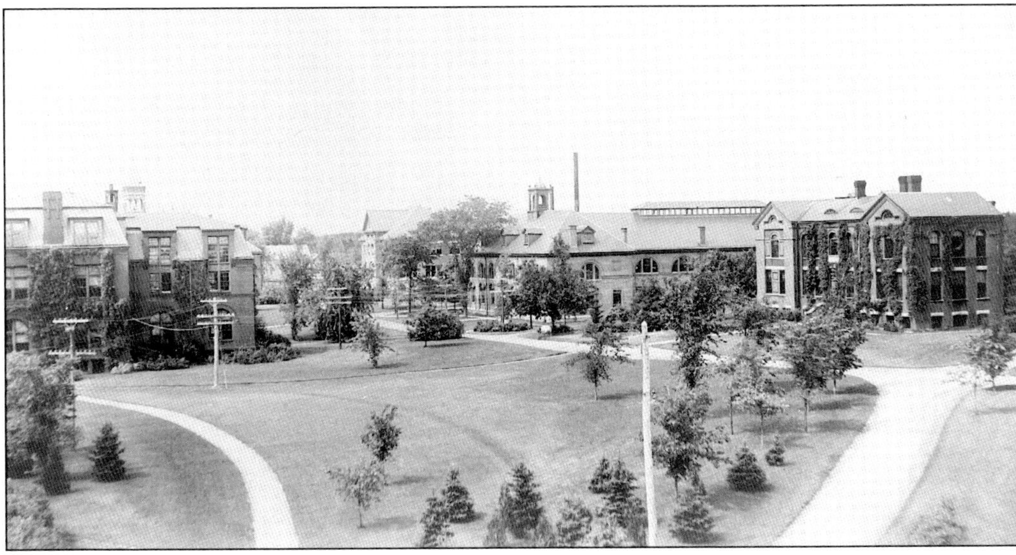

A VIEW OF THE CAMPUS MALL, C. 1905. The campus was getting "on line" with the emergence of telephone and telegraph poles prominent in this image. Tree planting and other horticultural enhancements begun under the Fernald administration are also becoming apparent.

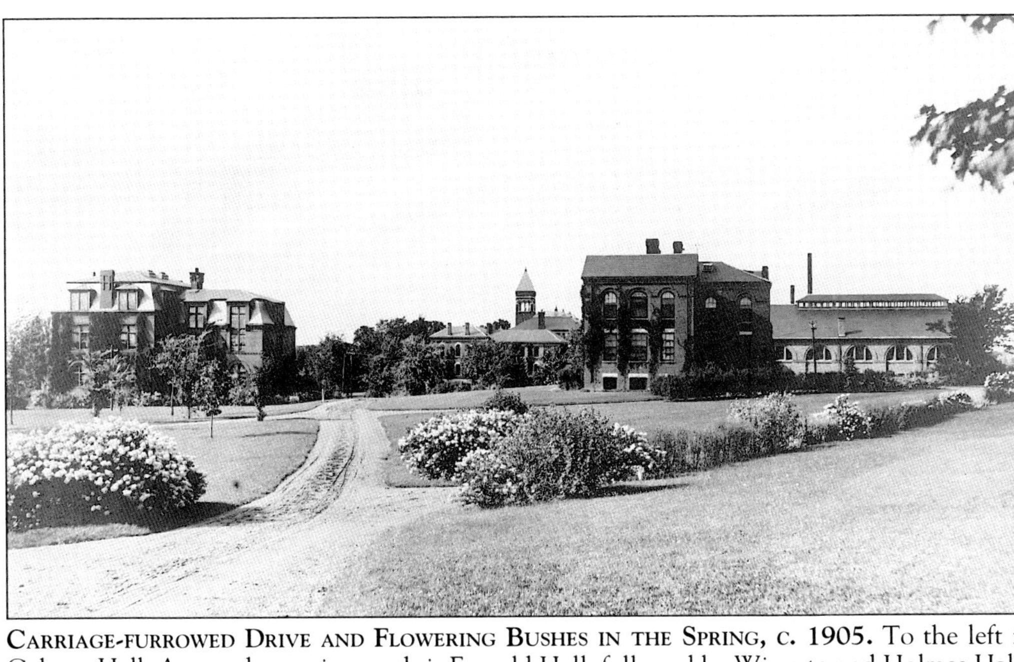

CARRIAGE-FURROWED DRIVE AND FLOWERING BUSHES IN THE SPRING, C. 1905. To the left is Coburn Hall. Across the carriage path is Fernald Hall, followed by Wingate and Holmes Hall. To the right is the newly completed Alumni Hall.

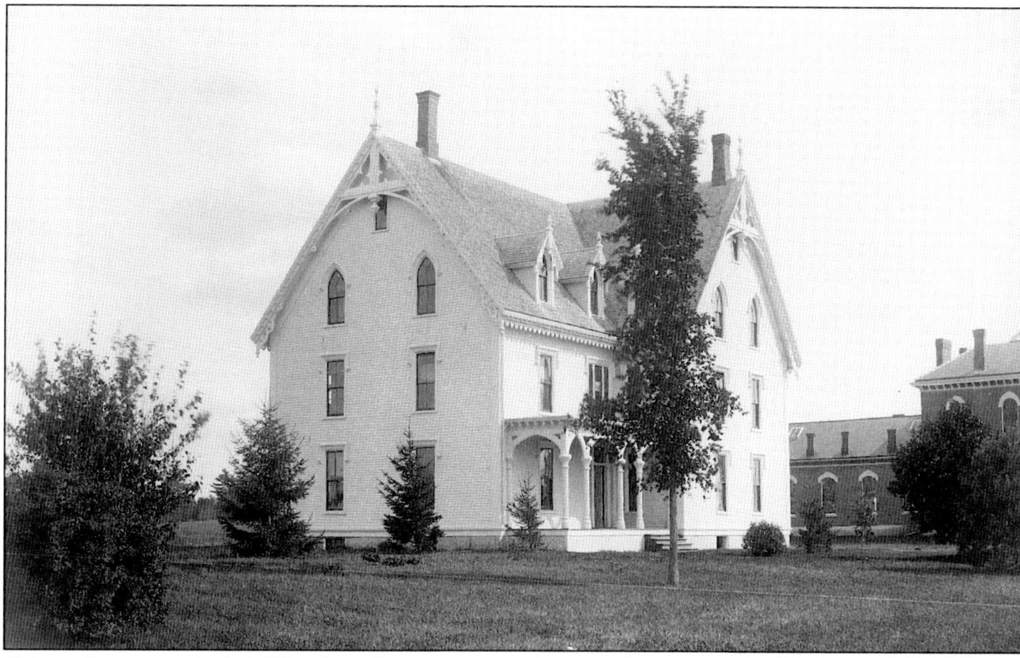

WHITE HALL, C. 1875. This building appears prominently in most early-campus photographs. It was the first building on campus constructed by approval of the trustees and was used as a classroom, male dormitory, and office space for the president.

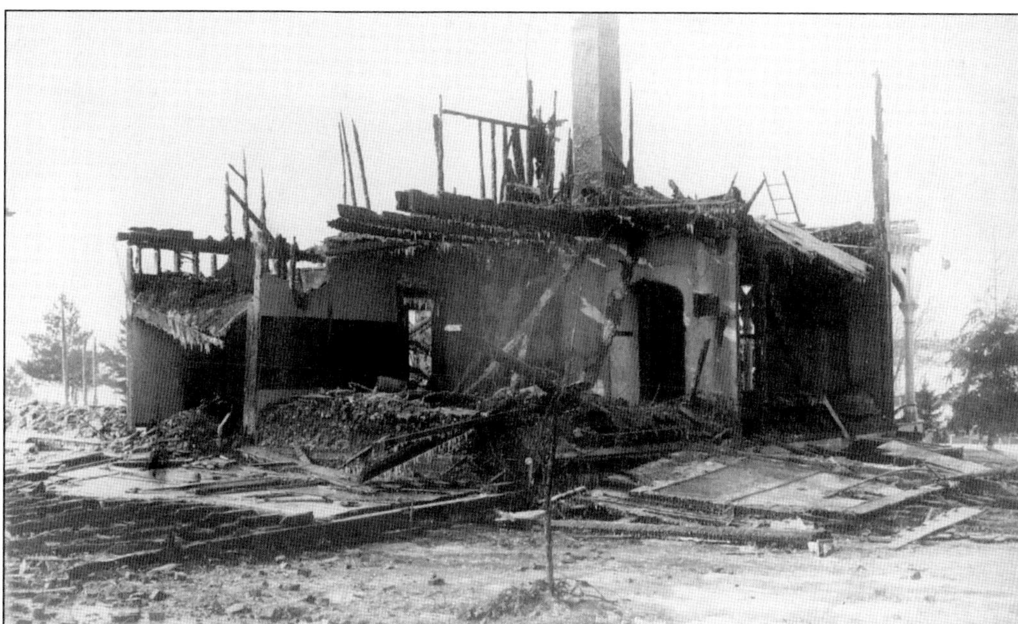

WHITE HALL, DESTROYED BY FIRE, FEBRUARY 9, 1890. The college report of 1890 described the origins of the blaze as being an over-heated wood stove in one of the dormitory rooms. The fire broke out at 11:00 a.m., while occupants were in Orono attending church services. Despite efforts from the Orono, Stillwater, and Old Town Fire Departments, the structure could not be saved and was later razed.

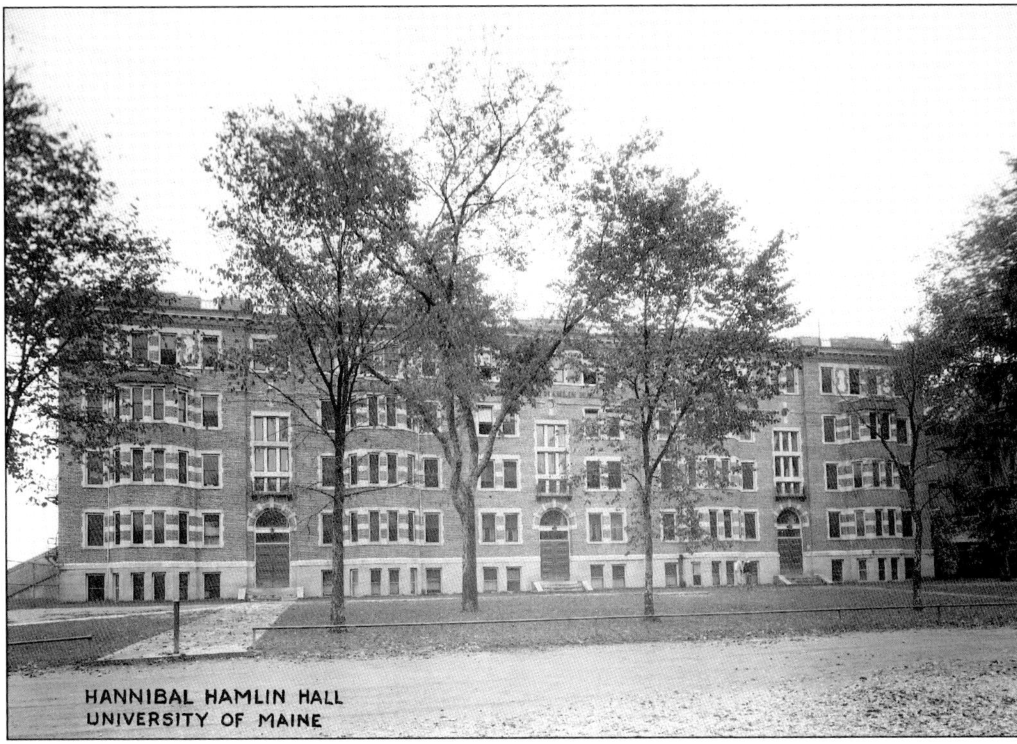

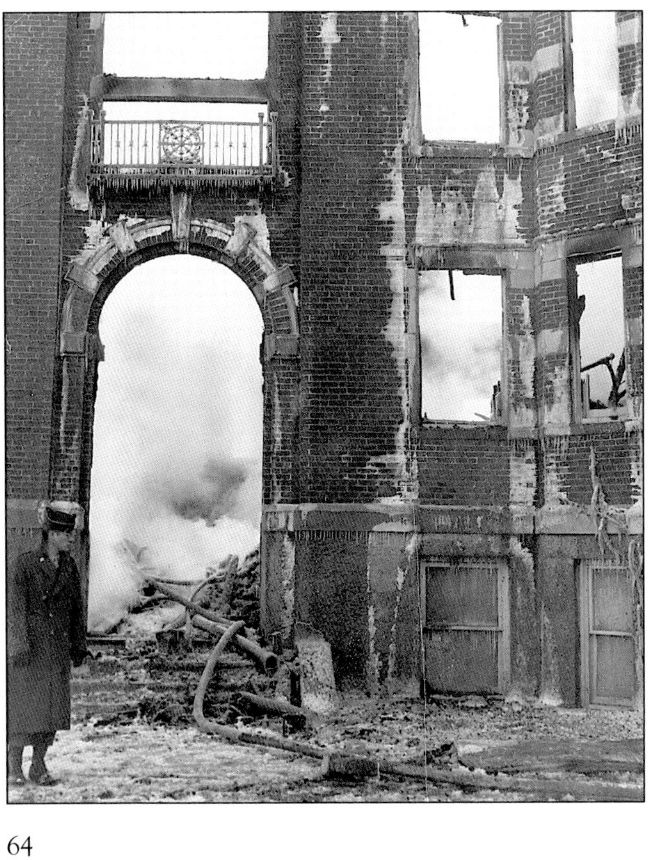

HANNIBAL HAMLIN HALL, C. 1915. Increasing enrollment created the necessity for a new, male dormitory on campus. This four-story building was named in honor of Hannibal Hamlin, president of the first board of trustees. With each floor equipped with bath and toilet facilities as well as a full kitchen and dining room that could accommodate 300 people, former President Fernald said the facility was "bordering on luxury."

OFFICERS OUTSIDE A CHARRED HANNIBAL HAMLIN IN FEBRUARY OF 1944. Despite its claim to be constructed of "fire-proof walls," the building burned in February of 1944. Used to house soldiers during WW II, two enlisted men lost their lives in the blaze and several others were severely injured.

WINGATE HALL ON A WINTER'S DAY IN 1897. The rivalry and race for one-upmanship between classes are evident from a view of the top of this image. Wingate was used at that time as an engineering building with laboratory space on the third floor.

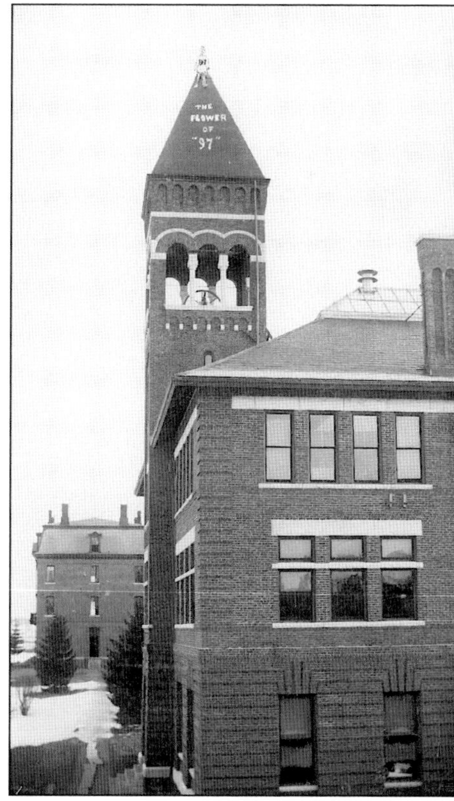

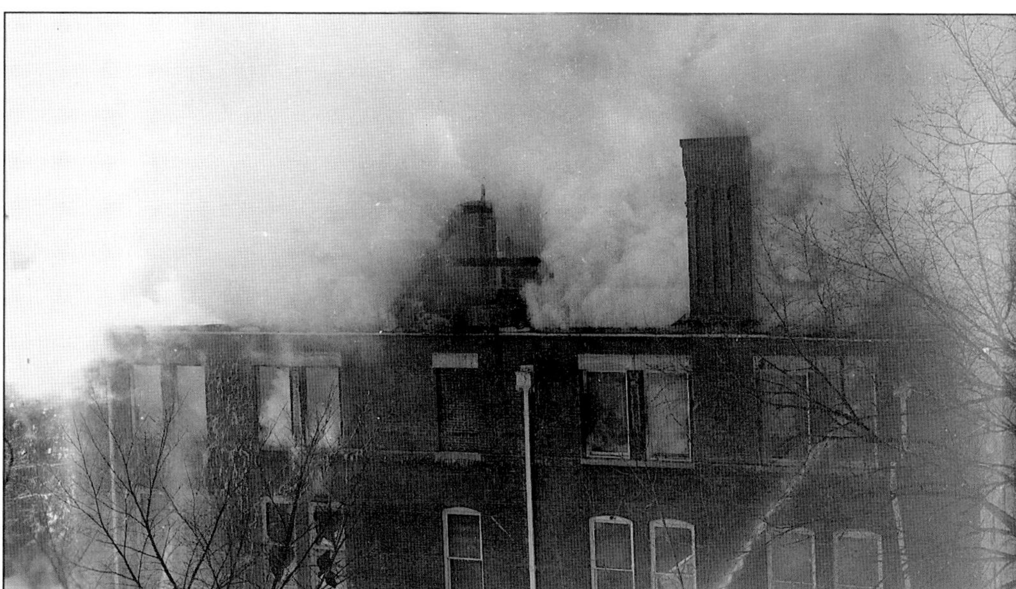

FIRE REVISITS THE ORIGINAL SITE OF WHITE HALL. In the winter of 1946, a fire ravaged through Wingate Hall, destroying the third floor and felling the tower, which have never been rebuilt.

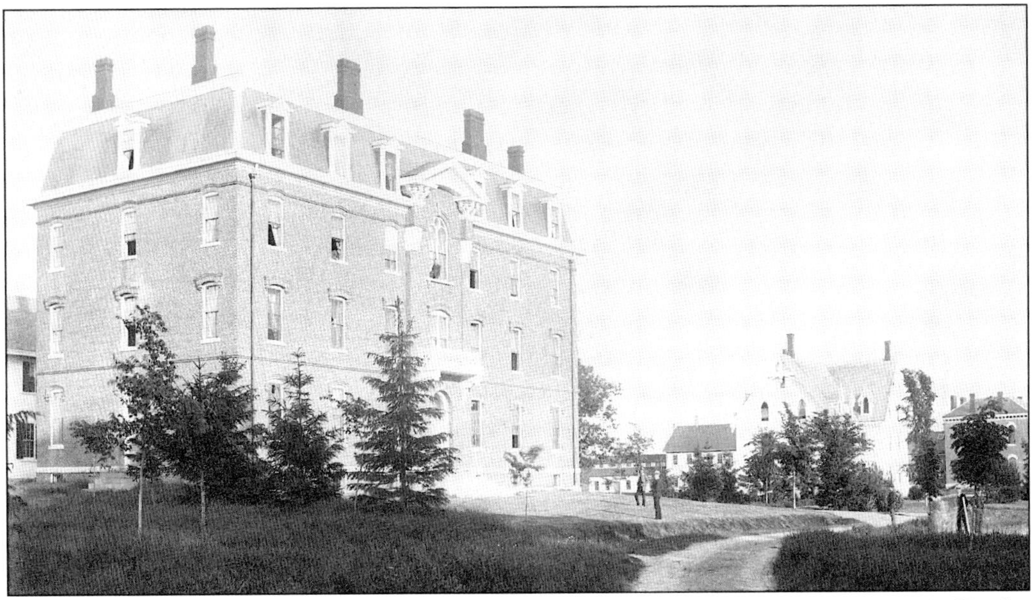

Students Gathering outside Brick Hall, Later Renamed Oak Hall, c. 1885. To the right stands White Hall, with Fernald Hall in the distance. The building, constructed in 1871, was aptly named Brick Hall, being composed almost entirely of bricks manufactured by students. Trustees hoped that the brick structure would be impregnable to fire.

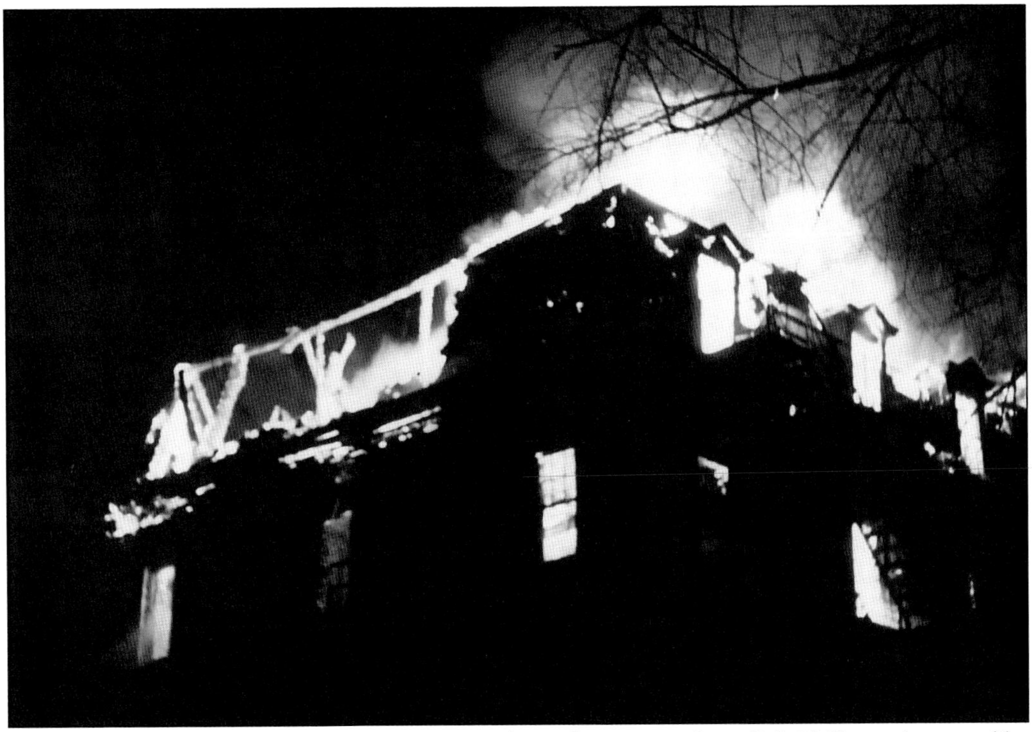

Oak Hall Burns, January 1936. Despite its hope for immortality, Oak Hall was destroyed by fire and replaced by a new dormitory on the same site and bearing the same name.

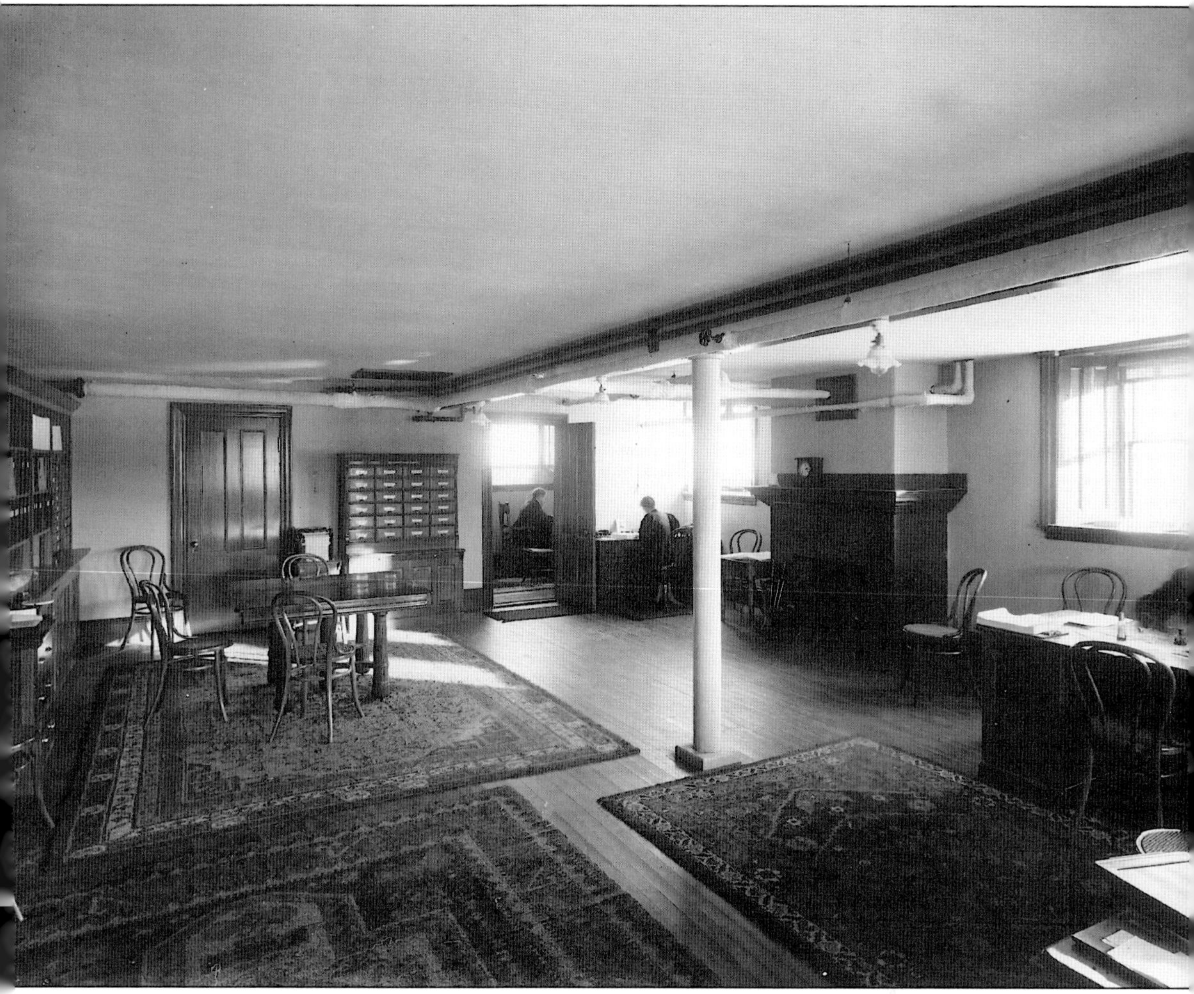

A View inside Coburn Hall, c. 1893. This image offers an interesting view of the president's facility in the basement of Coburn Hall. Note the functional decor enhanced by oriental rugs on the floor. The president's office was formerly located in White Hall, but after its destruction by fire, he may have sought a safer refuge. Seated and at work in the inner room is President Abram Harris. Harris may have been the first president to employ a secretary. She can be seen seated at her desk, in the background.

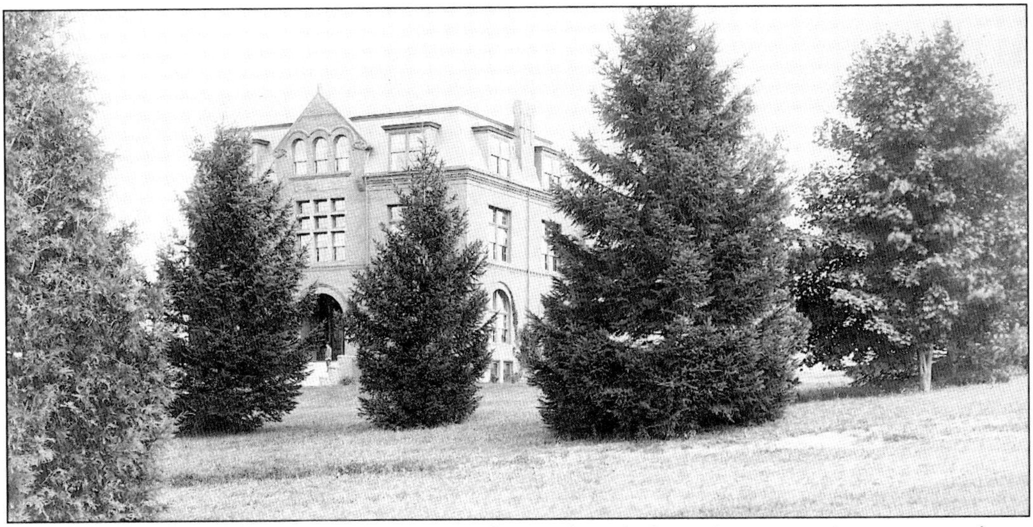

A LANDSCAPE OF COBURN HALL, C. 1900. The unidentified gentlemen on the steps may have been visiting the library on the first floor, a classroom on the second floor, or perhaps the president's office, which was located in the basement.

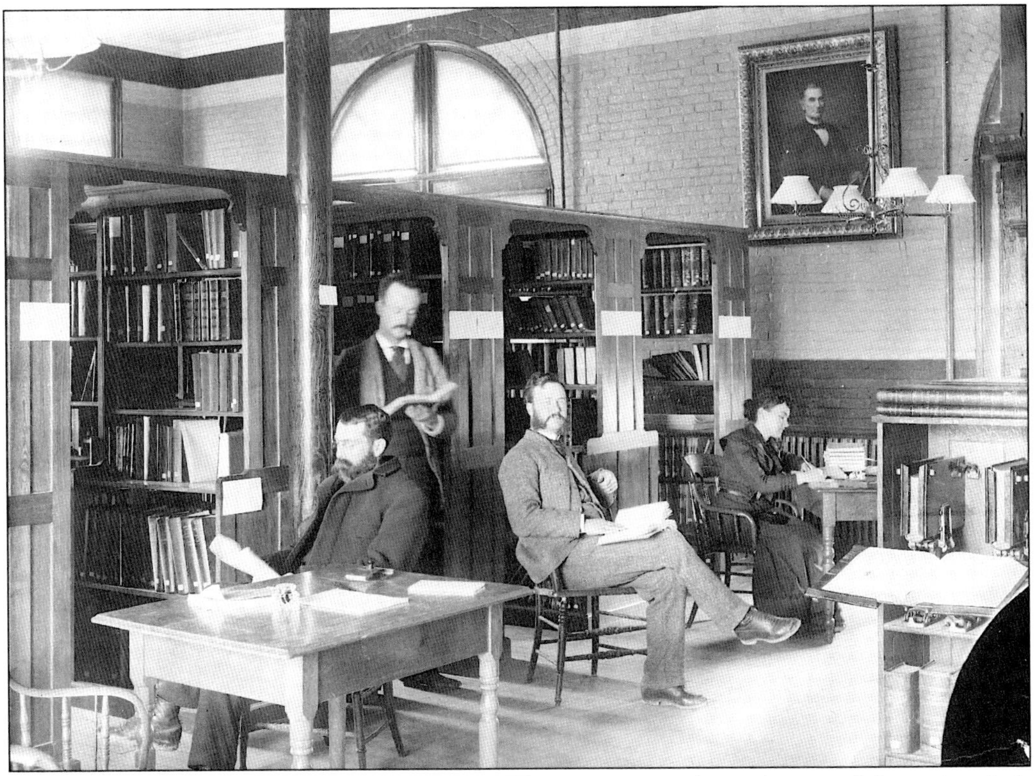

INSIDE THE COBURN HALL LIBRARY, C. 1895. This image provides a glimpse of the university's library space after it had been moved from Fernald Hall to Coburn Hall in 1888. Pictured here, from left to right, are Professor Horace Estabrooke (seated left), student Frank Dammon, Professor Allen Rogers (seated), and librarian Harriet C. Fernald, who introduced the Dewey Decimal System to the library.

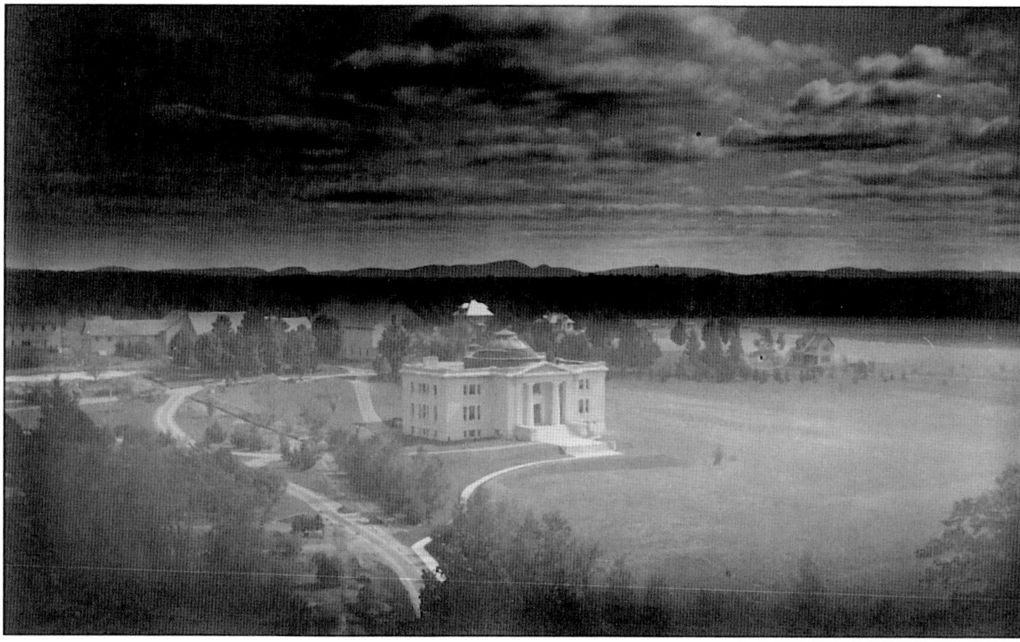

Carnegie Hall Library, c. 1910. This view, perhaps taken from atop the President's House, shows the new library in Carnegie Hall, shortly after its completion in 1910. In the background are the University Barns. The bottom image shows the interior of the library, c. 1920; it did not change appreciably over the next 40 years. The library remained in Carnegie Hall until the Folger Library was completed after the end of WW II. Today, Carnegie Hall houses the art department and gallery.

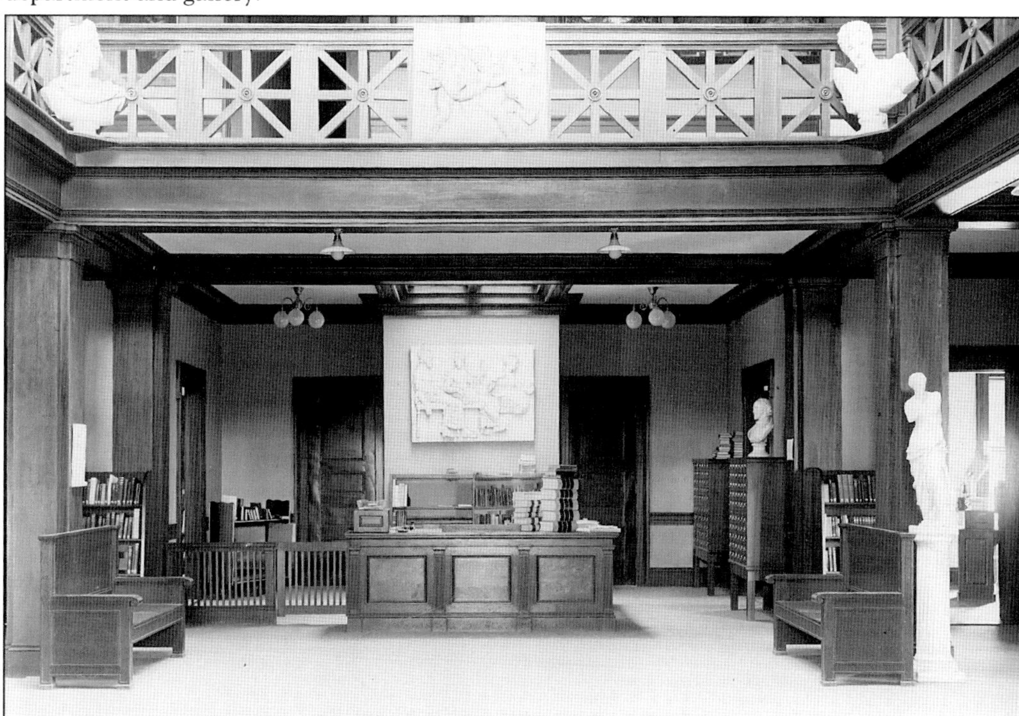

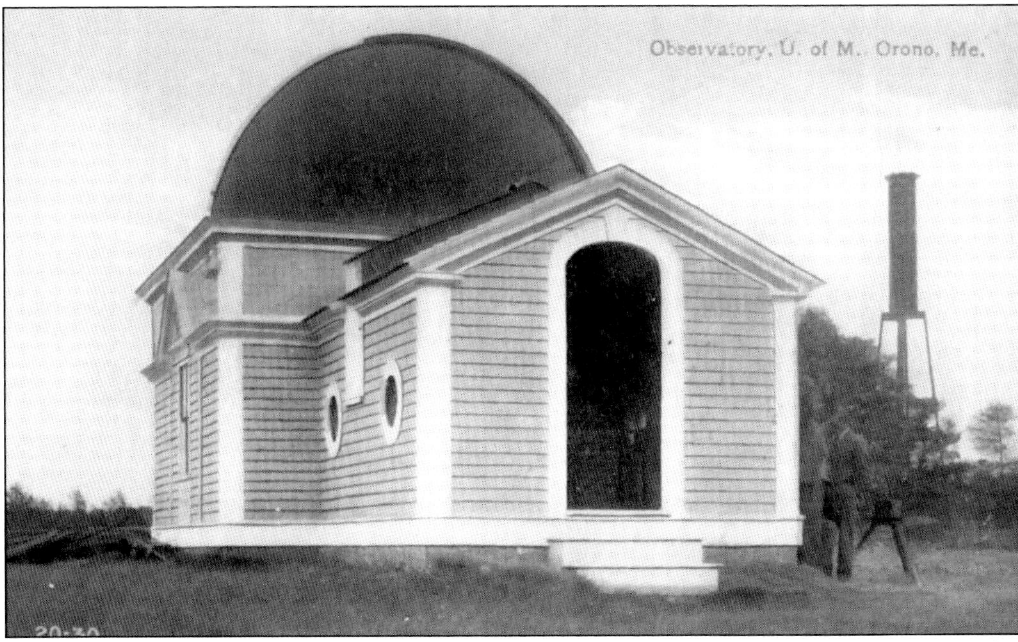

The University Observatory, c. 1905. The stand pipe in the background was used at that time as a precaution in the event of fire. In December of 1890, an Alvan Clark 8-inch refractory telescope was mounted in the observatory, making it the most efficient astronomical laboratory in the state. Courses in astronomy were first taught by Professor Hart and later by Dr. Fernald.

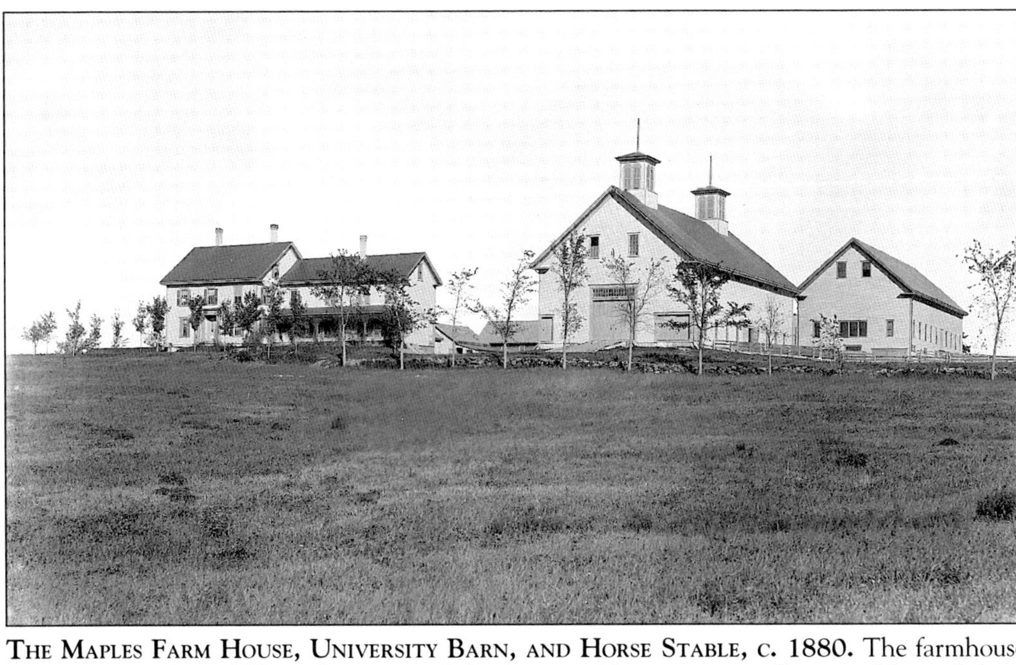

The Maples Farm House, University Barn, and Horse Stable, c. 1880. The farmhouse was constructed in 1877 on this site, and the horse stable was eventually moved here. It later served as the residence of Professor Walter and Elizabeth Balentine, who graciously offered the residence to the Fernalds after the President's House was damaged by fire in 1893.

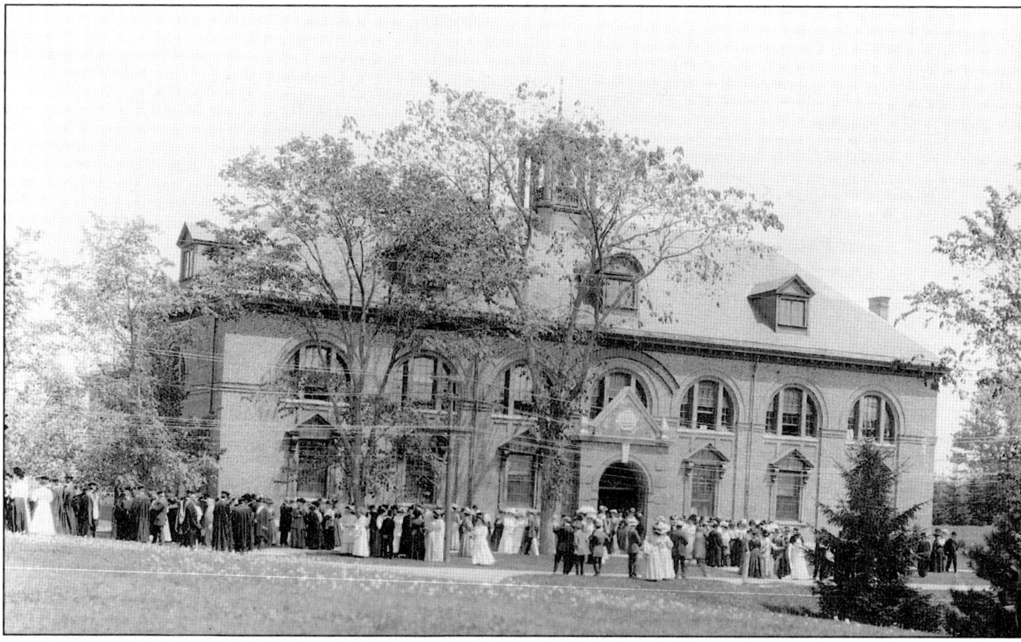

An Early Gathering outside Alumni Hall, c. 1901. The image is possibly that of the building's dedication, which took place in 1901. The two-story building, funded primarily from contributions by alumni, was designed to be a drill hall for the Coburn Cadets and a gymnasium for athletics and physical education classes. The first floor housed administrative office space.

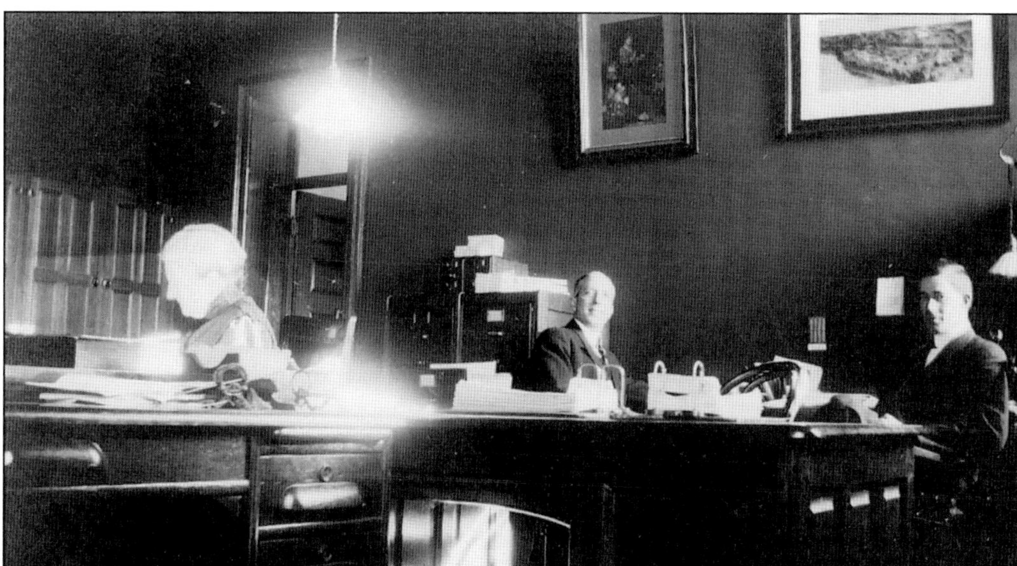

A View inside the First Floor of Alumni Hall, c. 1912. Shown in this photograph of the registrar's office are Elizabeth Balentine (registrar), Edgar Wingard (director of athletics), and James Gannett (commercial secretary).

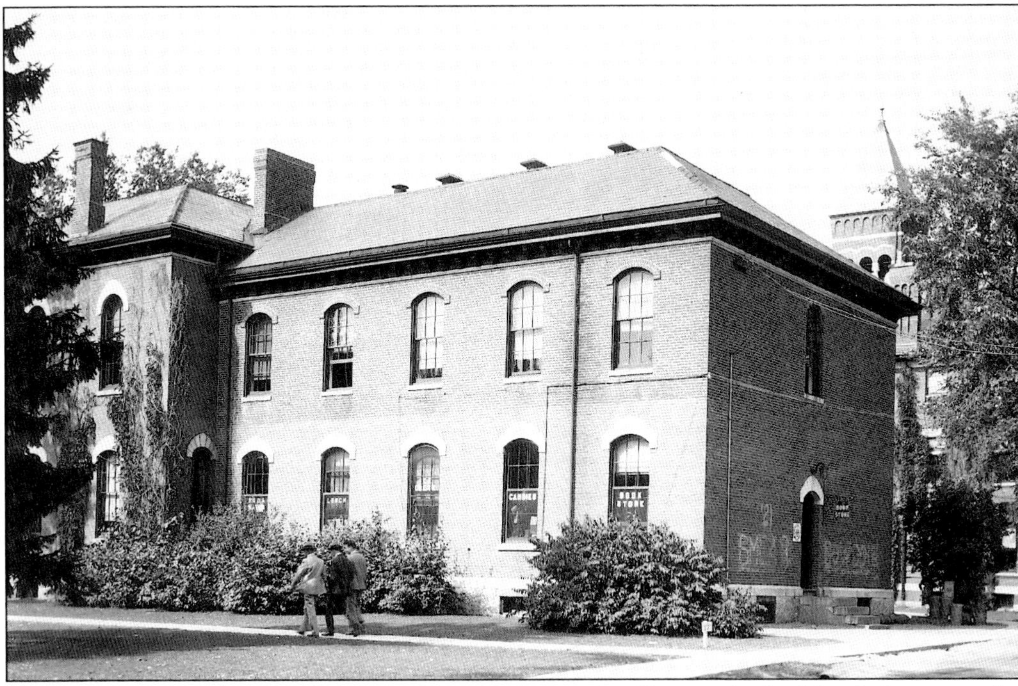

The Pathway alongside Fernald Hall, c. 1920. Graffiti on the building's front signifies the campus was gearing up for an athletic match with interstate rival Bowdoin. On November 2, 1895, fire damaged, but did not destroy, this historic building originally known as Chemical Hall. The building was renovated in 1896 and renamed Fernald Hall in honor of former president Merritt Caldwell Fernald.

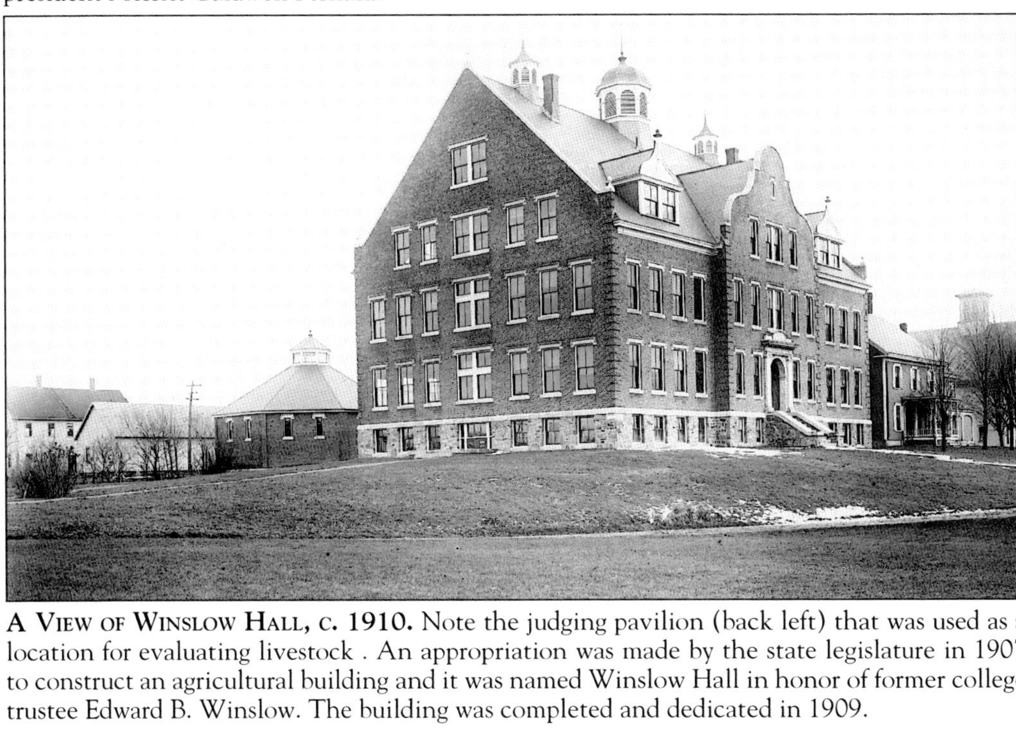

A View of Winslow Hall, c. 1910. Note the judging pavilion (back left) that was used as a location for evaluating livestock . An appropriation was made by the state legislature in 1907 to construct an agricultural building and it was named Winslow Hall in honor of former college trustee Edward B. Winslow. The building was completed and dedicated in 1909.

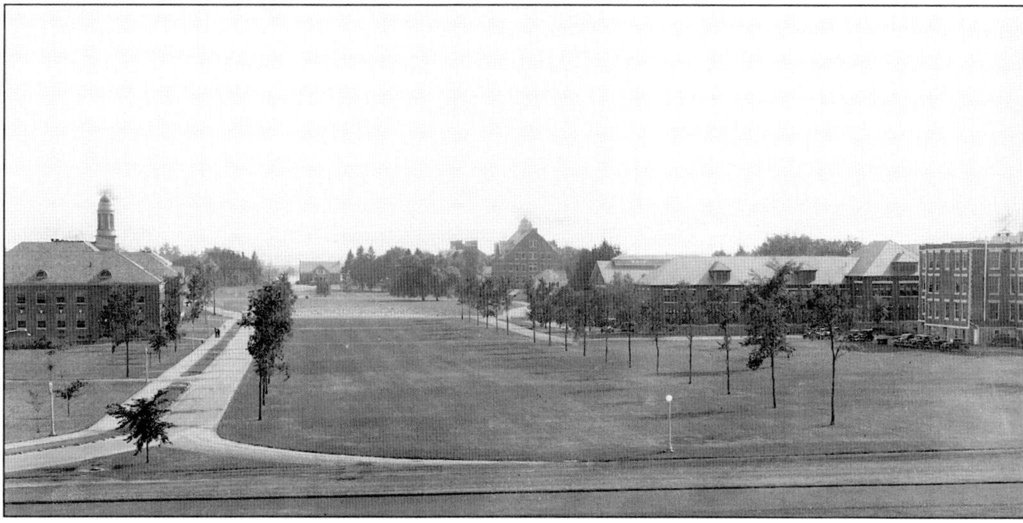

A 1930s View of the Campus Commons, with Folger Library Conspicuously Absent. The Clapp Building is shown in the center, behind the site on which the Folger Library now stands. In 1866, the board of trustees engaged noted landscape architect Frederick Law Olmstead to draft a plan for the college grounds that was ultimately rejected. In 1933, a new plan was developed by the Olmstead brothers' firm, descendants of Frederick Law Olmstead, for a new campus plan with the commons as a focal point.

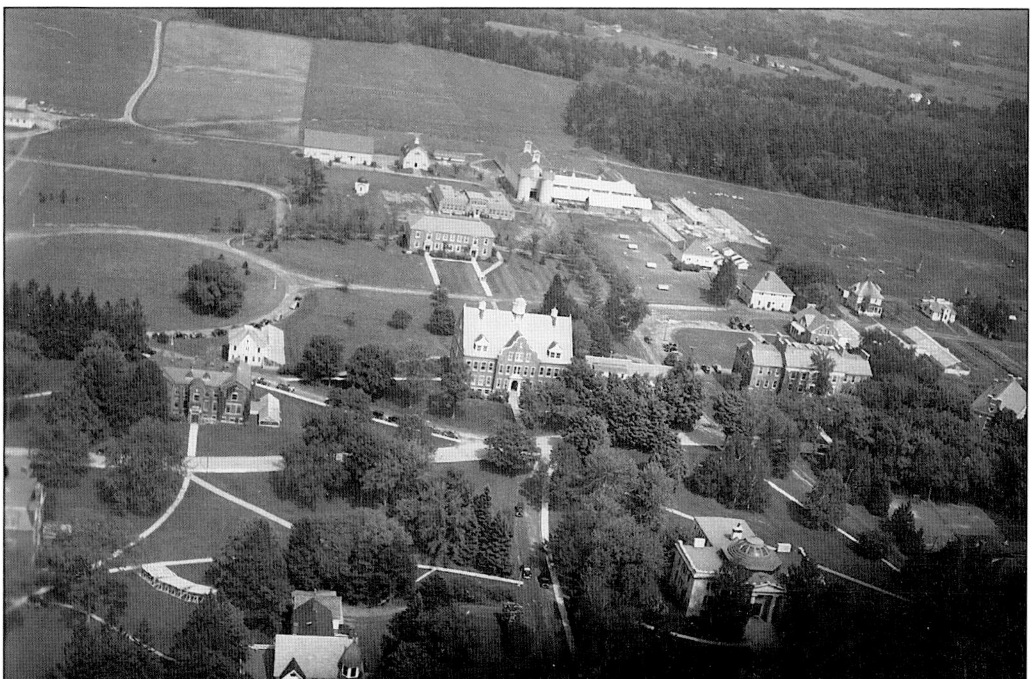

An Aerial Photograph of the Picturesque Campus, c. 1930. From left to right are Holmes Hall, Winslow Hall, Carnegie Hall, and the President's House.

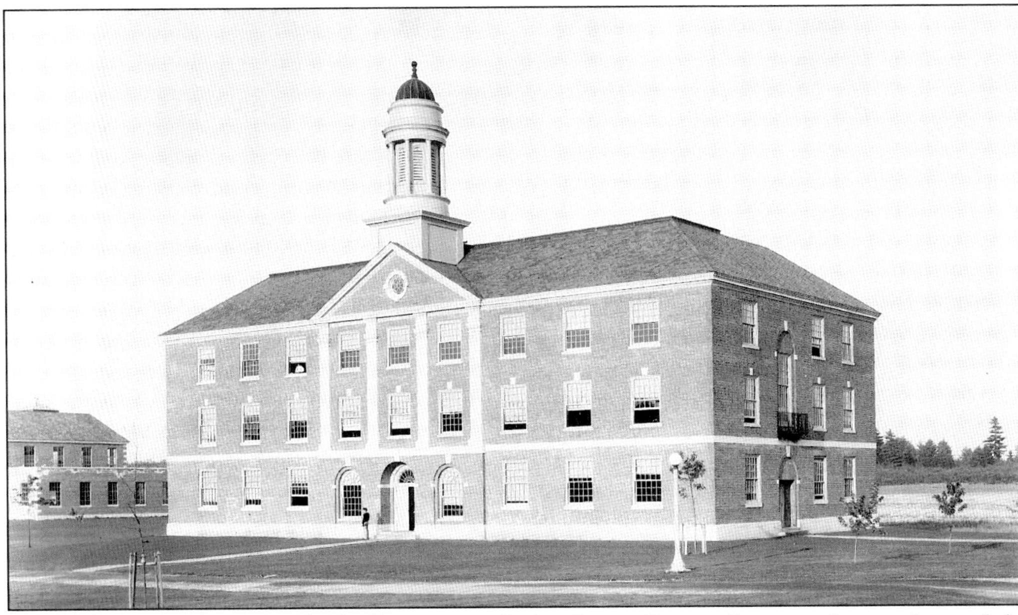

STEVENS HALL, C. 1925. The hall was named after James Stacey Stevens, former dean of the College of Arts and Sciences. Built in 1924, Stevens Hall was the original building for the College of Arts and Science. North and south wings of Stevens Hall were added at a later date and the entire building was dedicated on June 9, 1934.

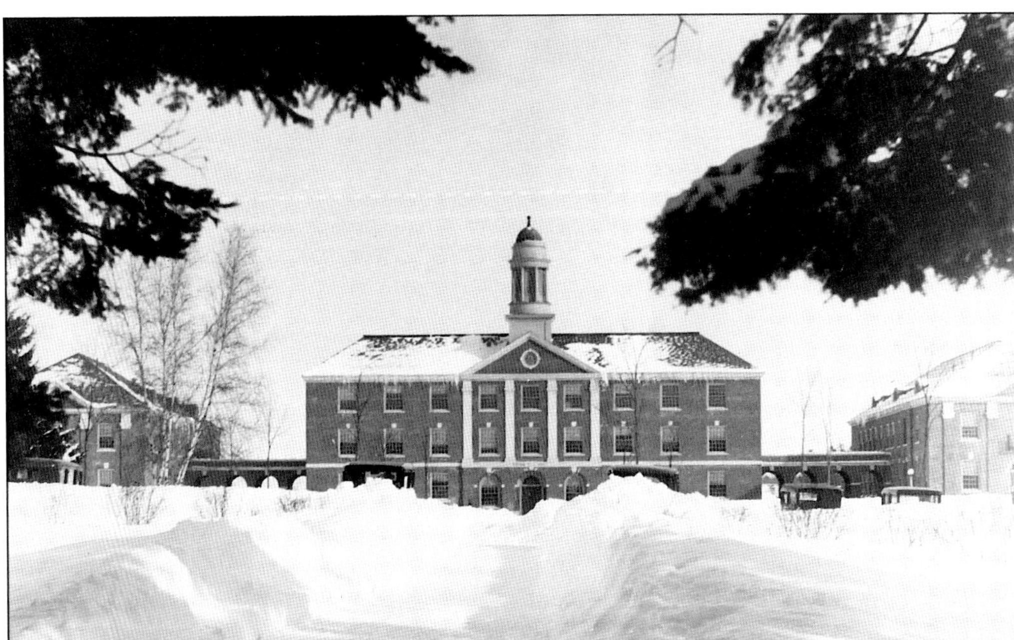

A COMPLETED STEVENS HALL WITH WINGS ADDED, C. 1935. Drifting snow banks seem to cover the first floor of Stevens and rise above the level of the automobiles bound in the parking lot.

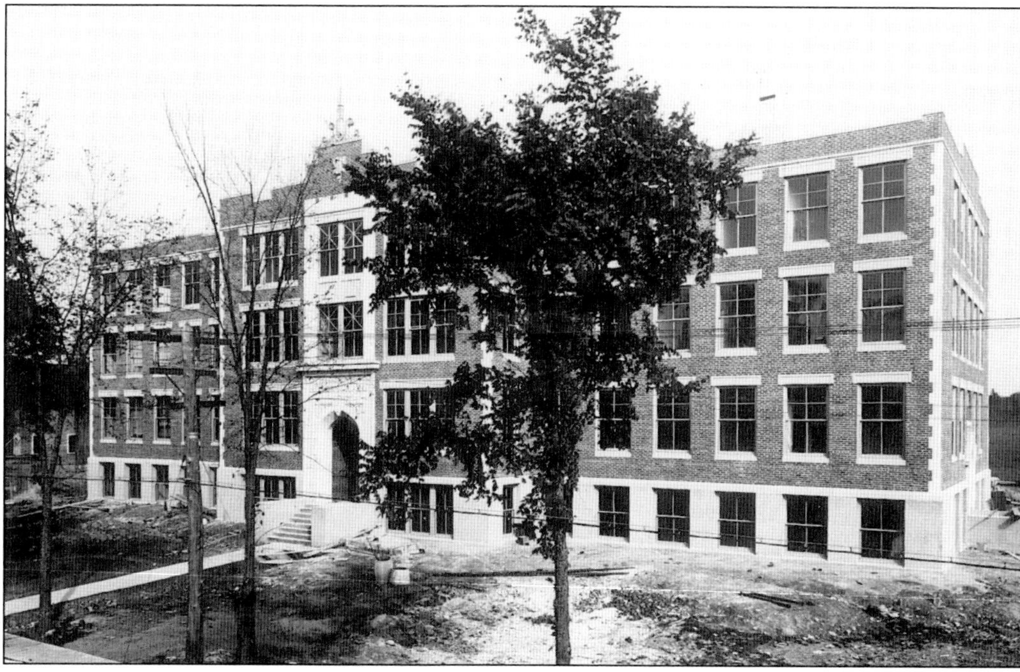

A VIEW OF AUBERT HALL SHORTLY AFTER ITS COMPLETION IN 1914. The building was named in honor of Alfred B. Aubert, the first professor of chemistry at the college, and it first served as the chemistry and physics building. Like many other buildings on campus, the structure has been added to and modified over the years.

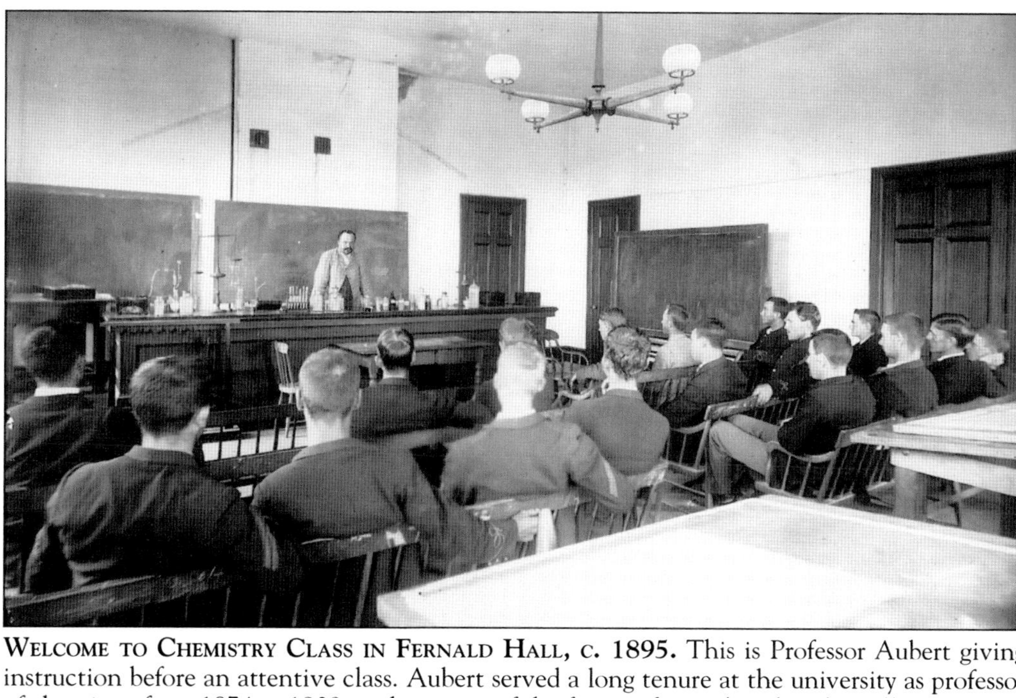

WELCOME TO CHEMISTRY CLASS IN FERNALD HALL, C. 1895. This is Professor Aubert giving instruction before an attentive class. Aubert served a long tenure at the university as professor of chemistry from 1874 to 1909, and was one of the first professors hired at the college.

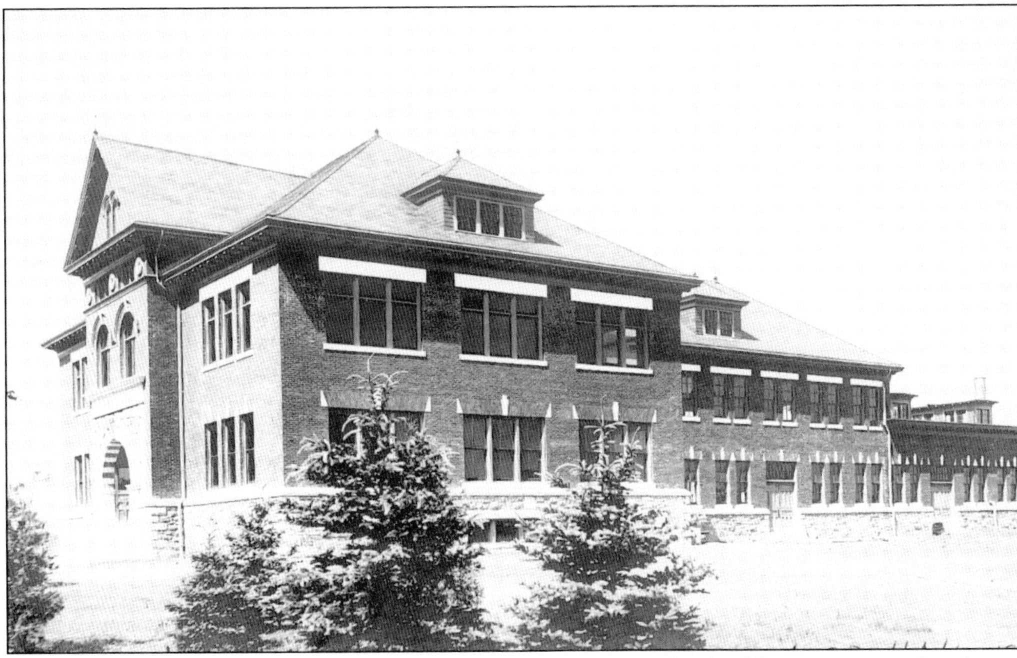

LORD HALL, SHORTLY AFTER ITS CONSTRUCTION IN 1904. The building was named in honor of Hon. Henry Lord, president of the board of trustees and an advocate of the university in the Maine Legislature. Its construction marked an effort to provide each major division of the college with a building.

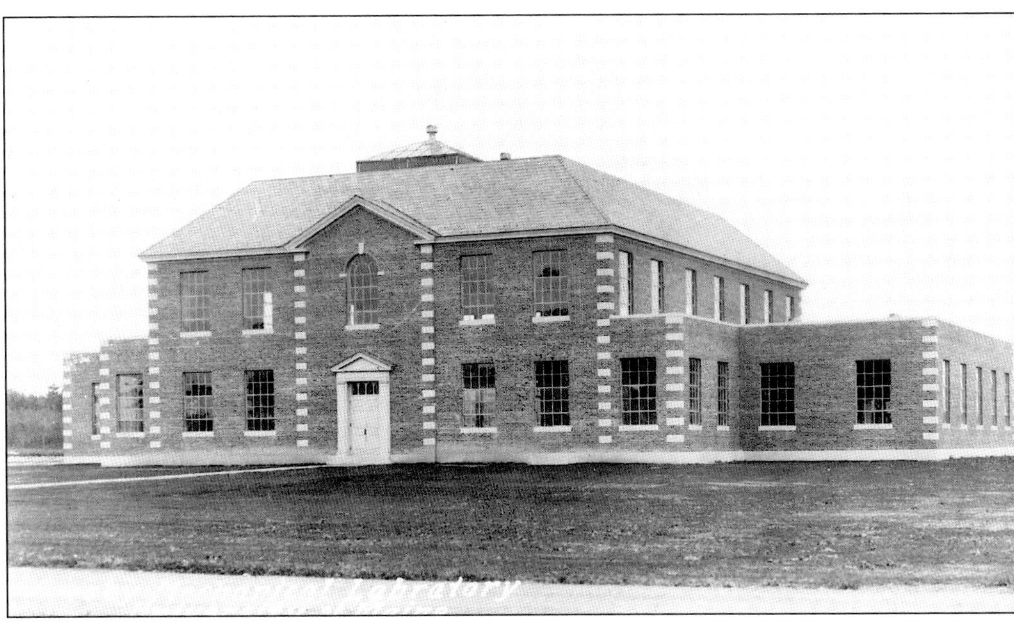

A VIEW OF THE CROSBY LABORATORY, C. 1930. An endowment of $400,000 was left by alumnus Oliver Crosby (class of 1876) to the school in 1923. The money was used to build a laboratory named for Crosby that was not completed until 1926.

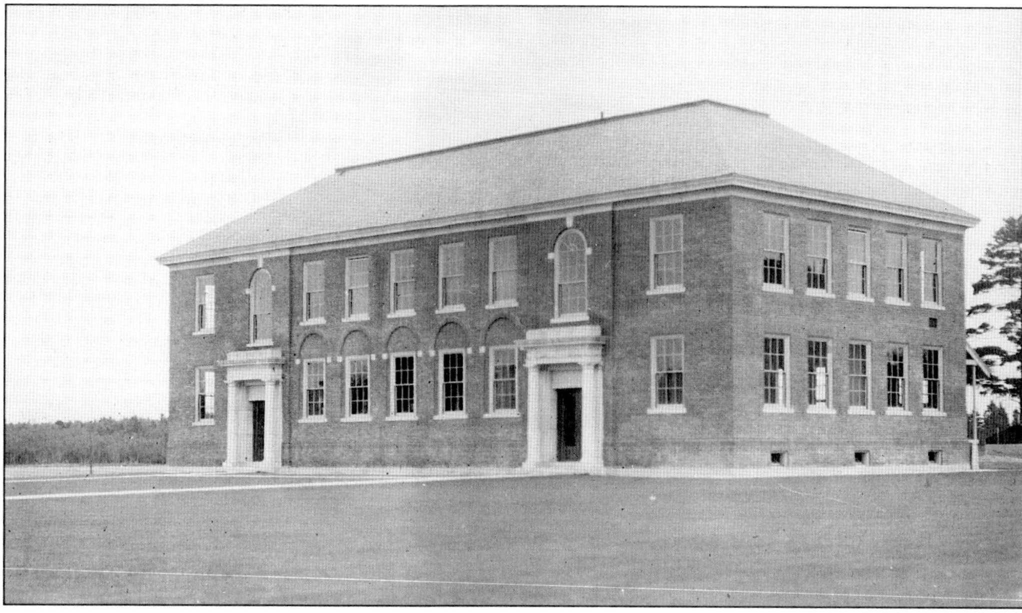

ROGERS HALL, SEPTEMBER 6, 1928. Named after Professor Lore Rogers, the building was first used as a laboratory for mechanical engineers.

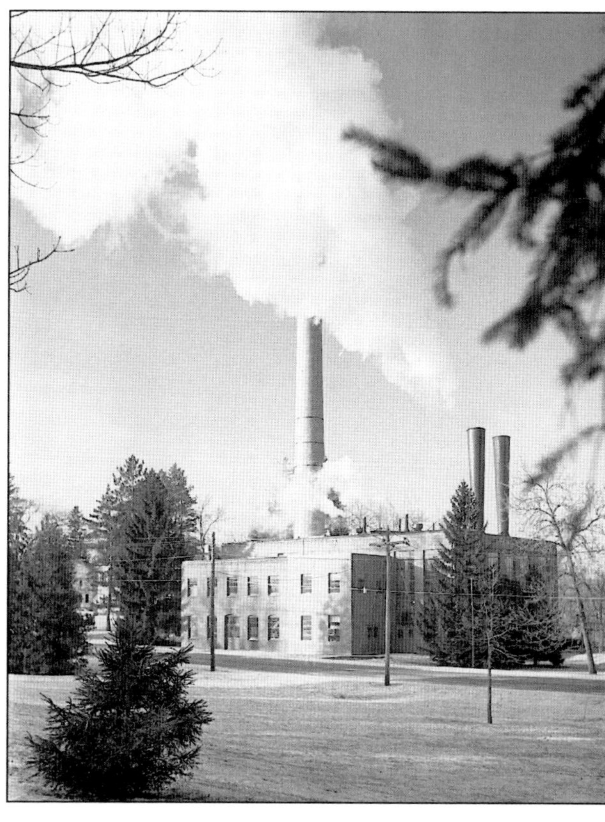

A VIEW OF THE CAMPUS HEATING AND POWER PLANT. Since 1907, this has been the best friend of many students on cold winter nights. In 1899, the university made the decision to move away from wood and coal furnaces to heat campus buildings. A pumping station was installed by the Stillwater River to produce steam heat, which was piped around campus.

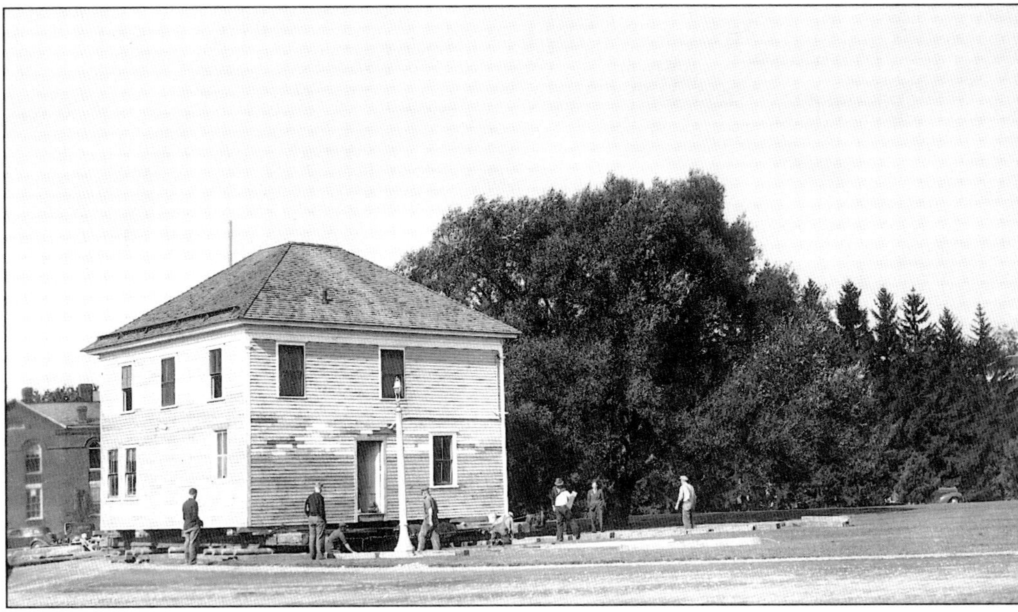

AN AGRICULTURAL BUILDING ON THE MOVE, C. 1935. During the university's first 70 years, several campus buildings were uprooted and relocated, including fraternity houses, barns, and faculty lodgings.

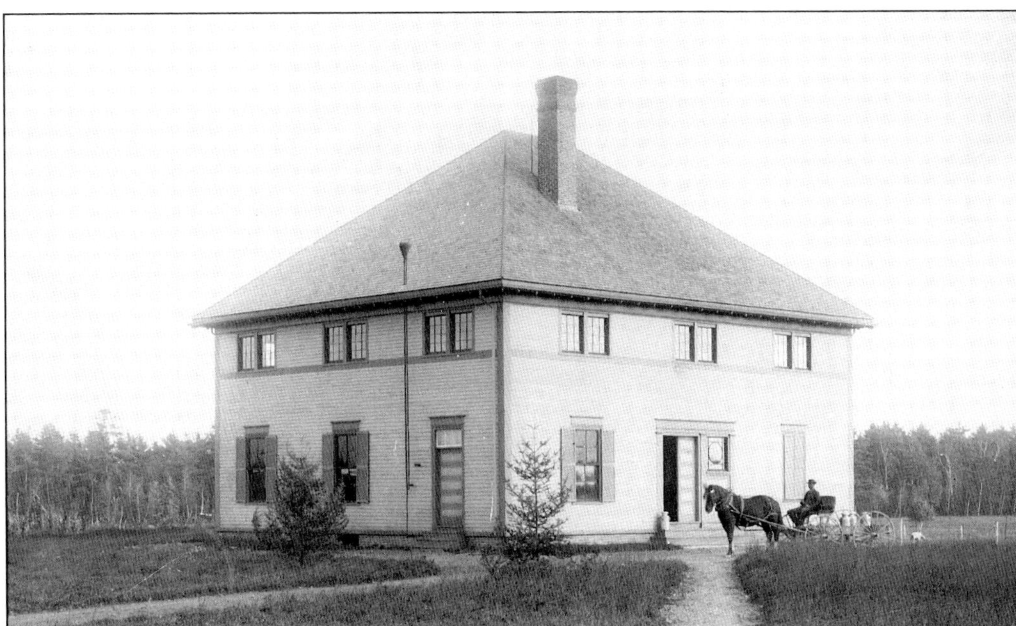

A HORSE-DRAWN CARRIAGE OUTSIDE THE DAIRY AND CREAMERY BUILDING, C. 1880. From its earliest days, a major objective of the college has been to promote agricultural research, expanding the scope of the university well beyond the Orono campus. The Highmoor Farm in Monmouth, the Aroostook Farm in Presque Isle, and the Blueberry Farm in Jonesboro have all contributed to this original goal.

Four

Sports

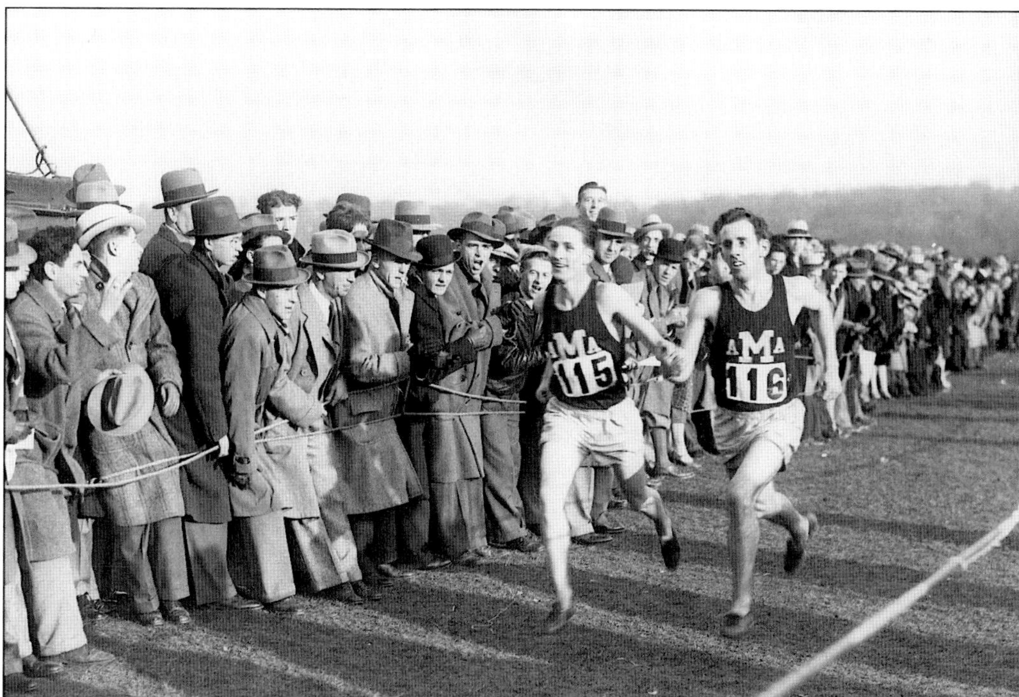

MAINE TRACKMEN FRANCIS LINDSAY AND HENRY RICHARDSON ARE CHEERED ON IN A DEAD-HEAT RUN TO THE FINISH AT AN INTERCOLLEGIATE TRACK MEET ON NOVEMBER 25, 1929. Sports have long played a significant role in the lives and development of students at the university. An early record states that boxing was the first sport participated in by U. Maine students. A form of Rugby was played by early students and may have been the second, followed by baseball and football. From the humble origins of using borrowed equipment and playing on primitive athletic fields marked out by students, athletics has evolved on campus. From informal games, often between faculty and students, to intercollegiate matches, athletic competition has and continues to play a prominent role in campus life.

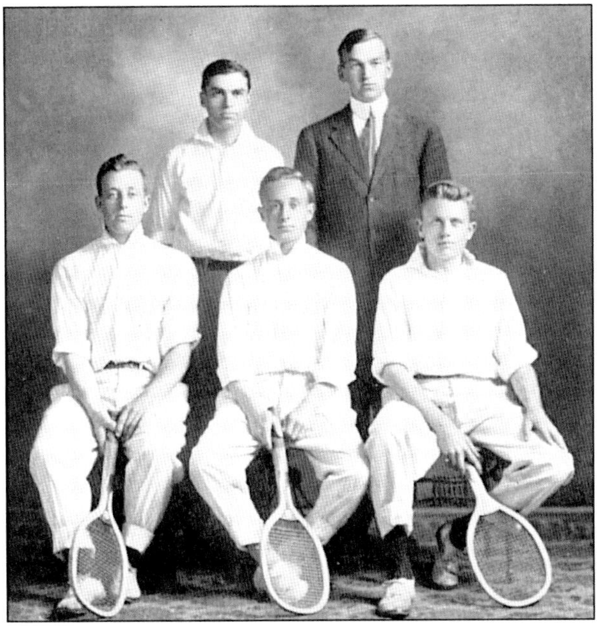

THE MEN'S VARSITY TENNIS TEAM OF 1910. Tennis as a club, intramural sport, and intercollegiate varsity sport has been played on the Maine campus for more than a century. Beginning in 1905, the University of Maine fielded a tennis team that has played a consistent schedule except for interruption during WW I and in the 1920s. Women's varsity tennis did not start until 1975.

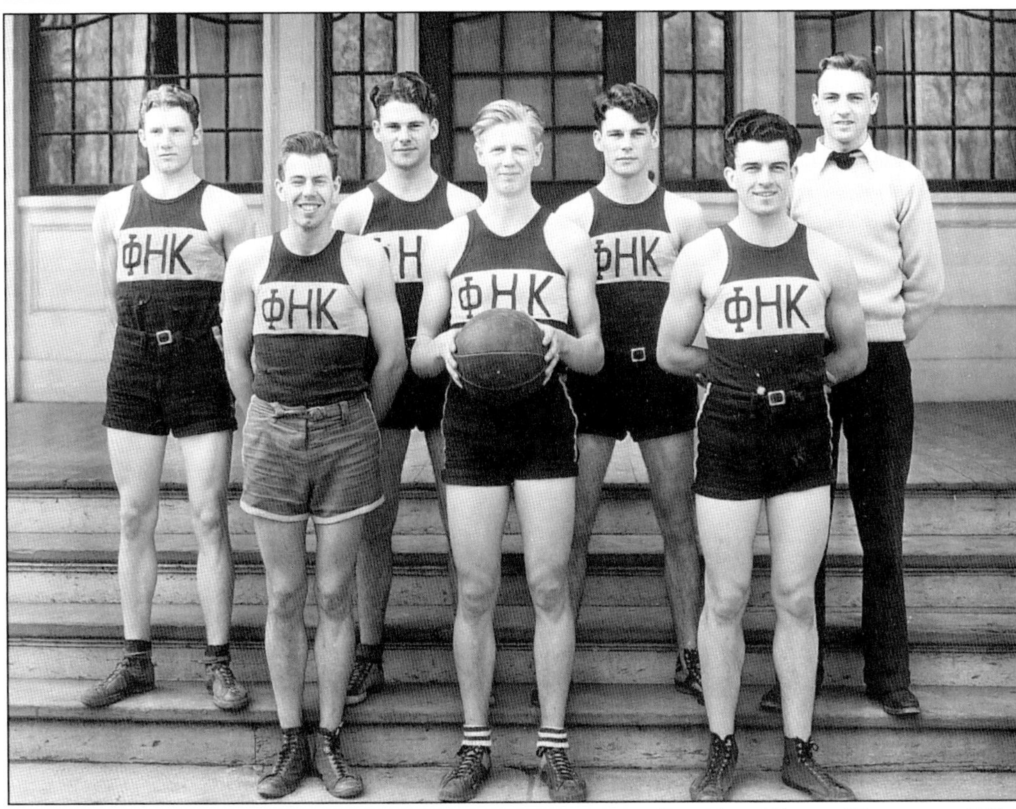

A FRATERNITY BASKETBALL TEAM POSES IN FRONT OF THE PHI ETA KAPPA HOUSE IN 1931. Intramural sports have been a part of college life since the 1880s, spawning rivalries between classes and fraternities. Although games between faculty and students occurred frequently, athletics were frowned upon by early administrators, fearing they detracted from academics.

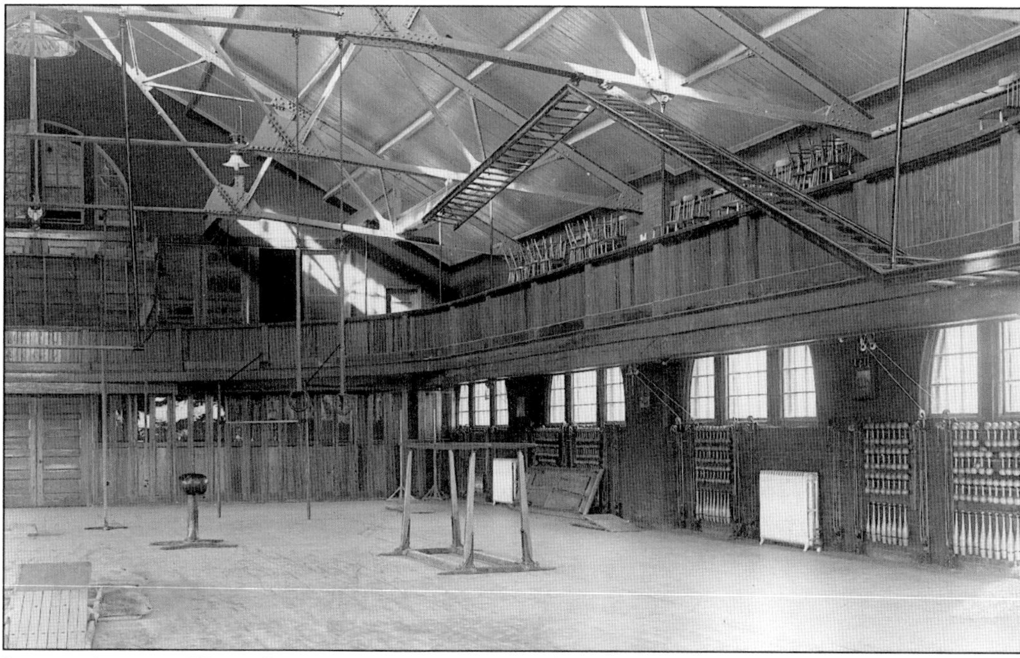

Inside Alumni Hall Gymnasium in 1916. Built almost entirely by funds from university alumni, the facility quickly became a mecca for student activities as well as athletic events. Dances, chapel services, political rallies, and athletic events were held here. The second-floor space was actually the college's second gymnasium; the first was a converted forge shop that was built in 1882.

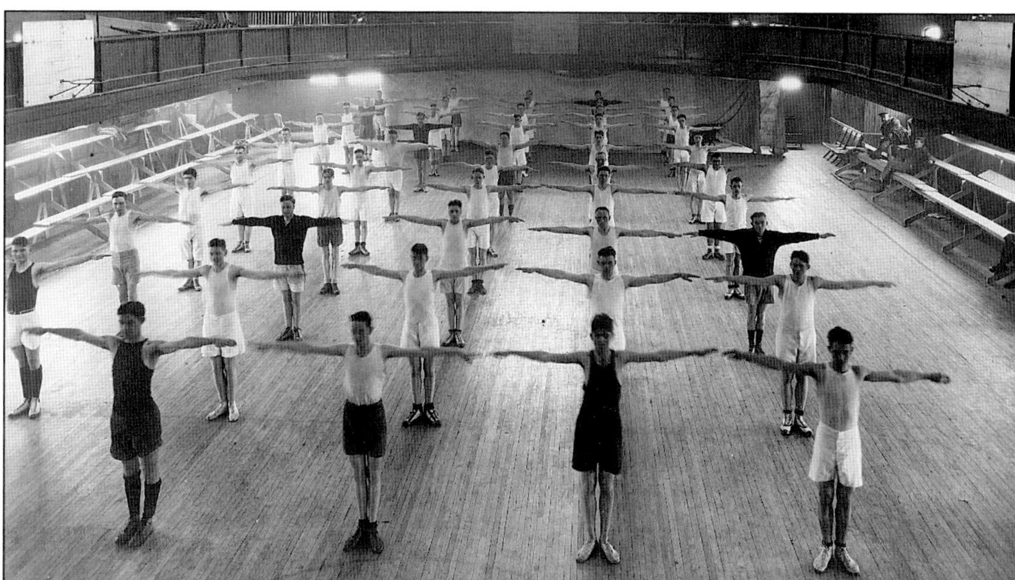

A Physical Education Class in the Gymnasium at Alumni Hall, c. 1920. The presence of the basketball rim and backboard as well as a marked floor and bleachers show that games were being played at this time. In 1906, physical education became a requirement and a full-time instructor was hired. The 1901 *Prism* acknowledged that "there is no better preventative of nervous exhaustion than regular, unhurried, muscular exercise."

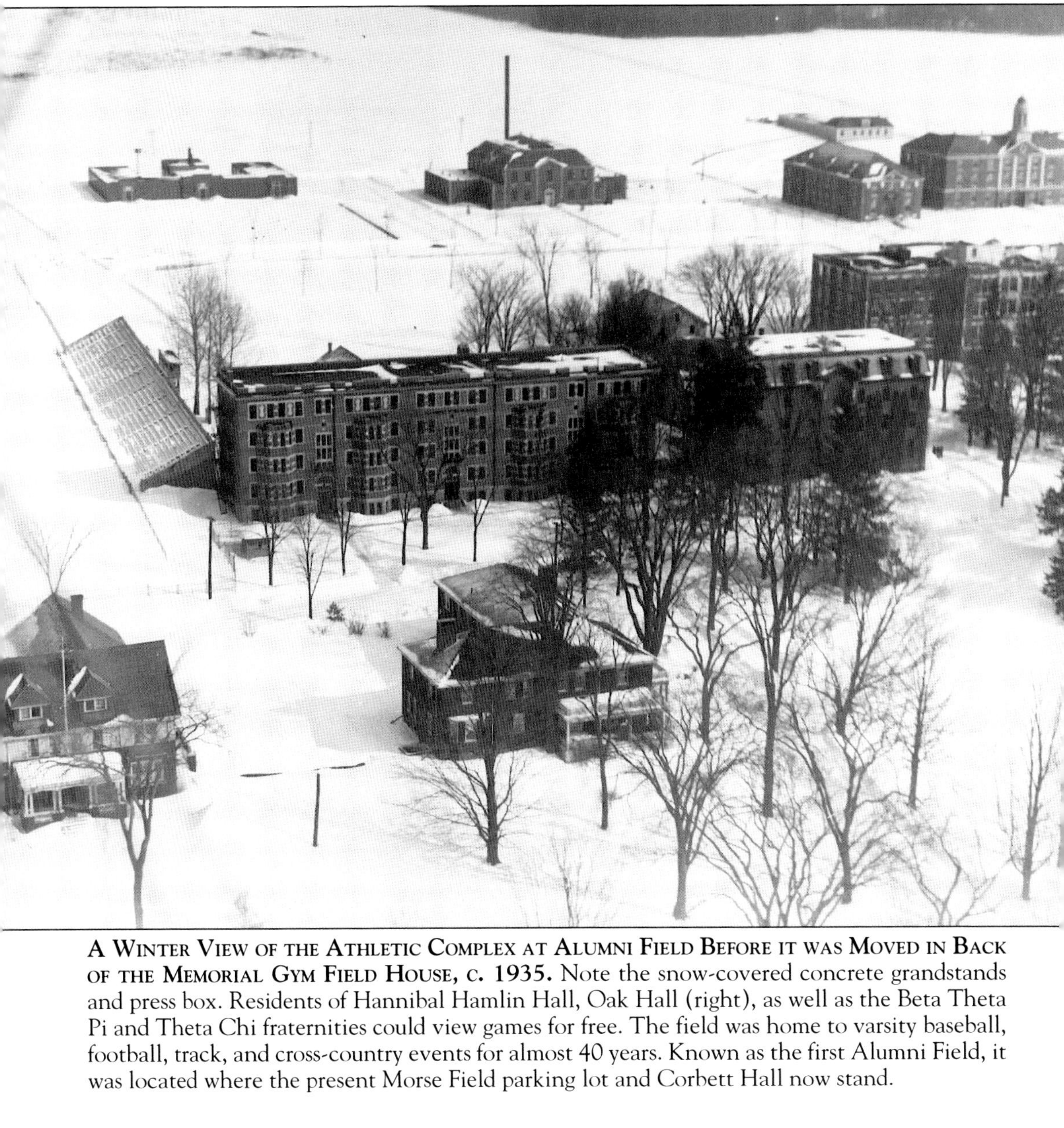

A Winter View of the Athletic Complex at Alumni Field Before it was Moved in Back of the Memorial Gym Field House, c. 1935. Note the snow-covered concrete grandstands and press box. Residents of Hannibal Hamlin Hall, Oak Hall (right), as well as the Beta Theta Pi and Theta Chi fraternities could view games for free. The field was home to varsity baseball, football, track, and cross-country events for almost 40 years. Known as the first Alumni Field, it was located where the present Morse Field parking lot and Corbett Hall now stand.

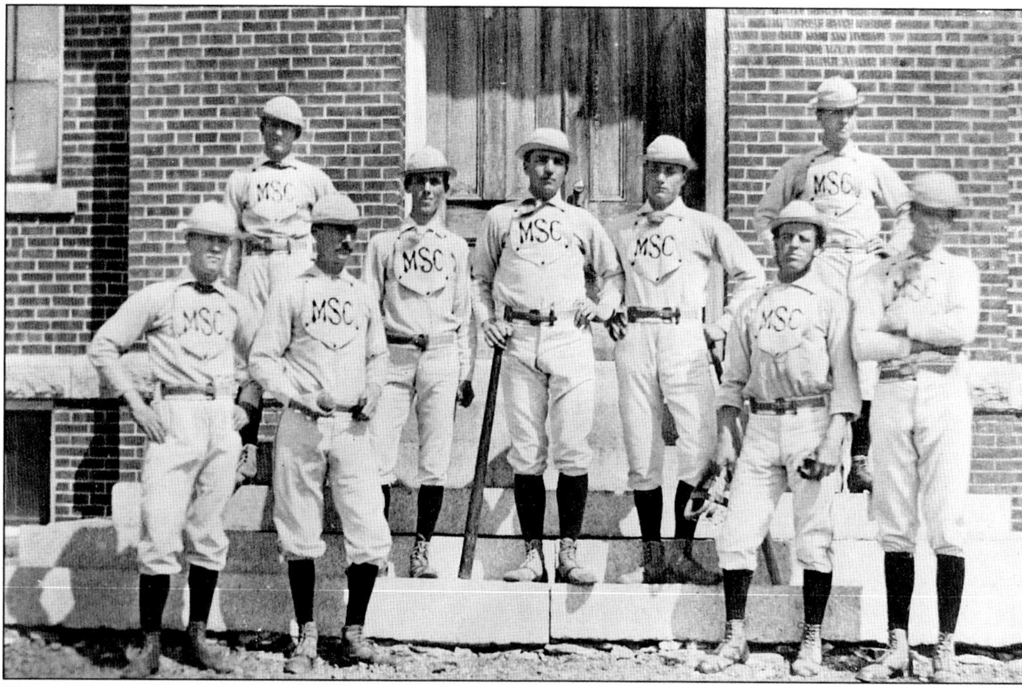

THE MAINE STATE COLLEGE BASEBALL TEAM DURING ITS INAUGURAL CAMPAIGN IN 1881. Baseball stands as the oldest sanctioned sport at the university. The first official game was played in 1881, but there is record of intramural activity before that. In 1885 an interstate league was formed with a nine-game schedule; however, lack of intercollegiate opponents nearly canceled the program in 1886. Early opponents included area high schools, YMCAs, and semi-pro teams.

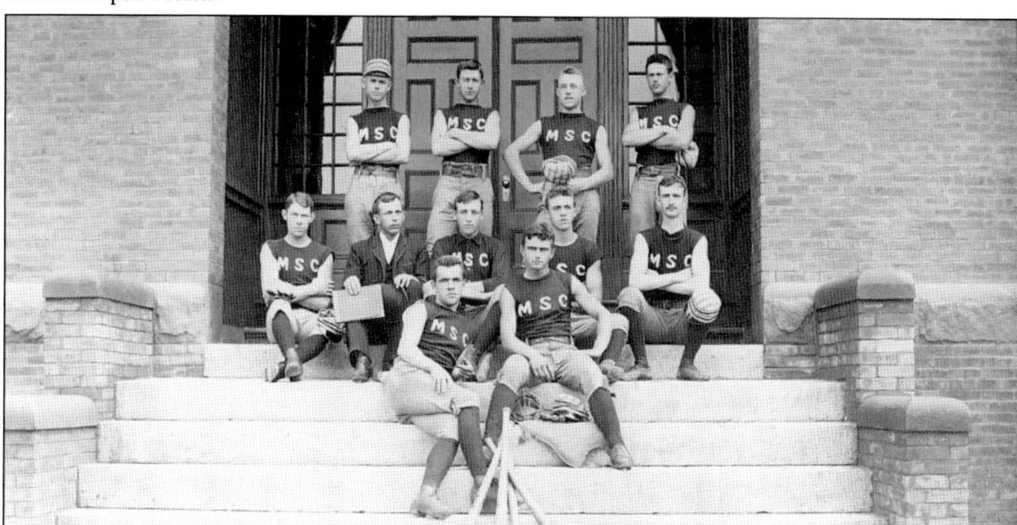

THE MAINE STATE COLLEGE BASEBALL TEAM, OUTSIDE OF COBURN HALL IN 1891. The catcher's mask and chest protector are recent innovations to the sport. Maine chalked up its first intercollegiate victory in 1881, a 15-5 victory over archrival Colby. Coached by students until 1894, the team practiced on a field where Aubert Hall now stands and played its home games at Maple Wood Park in Bangor.

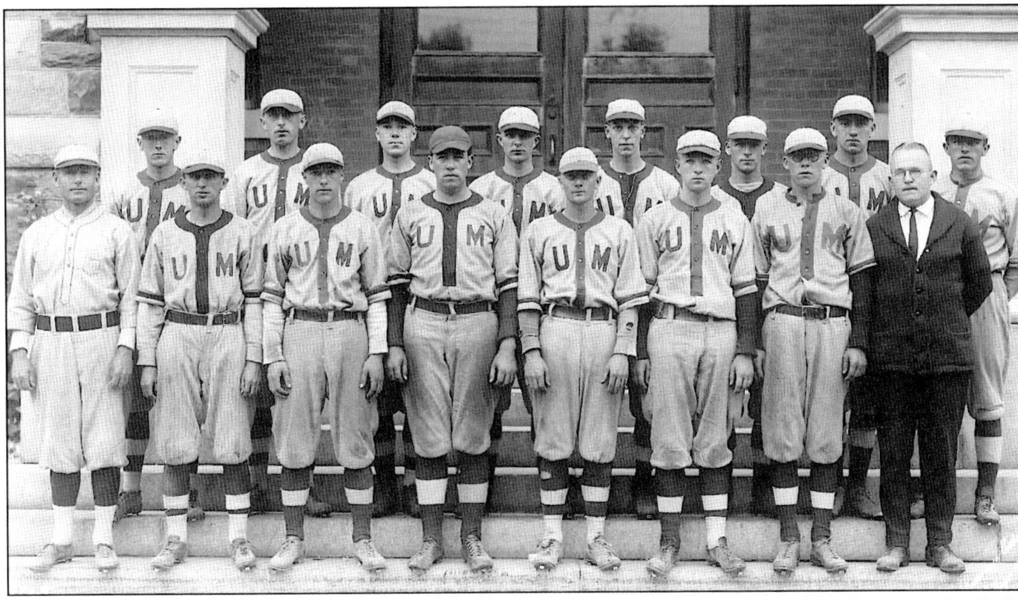

The University of Maine Baseball Team in the early 1900s. In 1902, the team had the rare opportunity to travel to the Polo Grounds in New York City, to face John McGraw's New York Giants in an exhibition game. Before losing, the Maine team made a good showing against the professionals. After 1900, Maine baseball teams began to travel out of state and played Ivy League schools such as Brown and Harvard as well in-state rivals Bowdoin, Bates, and Colby.

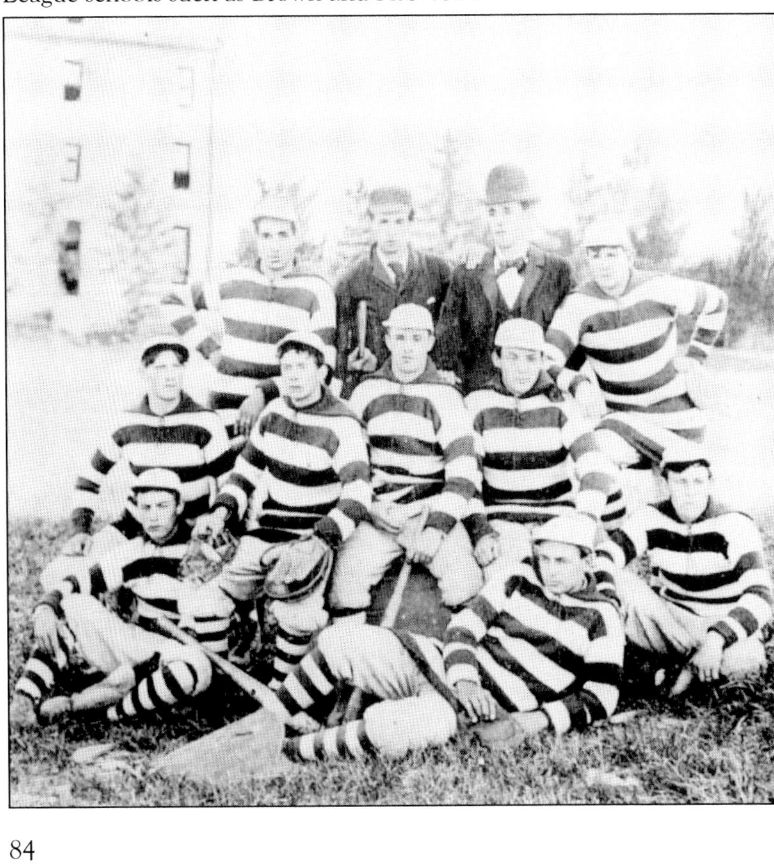

Jail Break? The Maine State College baseball team appears in stripes in 1895. They were winners of the Maine Intercollegiate Pennant that year. Popular as a sandlot sport on campus, administration considered baseball to be a distraction and begrudged practice times and proposed away-game schedules.

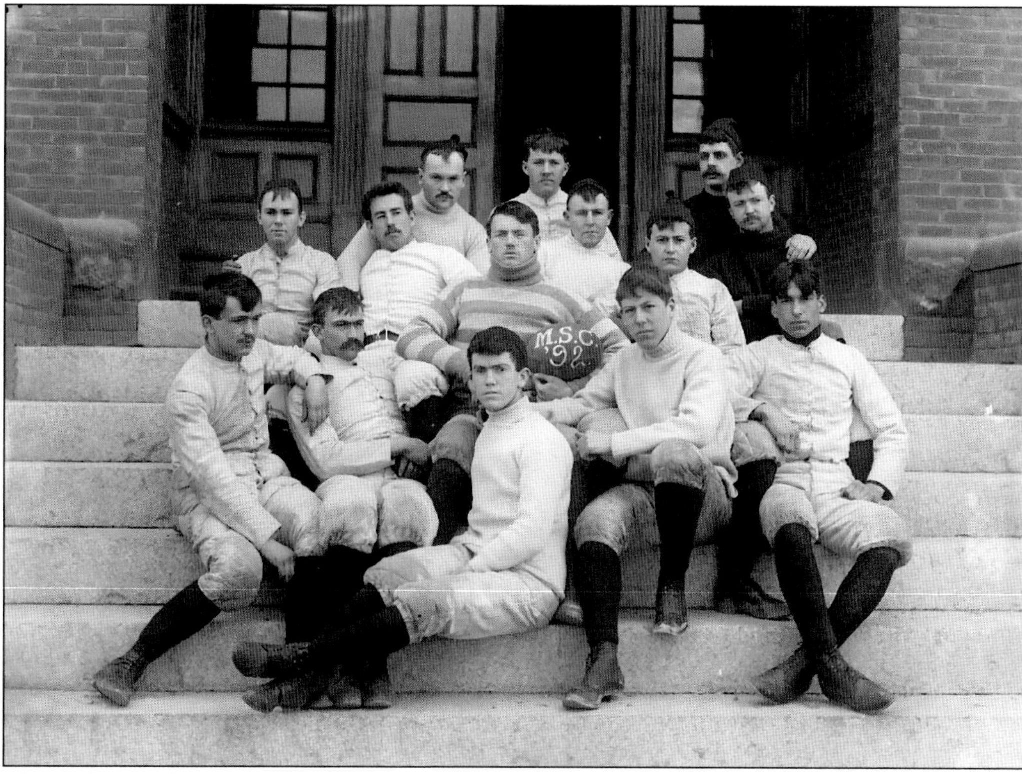

MAINE STATE COLLEGE'S FIRST FOOTBALL TEAM, OUTSIDE COBURN HALL IN 1892. Although the sport was played earlier on campus, the first organized team appeared in 1890 and played its first official game against Bangor High School, a 14-0 loss. The football schedule in the 1890s included games against Colby, Bates, Bowdoin, Edward Little High School, MCI, and New Hampshire State College.

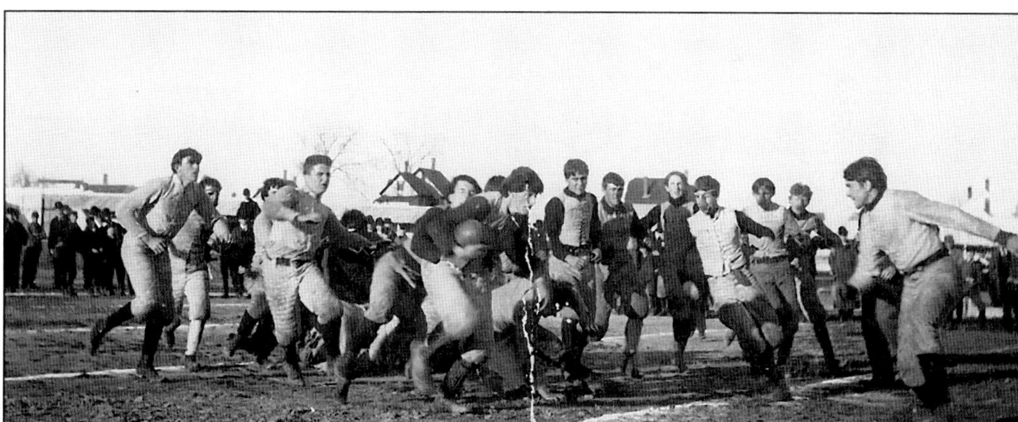

MAINE MEN IN ACTION AGAINST AN UNKNOWN OPPONENT IN 1894. Early contests were measured by two 20-minute halves. A touchdown was worth three points as was a drop kick between the goal posts. Protective equipment was limited to nose and shin guards, laced canvas jerseys, and pants. With the lack of protective equipment and increased intensity among rivals, President Roosevelt called for a meeting of college leaders to make rule changes that made the game safer.

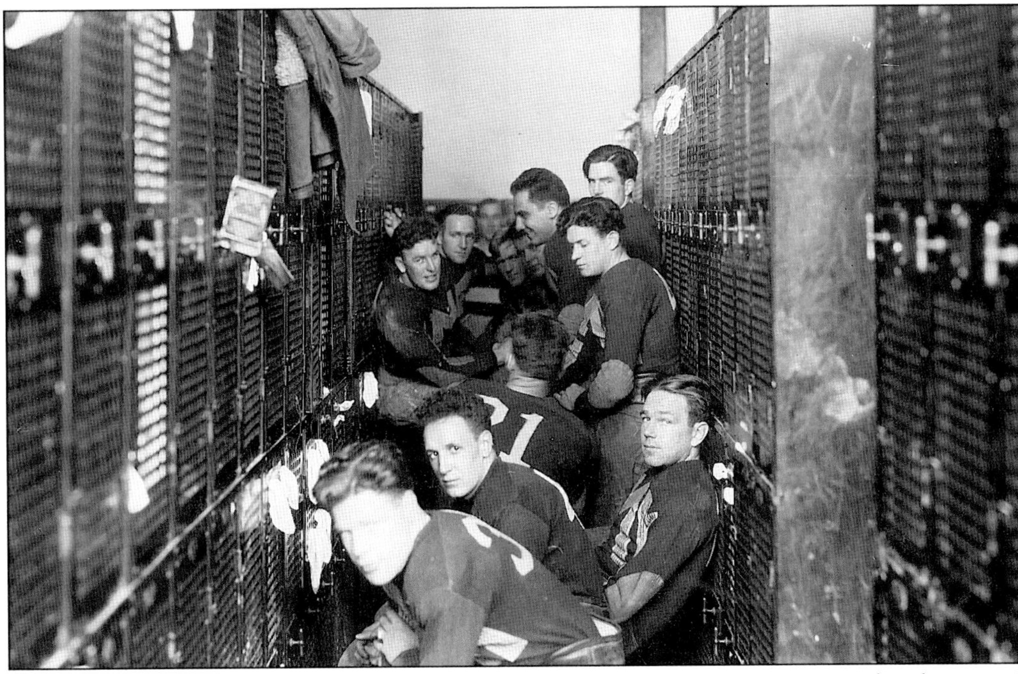

Cramped Quarters: A Maine Opponent Dressing Before a Game in 1928. The photograph was taken at the locker room in Alumni Hall where opposing teams dressed. This image demonstrates the need for more functional space. Help was on the way, with the completion of the Memorial Gymnasium facilities by the mid-1930s.

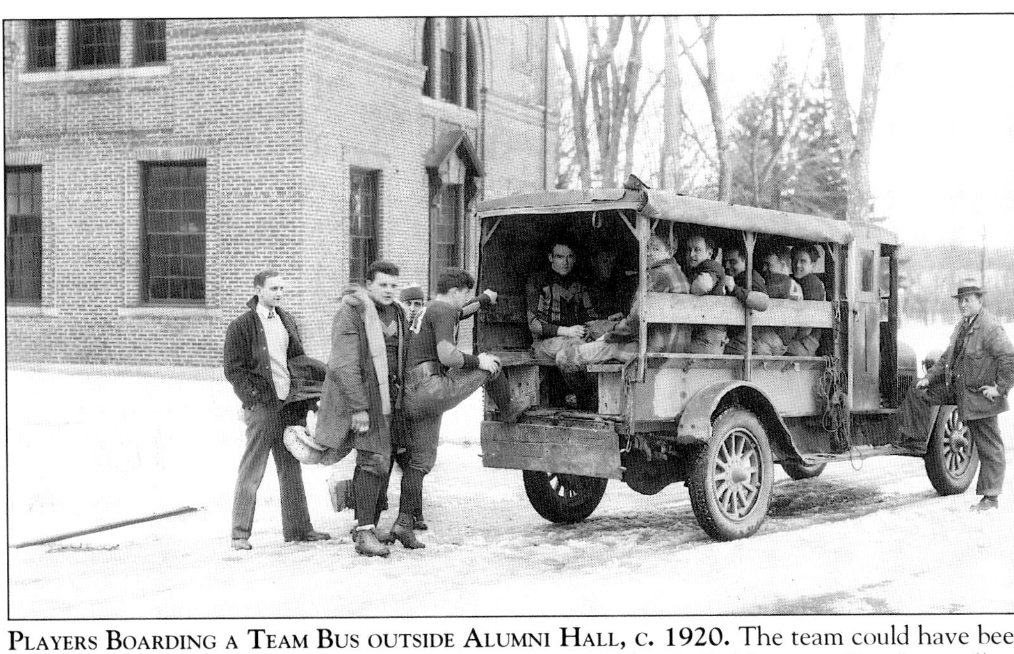

Players Boarding a Team Bus outside Alumni Hall, c. 1920. The team could have been en route to an away game since games played at the first Alumni Field were well within walking distance. Players could also change for games and practices in Oak Hall and fraternity houses, which provided some of the few hot baths on campus.

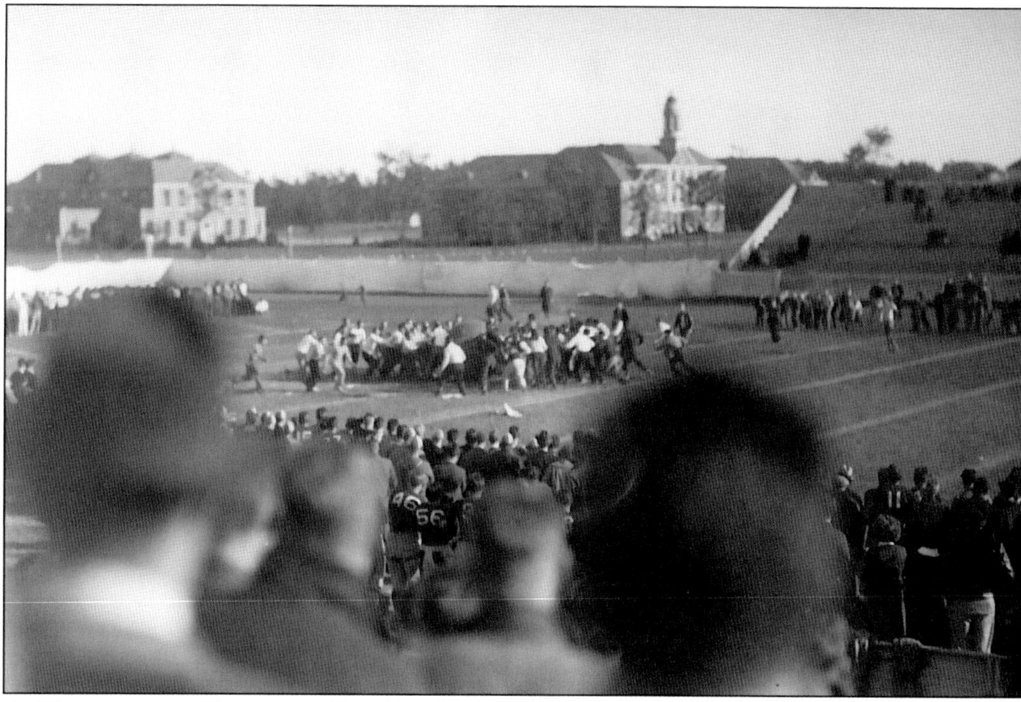

A Homecoming Football Game in the 1930s. Note Steven Hall near the center of the photograph. Homecoming games have been played at Alumni Field since 1931, often against traditional rivals Colby and Bowdoin. Maine Night, designed to create a pep rally atmosphere before such games, was dismissed and tabbed "A night for artificial spirits and liquid indulgence."

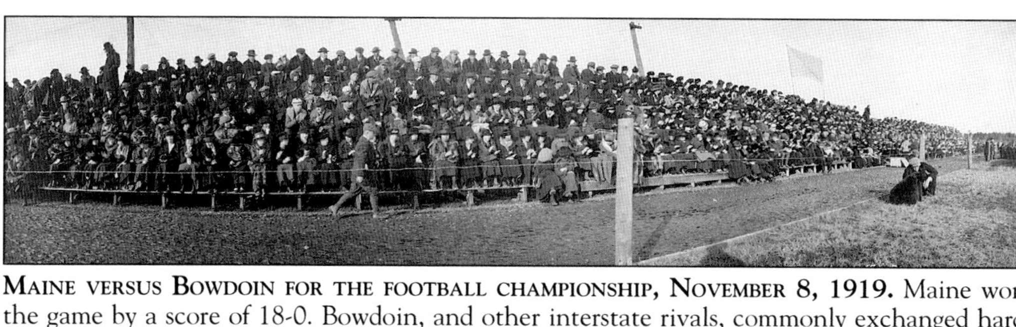

Maine versus Bowdoin for the football championship, November 8, 1919. Maine won the game by a score of 18-0. Bowdoin, and other interstate rivals, commonly exchanged hard feelings as sentiments ran high—inciting property damage, graffiti around campus, and unruly student demonstrations. The team was encouraged by its mascot, Bananas (seen on the right).

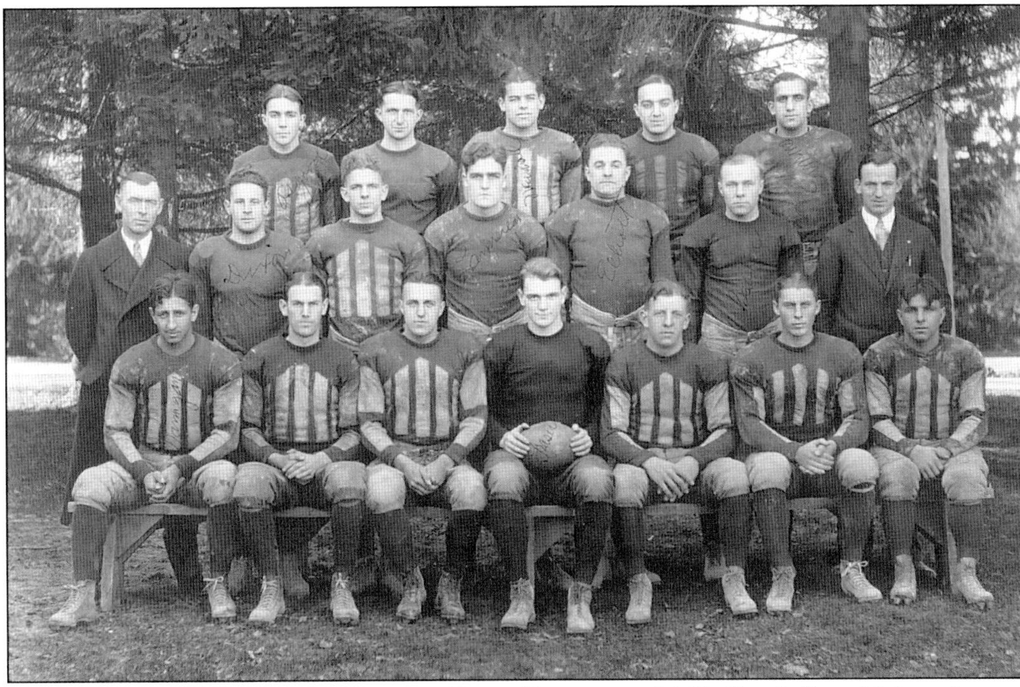

The Maine Black Bears Pose for a Team Photo, c. 1925. Football at Maine changed dramatically under the leadership and innovation of Coach Fred Brice, seen here in the second row to the far left. The university football team became known as the Black Bears in 1916, with the gift of a black bear cub that was adopted as the team's mascot.

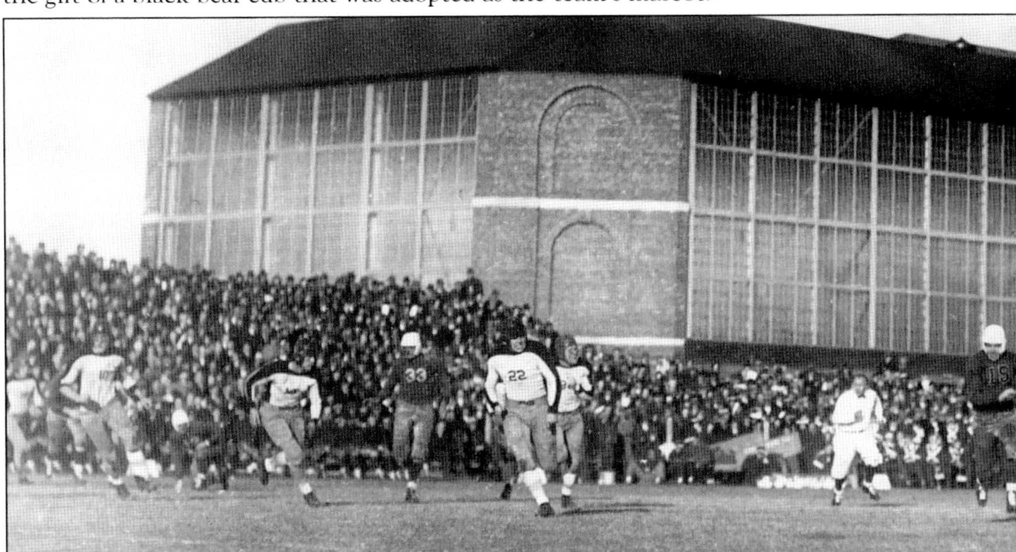

Maine Playing in front of the New Memorial Field House, c. 1930. Coach Brice brought many firsts to football in the state. U. Maine was the first team to wear numbers on both sides of their jerseys and the first to play under the lights. They were the first to have a game broadcast on the radio as well as the first team to have coffee and hot dogs served during halftime. Maine was said to have been one of the pioneers in the use of the forward pass, which was legalized in 1906.

FRED M. "FOXY FRED" BRICE, AS HE APPEARED C. 1930. Brice put football at Maine on the map with his teams won MSS titles ten times during his 20-year career. He also coached varsity basketball and baseball at Maine for a shorter duration. Brice happened upon coaching almost by accident. Gassed on the battlefield during WW I, doctors advised him to spend as much time outdoors as possible, so he took up coaching.

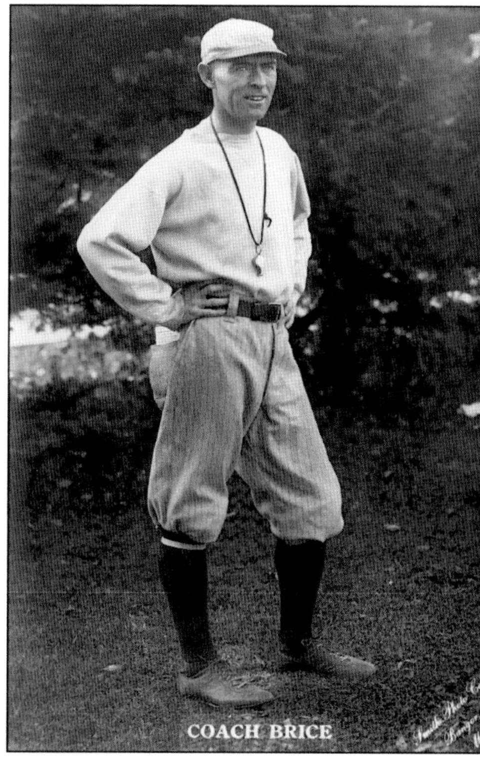

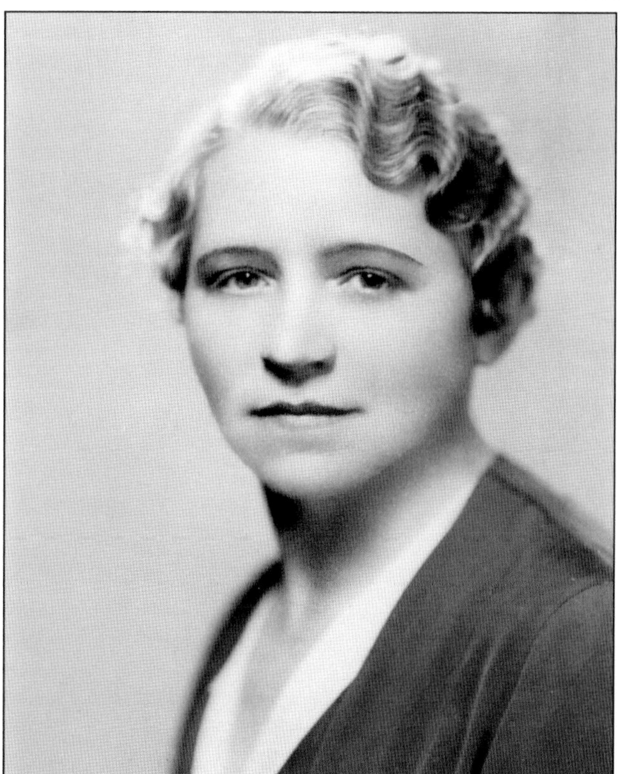

HELEN LENGYEL—COACH, ATHLETIC DIRECTOR, AND PIONEER IN WOMEN'S ATHLETICS. Lengyel came to the university in 1925 and did much to close the gender gap in athletics occurring on campus. She facilitated intramural programs for women, resurrected the women's basketball program, and coached the field hockey team. In 1963, an athletic facility was named Lengyel Gymnasium in her honor.

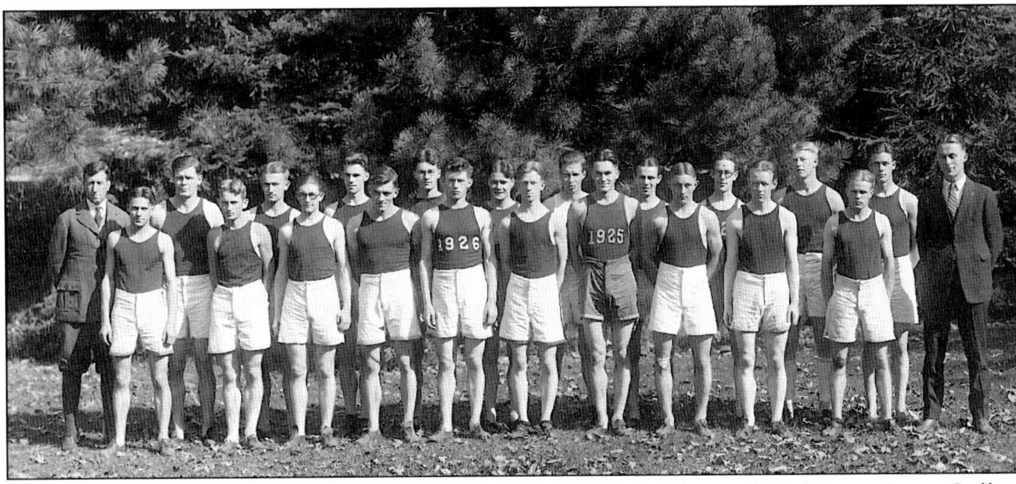

THE 1925–1926 TRACK TEAM, OUTSIDE THE FIELD HOUSE, FALL 1925. Maine State College held its first-ever track meet in Orono in 1894. The next year, the self-supported team traveled to Waterville to face Colby for its first intercollegiate meet. In 1897, a quarter-mile cinder track was built on campus as part of the first Alumni Field.

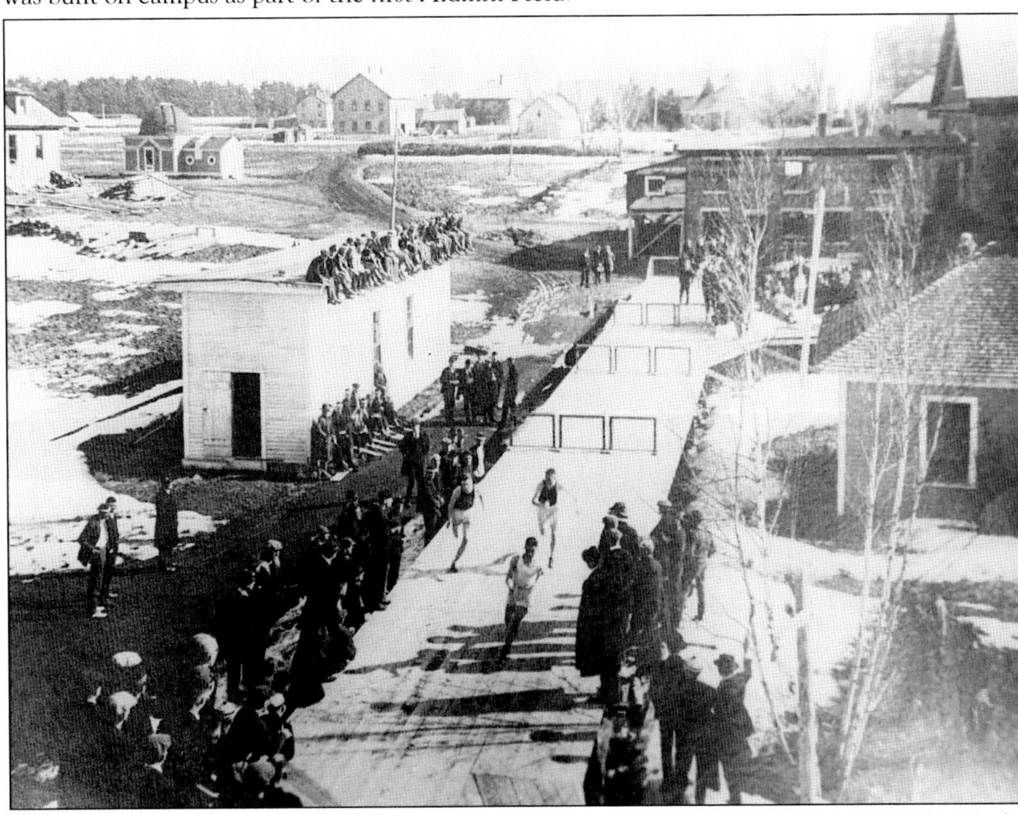

A SPRING TRACK MEET HELD ON CAMPUS IN 1922. The observatory to the far left helps to define the location of the track. Leading the pack is UMO trackman Seth Pinkham. In the years preceding WW I, Maine was a track-and-field powerhouse, winning several New England track championships. Maine track athlete Edmund Black won a bronze medal in the 1928 Olympic games.

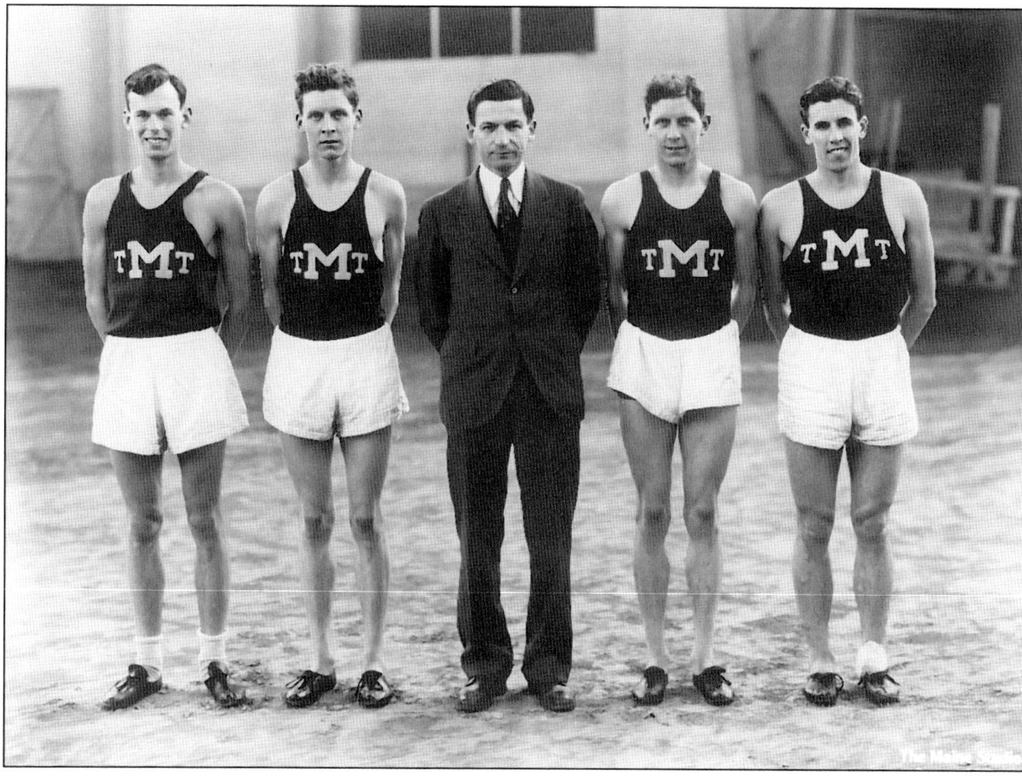

MEMBERS OF THE UNIVERSITY OF MAINE INDOOR TRACK TEAM, IN THE FIELD HOUSE IN 1934. Pictured, from left to right, are Joel Marsh, Ernie Black, Coach Jenkins, Ken Black, and Bill Cole. Indoor training for track was held initially in the limited space at Alumni Hall. The program welcomed the new accommodations at the Memorial Field House, which was built in 1925–26.

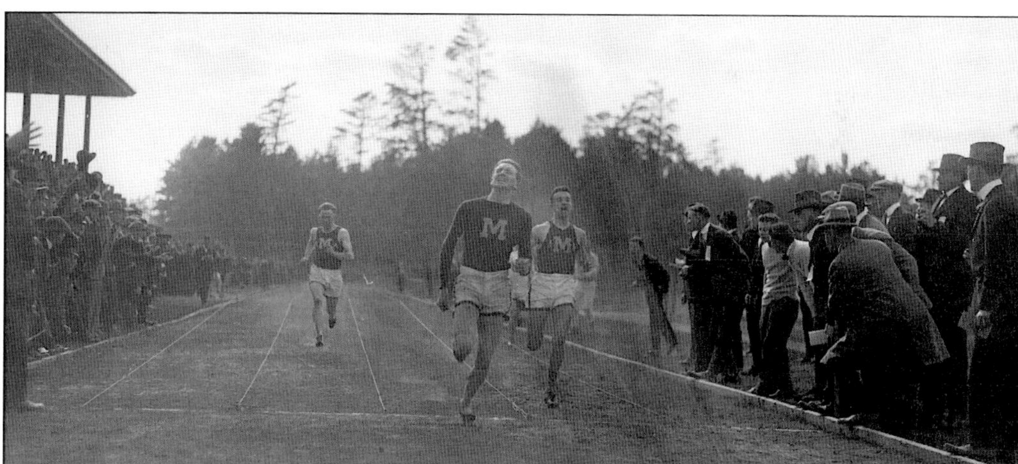

MAINE MEN FINISH STRONG, C. 1915. This meet may have been a cross-country event held in Orono, as the race would finish the last quarter mile on the cinder track around Alumni Field. The first organized cross-country meet held on campus took place on October 24, 1908. Runners commenced at the Old Town Post Office and followed the line of the electric railroad to campus before ending up at Alumni Field.

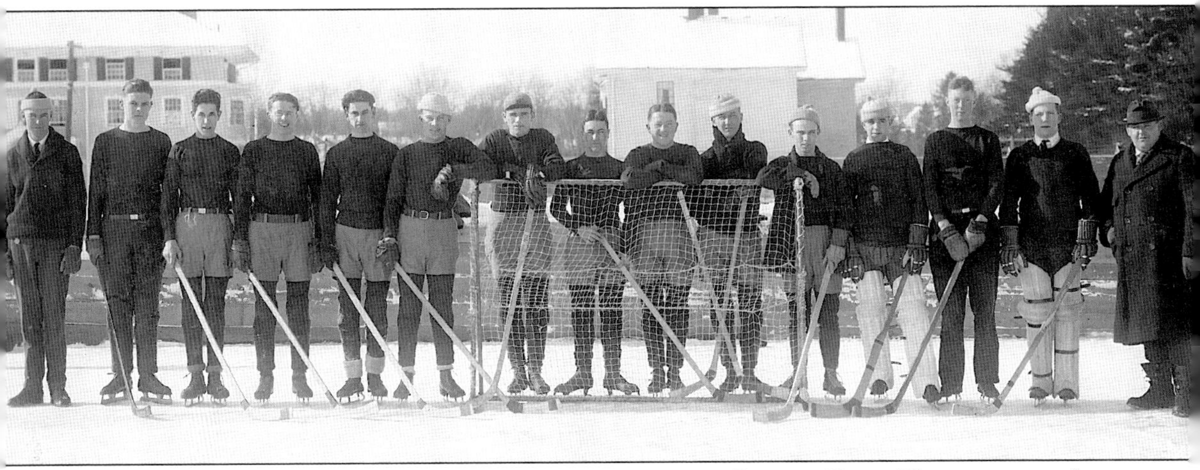

The U. Maine Ice Hockey Team of 1922–1923, on an Outside Rink. The sport grew from a club in 1906–07, when it played a limited schedule featuring local high schools and Bowdoin College. Hockey held club status until 1923, when it was first recognized as a varsity sport. Home games and practices were held outdoors on a rink where Corbett Hall is now located. Varsity hockey was discontinued at Maine in the 1930s due to health risks incurred by darkness and freezing temperatures. College officials prolonged the suspension until a suitable indoor facility was found. A $400,000 gift from university benefactor Harold Alfond reinstated the sport in 1976, when Alfond Arena opened. After its first season in 1977, U. Maine Hockey made a quick rise to national prominence, winning national championships in 1996 and 1999.

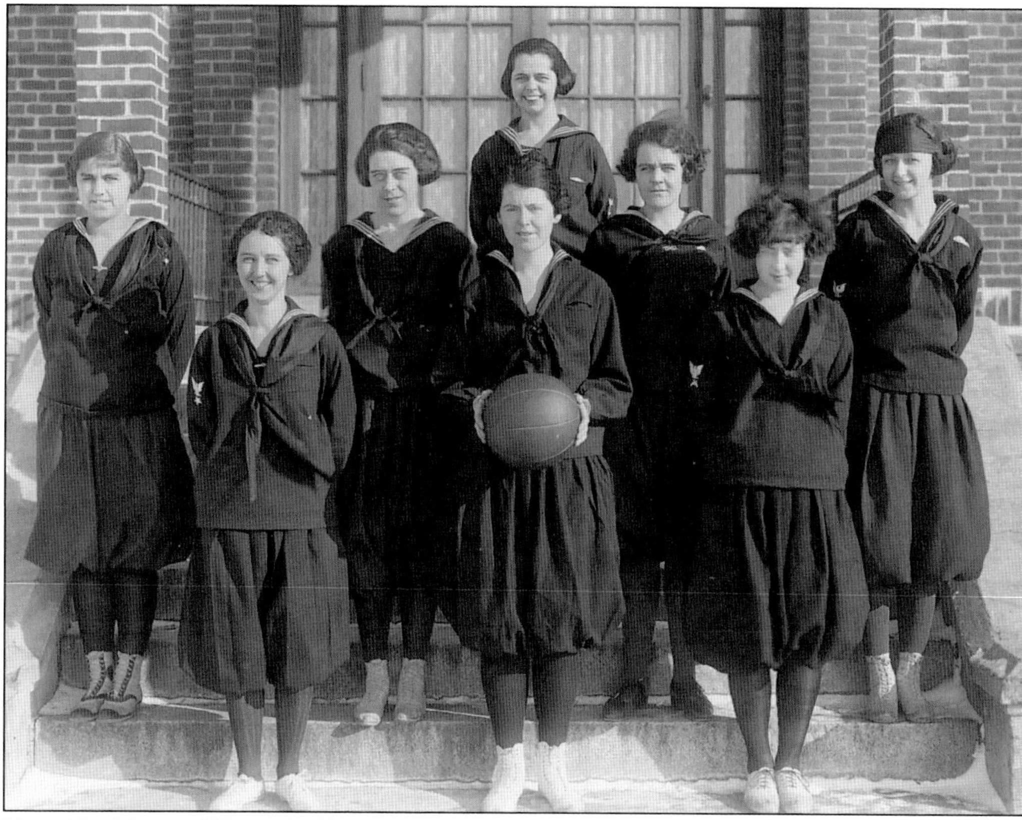

The U. Maine Women's Basketball Team of 1922–23. Standing, left to right, are Anna Sargent, Elizabeth Ring, Kay Denison, Daphne Winslow, Ruth Denison, Kay Hunt, and Kay Clark. The emblem on players' sleeves might signify an acknowledgment of lives lost in WW I.

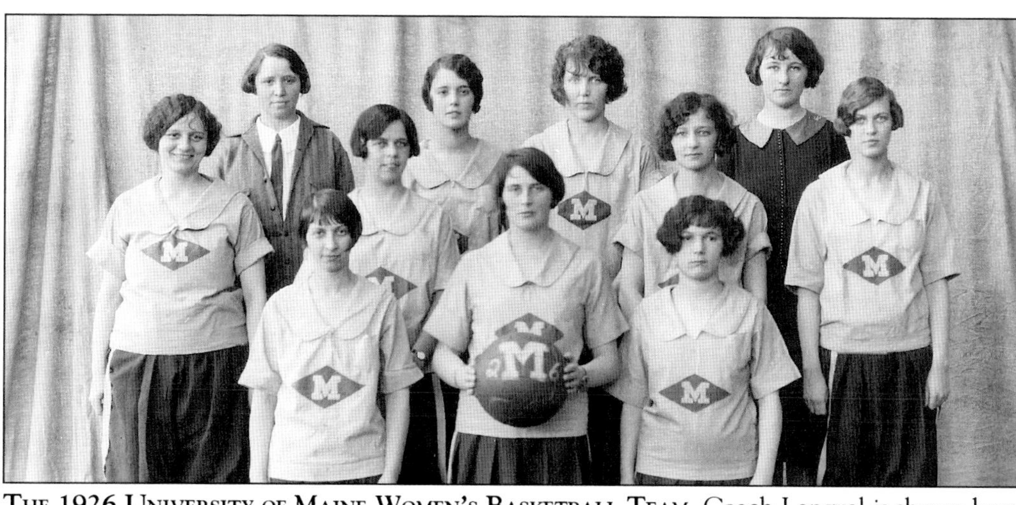

The 1926 University of Maine Women's Basketball Team. Coach Lengyel is shown here, standing at the top left of the photograph. Rules in the 1920s allowed women to play with six players, and positions included left forward, right forward, center, side center, left back, and right back.

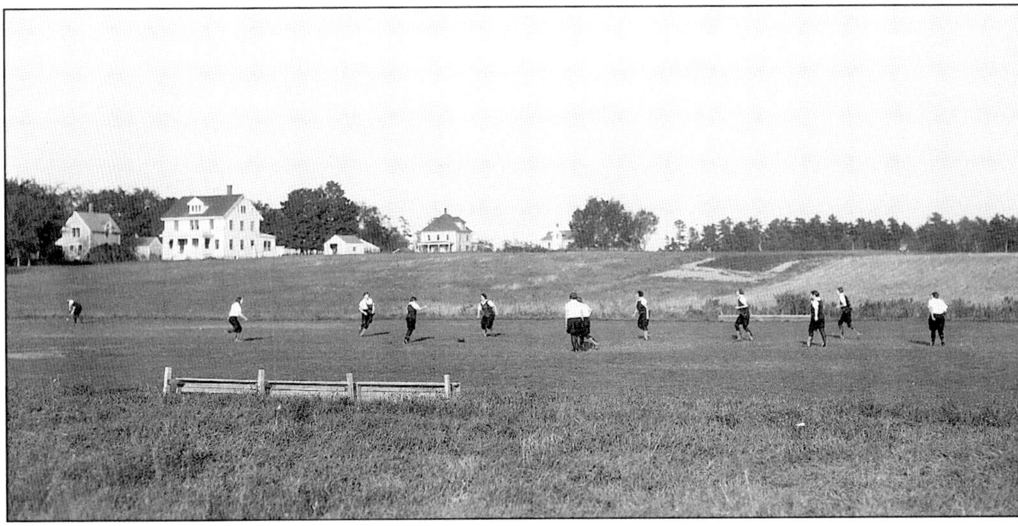

A c. 1930 Photograph of a Physical Education Class or One of the Interclass/ Intramural Programs Provided for Women Athletes. The game appears to be soccer or some variation of the sport.

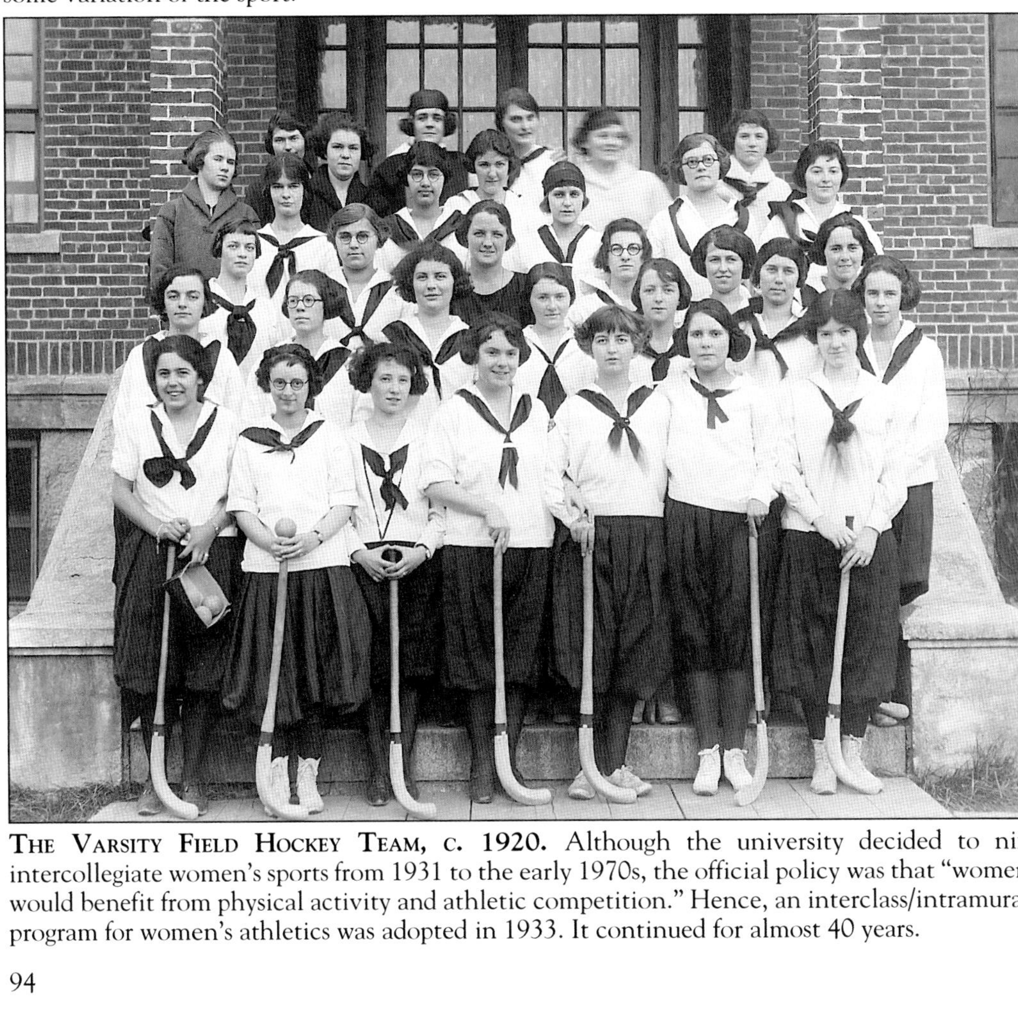

The Varsity Field Hockey Team, c. 1920. Although the university decided to nix intercollegiate women's sports from 1931 to the early 1970s, the official policy was that "women would benefit from physical activity and athletic competition." Hence, an interclass/intramural program for women's athletics was adopted in 1933. It continued for almost 40 years.

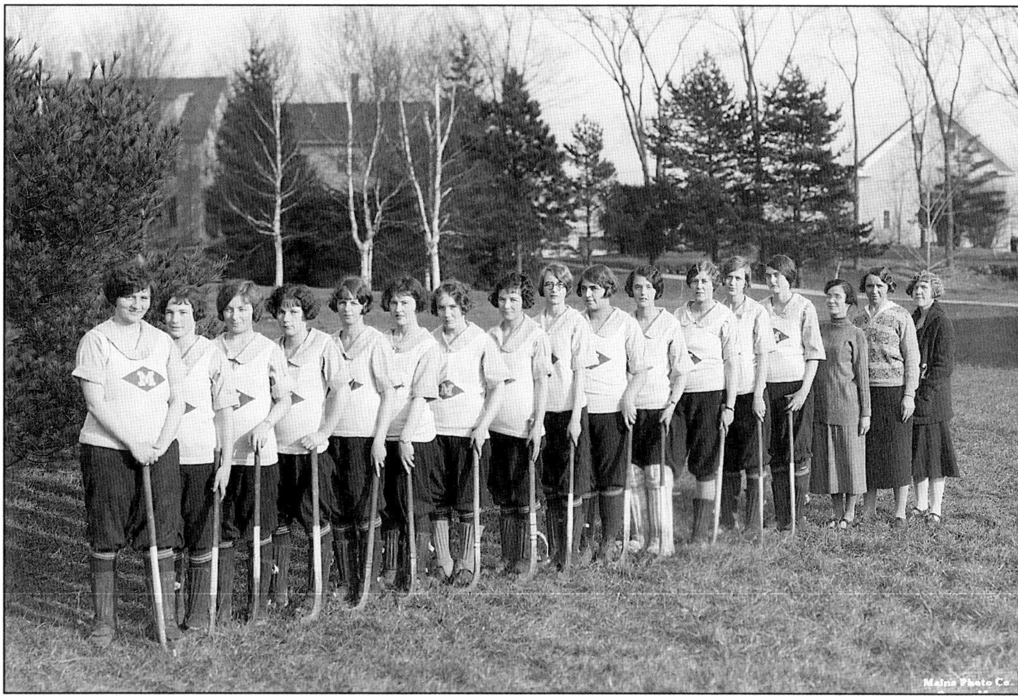

THE 1925–26 U. MAINE FIELD HOCKEY TEAM, COACHED BY HELEN LENGYEL. Women's sports flourished in the 1920s, mainly due to the vision and hard work of Helen Lengyel (far right, second from end).

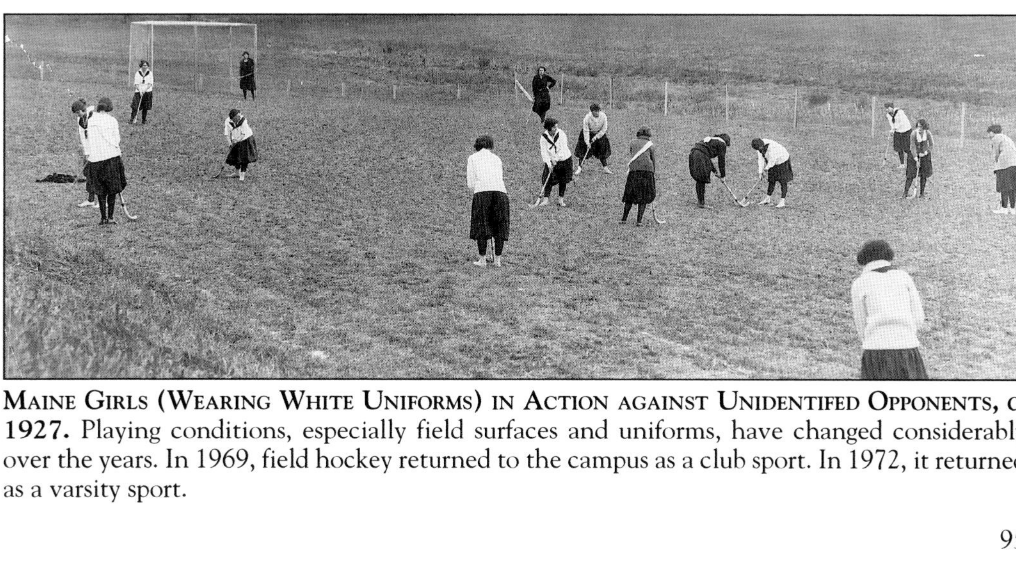

MAINE GIRLS (WEARING WHITE UNIFORMS) IN ACTION AGAINST UNIDENTIFED OPPONENTS, C. 1927. Playing conditions, especially field surfaces and uniforms, have changed considerably over the years. In 1969, field hockey returned to the campus as a club sport. In 1972, it returned as a varsity sport.

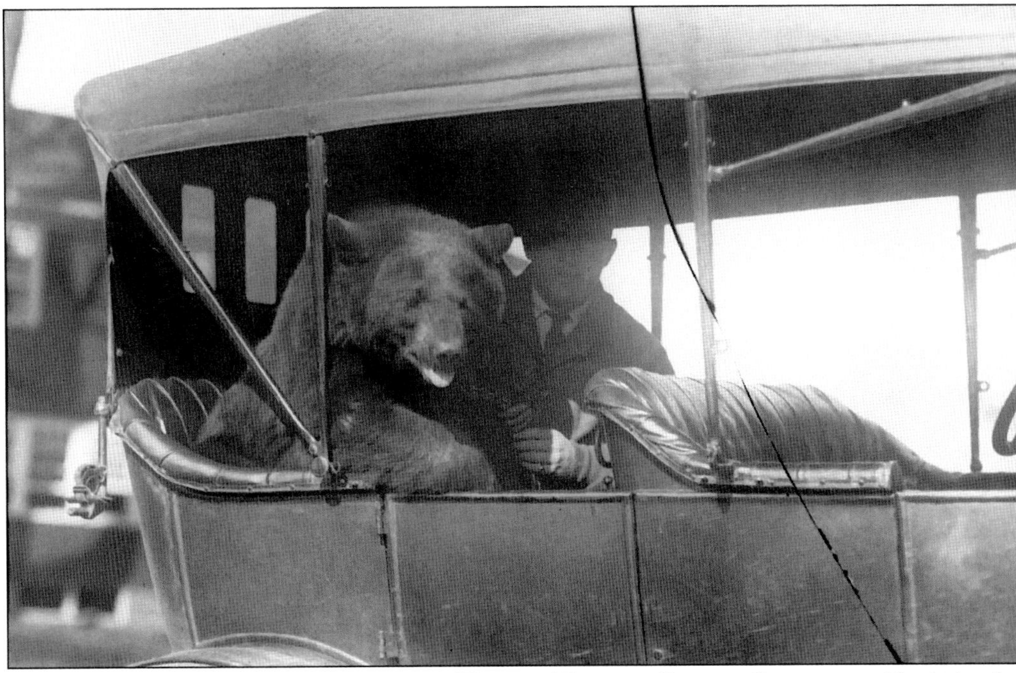

BANANAS IN THE BACK SEAT OF A MODEL T, WITH TRAINER GEORGE STACKPOLE. Tradition has it that Bolivar the elephant was the university's first mascot, captured from a downtown Bangor clothing exposition and forced to attended a football game in the early 1900s. In 1914, a black bear cub was donated to the university and became the official team mascot for all sports.

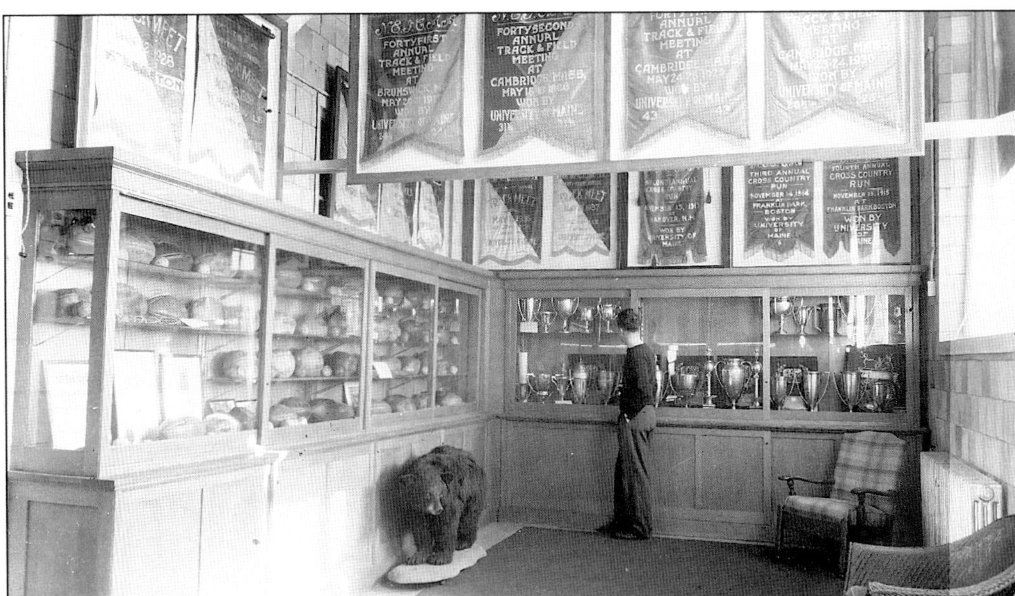

A STUFFED BANANAS, NOW PART OF THE TROPHY ROOM AT MEMORIAL GYMNASIUM, C. 1937. Bananas died of ptomaine poisoning, was sent to a taxidermist, and was placed in the Memorial Gymnasium trophy room. Bananas appeared in a Hollywood movie and was a favorite of the brothers at the Beta Theta Pi fraternity house, who gave him food and lodging.

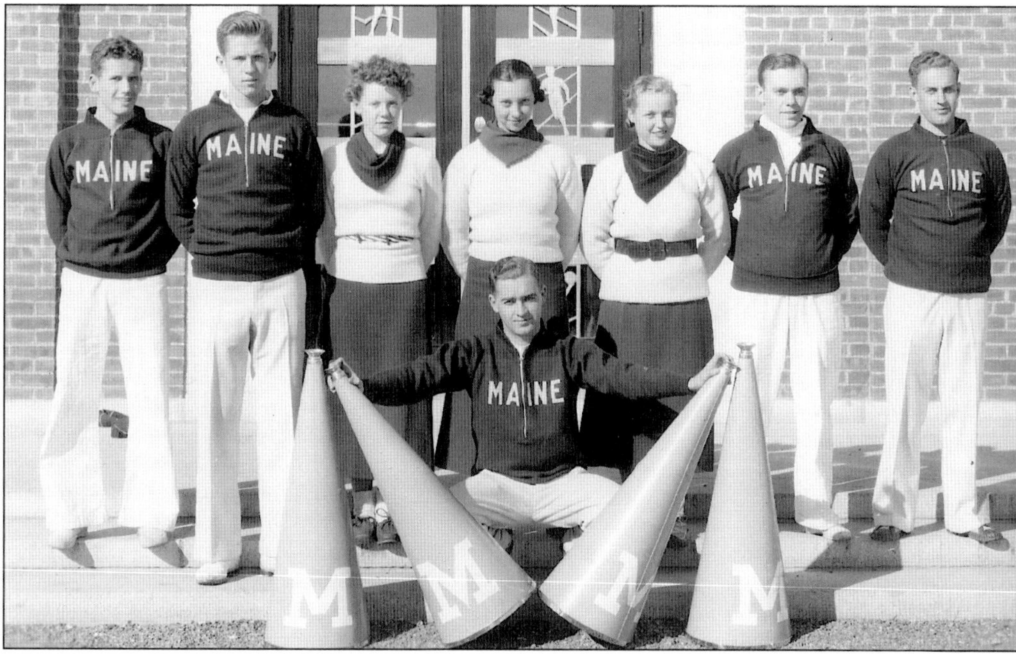

Cheerleaders Posing outside Memorial Gymnasium in 1935. In the front, with the megaphones, is head cheerleader Leo Murphy. According to records, cheerleaders began appearing at campus sporting events as early as 1913. Cheerleading would eventually turn into a sport of its own, with intercollegiate competitions held.

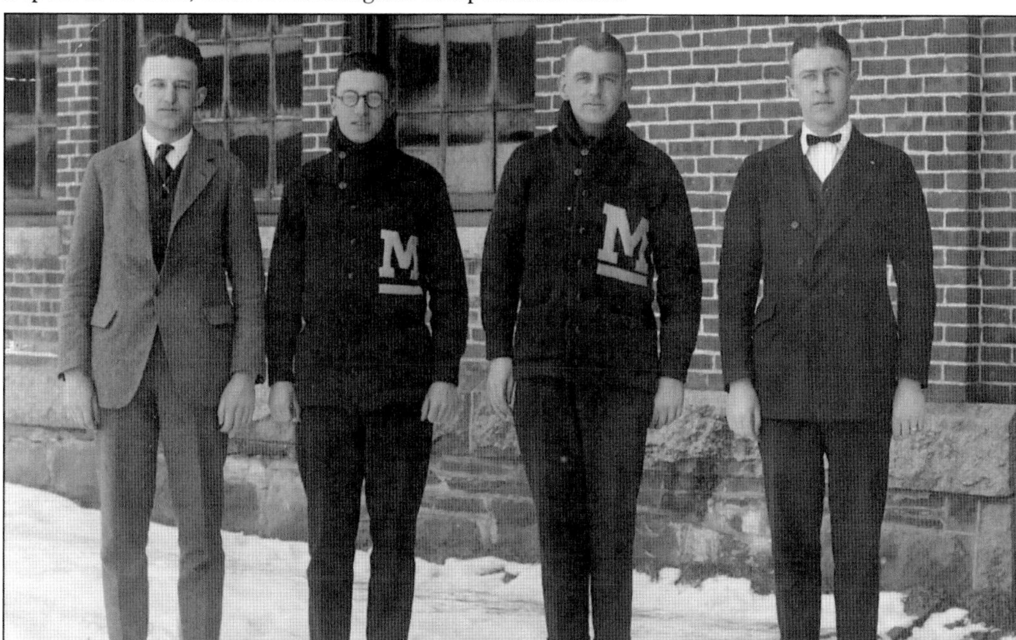

Sport Managers Pose outside Alumni Hall, Winter 1921. Student athletic managers, from left to right, are H.C. Crandall (basketball), H.W. Fifield (track), W.B. Cobb (football), and R.W. Graffam (baseball). Managers handled a wide variety of responsibilities, including being trainers, assistant coaches, and dealing with public relations.

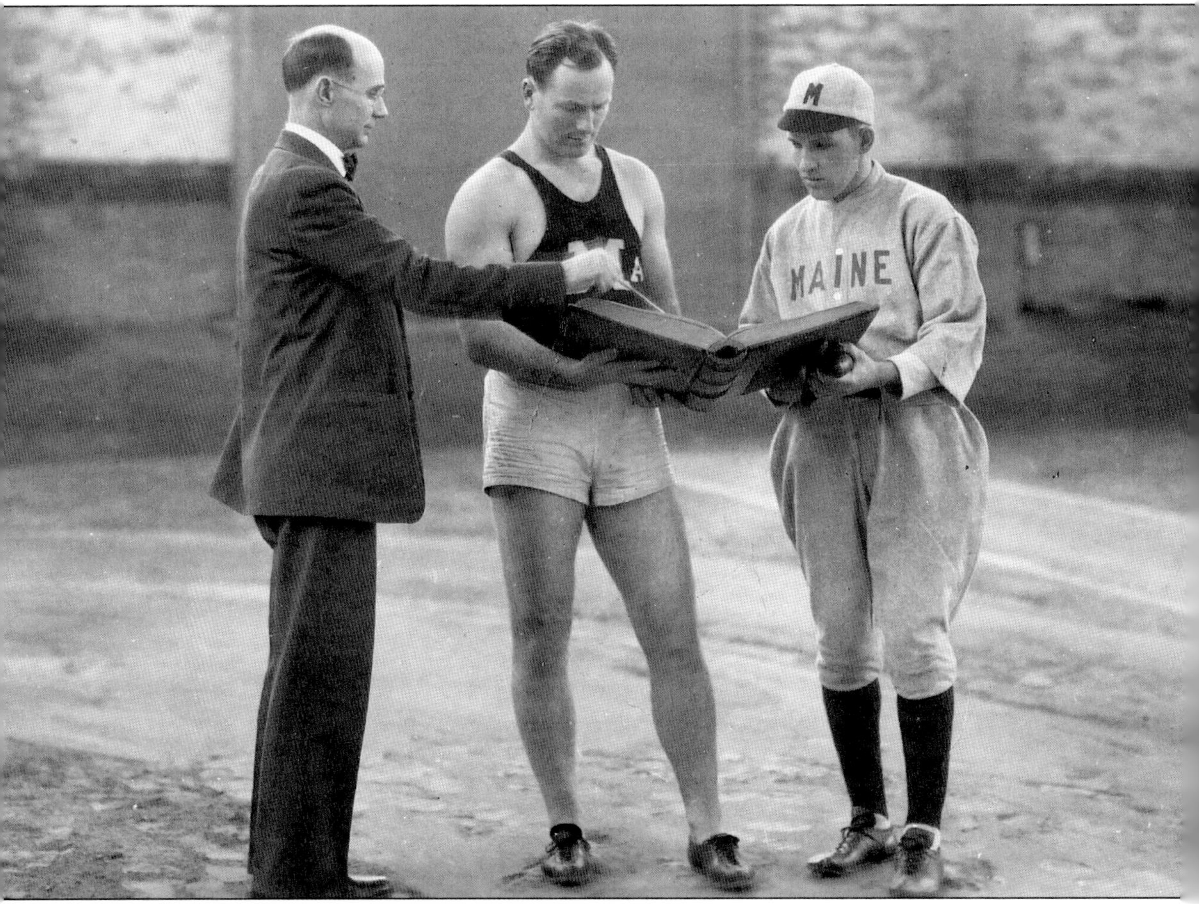

DEAN ARTHUR L. DEERING WITH EDMUND BLACK, CAPTAIN OF THE TRACK TEAM, AND CARL D. TRUE, CAPTAIN OF THE BASEBALL TEAM, INSIDE THE NEWLY COMPLETED MEMORIAL GYMNASIUM FIELD HOUSE. The men are examining "The Book of Builders," which was a record of those making contributions toward the completion of the facility and was probably a fund-raising gimmick. At the time of its completion, the armory and field house was reported to be the largest in the United States. It could accommodate five track-and-field events simultaneously and had a regulation baseball diamond.

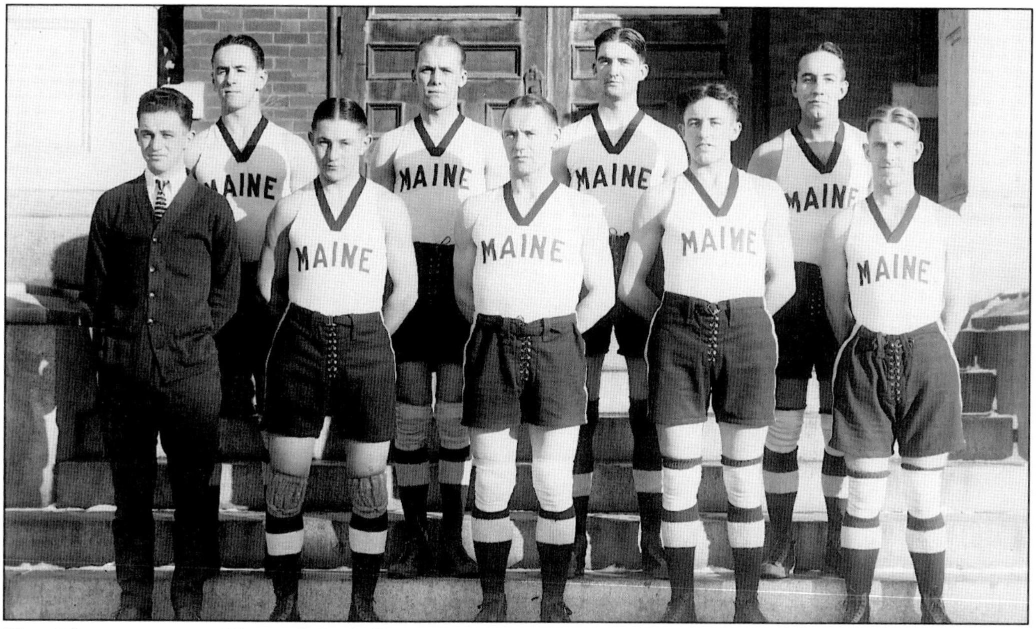

THE UNIVERSITY OF MAINE MEN'S BASKETBALL TEAM IN 1923: The first varsity season played at Maine was in 1901, ten years after Dr. Naismith invented the game. Basketball was discontinued as a varsity sport in 1910, but reinstated after WW I. The sport was again discontinued in 1929 due to lack of support, inadequate playing facilities, and the rough nature of the game. Interestingly, a student referendum upheld the ban and basketball did not return as a varsity sport until 1937.

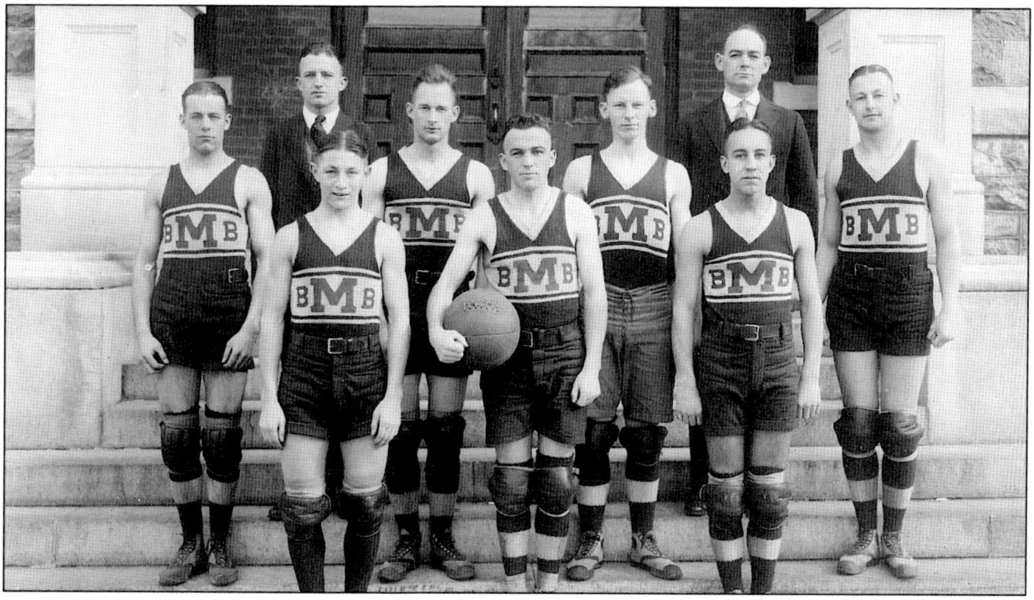

THE UNIVERSITY OF MAINE MEN'S BASKETBALL TEAM IN 1920. The photo is labeled as the first varsity basketball team after the sport was reinstated in 1920. Note the laced-up basketball. Manager Horace Crandall appears at top left and Coach James Baldwin appears at top right. The team was captained by Donald Coady (front row, on the right) and finished their season with a record of seven wins and six losses.

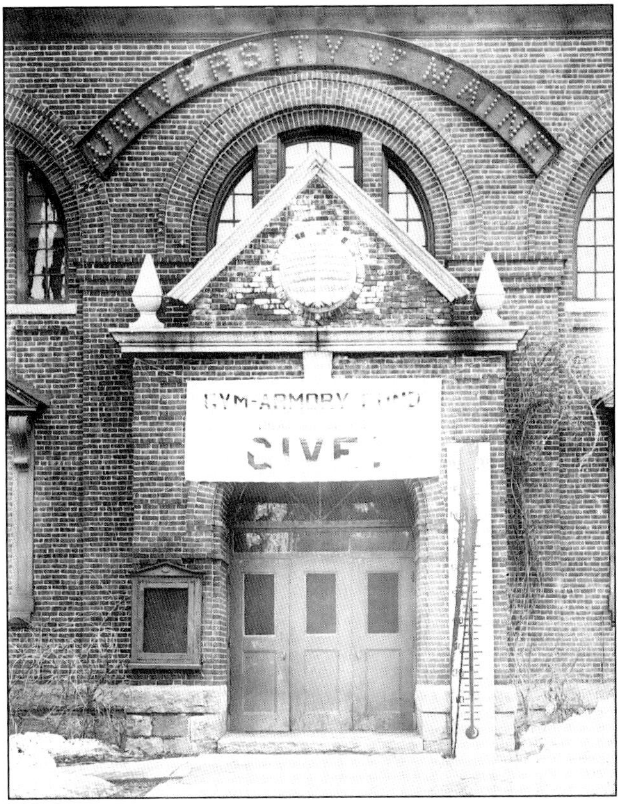

A SIGN OUTSIDE OF ALUMNI HALL, GAUGING THE PROGRESS OF FUNDS NEEDED TO COMPLETE THE MEMORIAL GYMNASIUM AND ARMORY IN 1925. The facility was completed and funded entirely by contributions from faculty, students, alumni, and other interested parties.

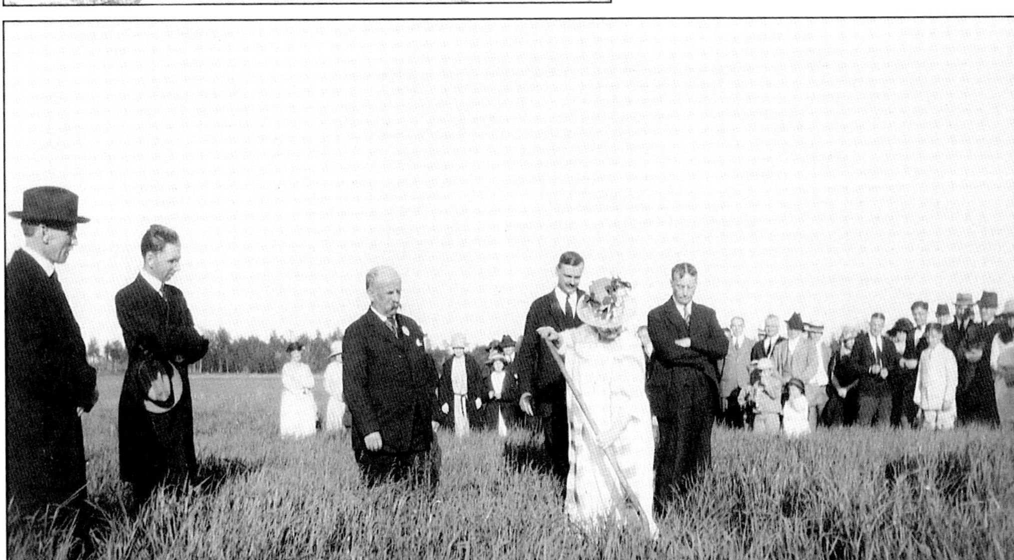

THE CEREMONIAL GROUND-BREAKING OF THE MEMORIAL GYMNASIUM AND FIELD HOUSE IN 1925. President Little and the board of trustees are pictured with an unidentified dignitary (the woman with the shovel). It is unlikely that the major project would have been undertaken without the influence and efforts of Little, a staunch advocate of athletics. Little pushed for a University Athletic Association, which was founded in 1923 to provide greater organization and guidance for intercollegiate athletics.

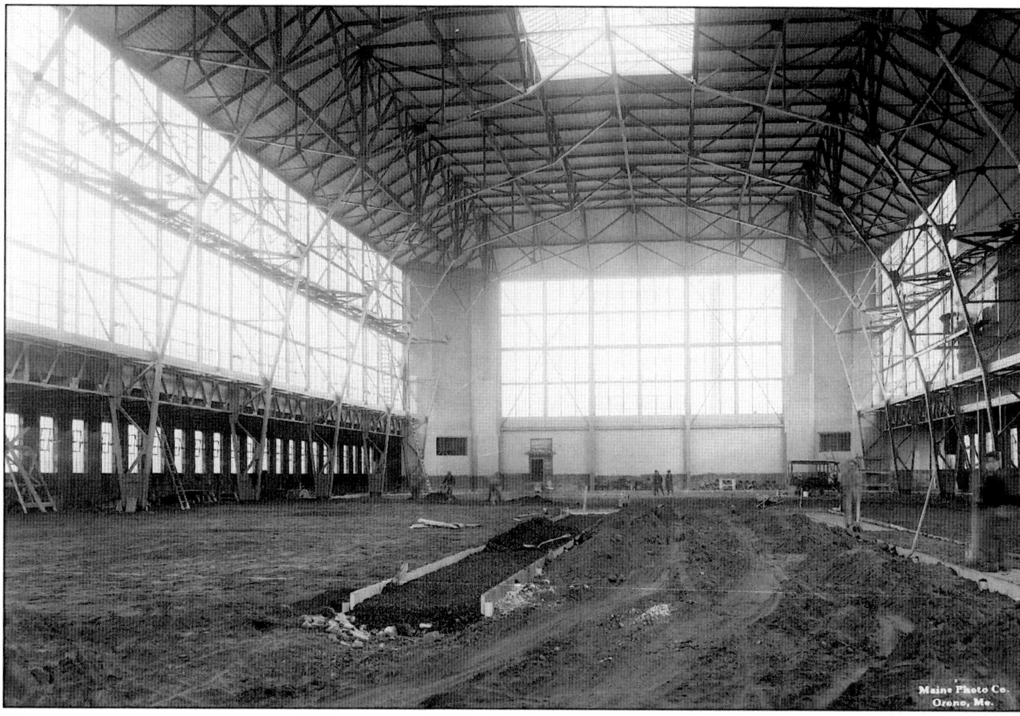

Construction inside the Memorial Gymnasium and Field House in 1926. The complex was named in honor of Maine students who lost their lives in the Spanish-American War and WW I. The inside was completed in time for the indoor track season of 1926–27.

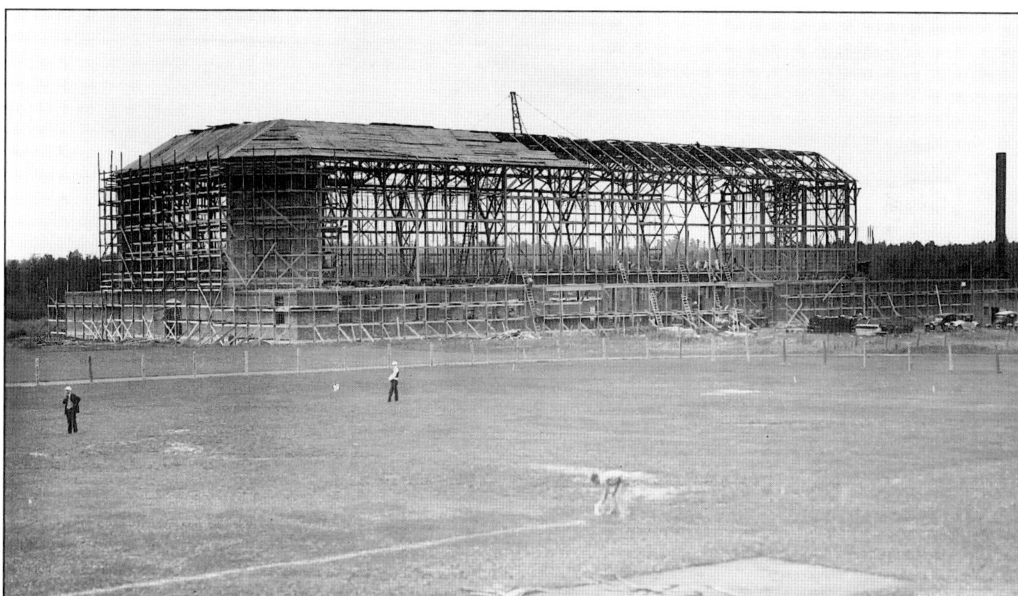

Construction of Memorial Gymnasium and Field House in Full Bloom, 1925. A new era in athletics began as the university opened the complex in 1926. The facility consisted of a field house, gymnasium, locker rooms, and office space, and was fully completed and dedicated in June of 1933. Later, an Olympic-size swimming pool was added.

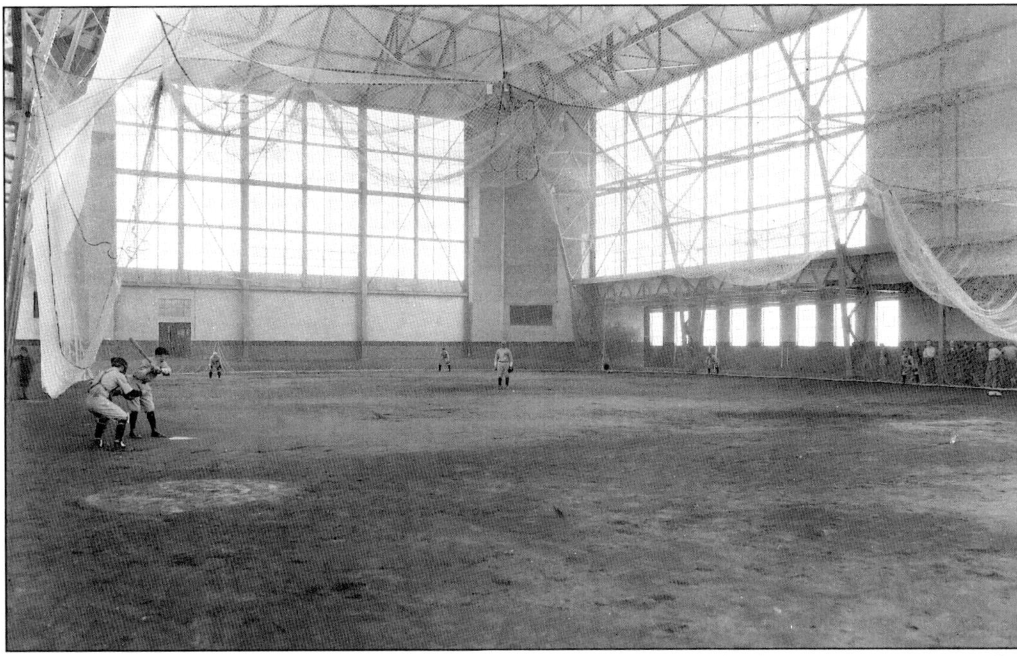

Baseball Practice inside the Field House, c. 1928. The indoor facility gave Maine men a big advantage over in-state rivals and other colleges when weather conditions forced indoor practices. The cramped space in the Alumni Hall was then given to the women's athletics program.

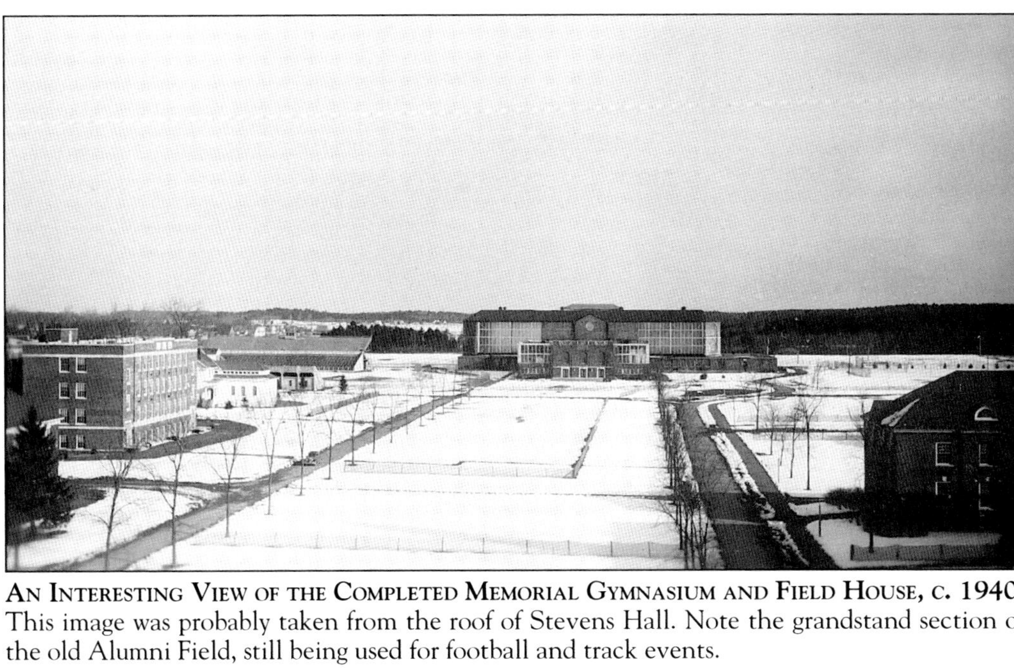

An Interesting View of the Completed Memorial Gymnasium and Field House, c. 1940. This image was probably taken from the roof of Stevens Hall. Note the grandstand section of the old Alumni Field, still being used for football and track events.

Five

Events and Organizations

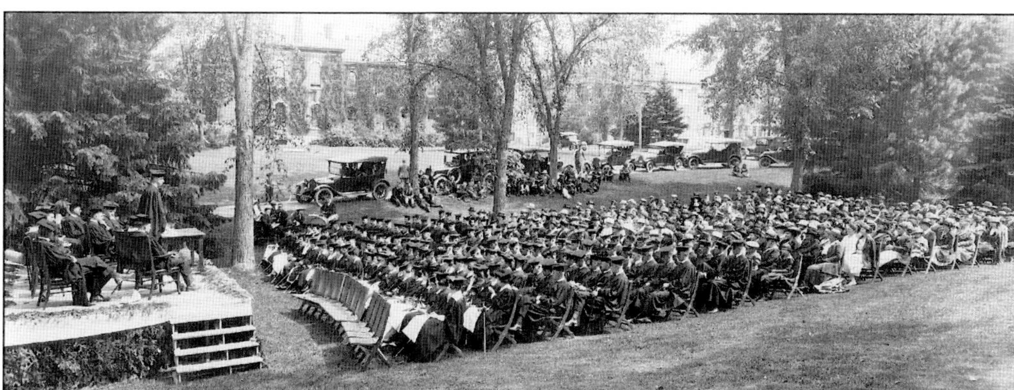

Commencement Exercises outside Alumni Hall, c. 1923. Graduates in caps and gowns are shown seated while spectators shade themselves under trees. Leading the proceedings was perhaps President Little or a student speaker. From new student orientation all the way through graduation exercises, events and organizations have provided a rich aspect for student lives. Fraternities and sororities encouraged comradeship among students, while honor societies gave scholars the opportunity to learn and serve. Just as important were events such as Homecoming, alumni picnics, Class Day, and other affairs that helped graduates retain a sense of their past as well as community with other alumni.

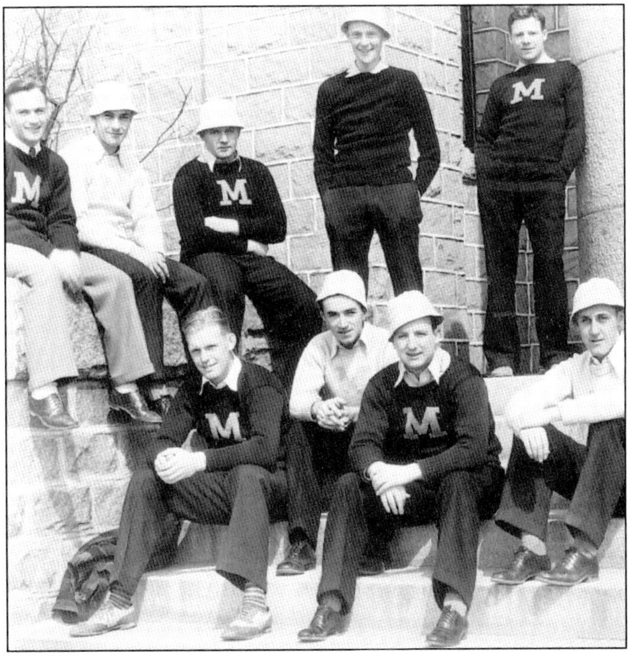

MEMBERS OF THE SENIOR SKULLS POSING FOR YEARBOOK PICTURES OUTSIDE CARNEGIE HALL IN 1931. Established in 1906, Senior Skulls was a society that honored young men on campus who had distinguished themselves in campus and community service. The goal of the society was to promote citizenship and leadership, but it was initially founded to promote goodwill among the fraternities at U. Maine. A spin-off of the group, the Sophomore Owls Society, was founded in 1910 to assist freshmen in adapting to campus life. Below, Senior Skulls (1939–1940) pose outside of Fernald Hall. Note the ribbons attached to some members, which may represent a fraternity pledge.

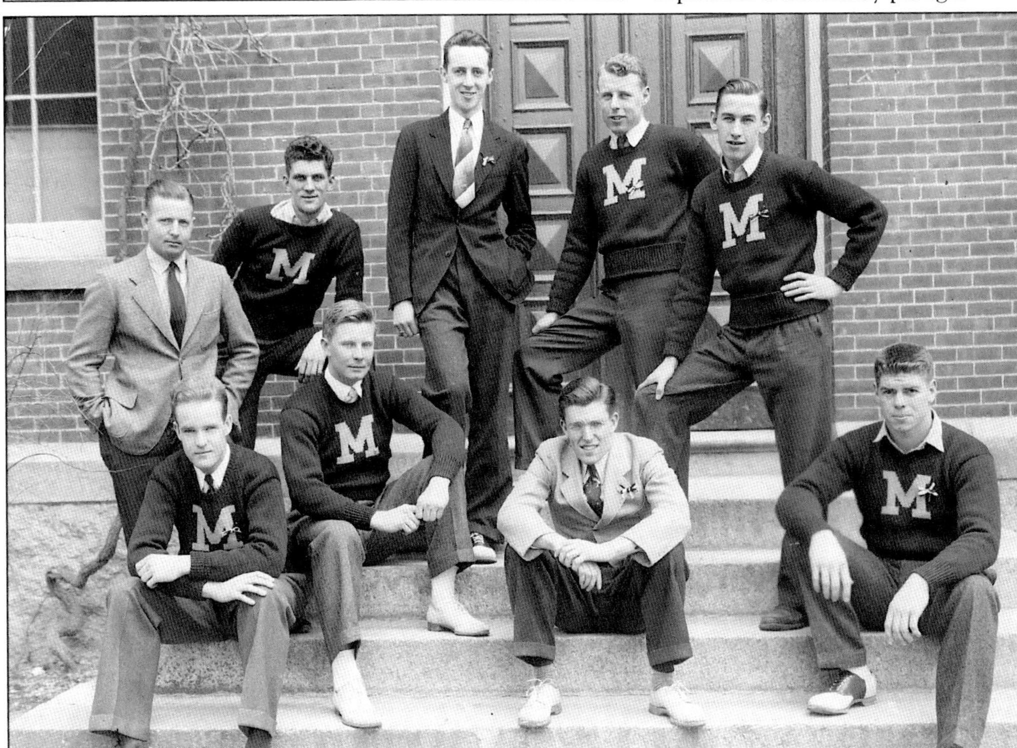

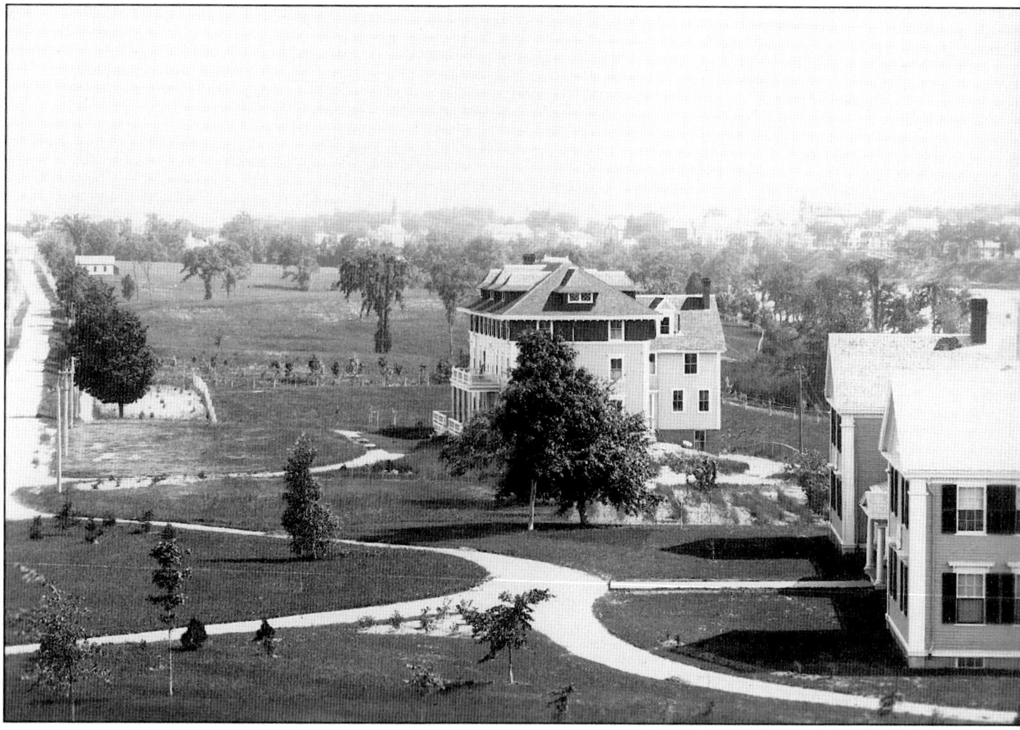

PHI GAMMA DELTA FRATERNITY HOUSE (CENTER), MOUNT VERNON HOUSE (RIGHT), AND ORONO (IN THE DISTANCE), C. 1910. The existence of fraternity life at the university can be traced back to 1874, with the establishment of the QTV fraternity. The first Greek letter fraternity, Alpha Sigma Chi, was established in 1878, with Beta Theta Pi following the next year. The idea spread, perhaps in an attempt to copy established traditions taking place at Bowdoin and Colby, or perhaps out of the need for young men to bond with others with similar interests. The emergence of fraternities also helped solve the housing problems related to increasing enrollments. When the Maine Legislature passed a bill authorizing guaranteed loans to fraternities looking to build their own houses, Fraternity Row emerged on College Avenue. Below, Phi Kappa Sigma, Phi Gamma Delta, and the Mount Vernon House appear in a *c.* 1905 photograph.

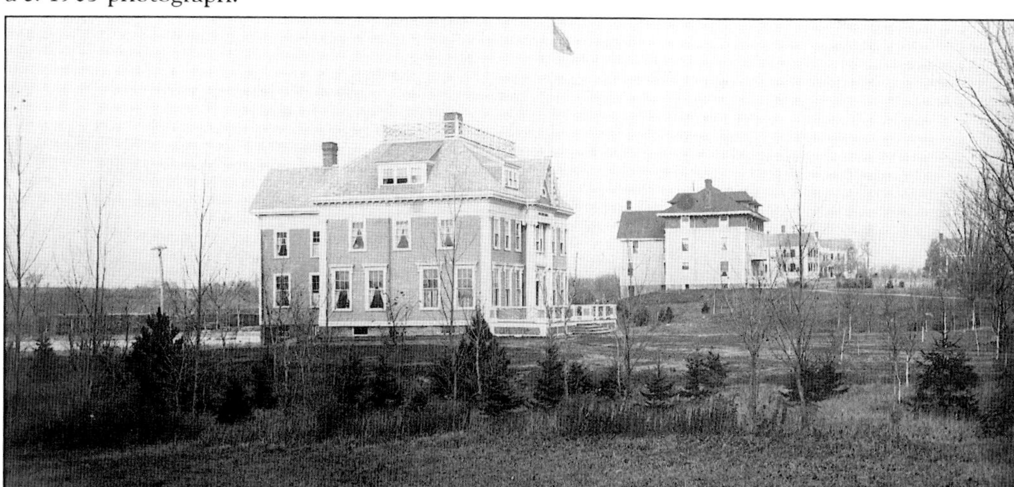

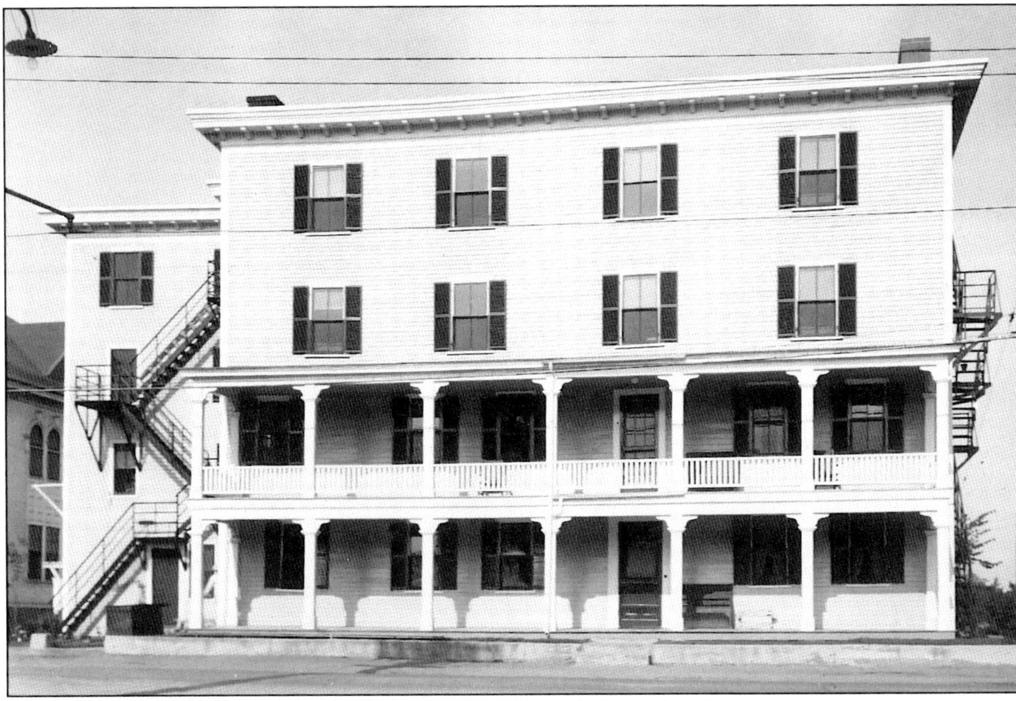

South Hall, Orono, c. 1935. This building provided another housing option to students. It opened initially as a cooperative self-help dormitory for women.

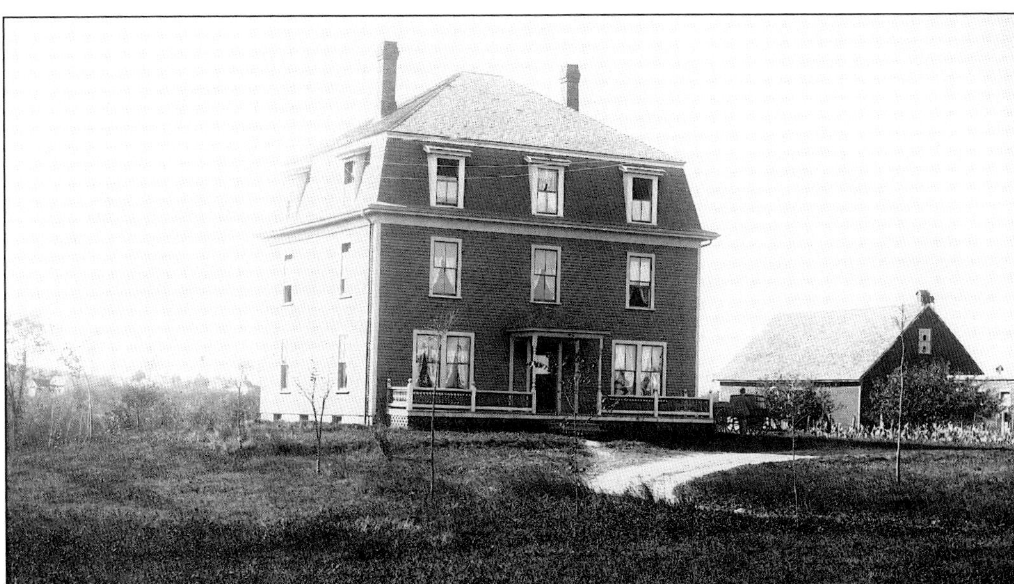

Spearen Inn, c. 1905. A local boarding house, the building was used as a student dormitory in 1903. It became a fraternity house in the 1920s for Sigma Phi Sigma and later Tau Kappa Epsilon.

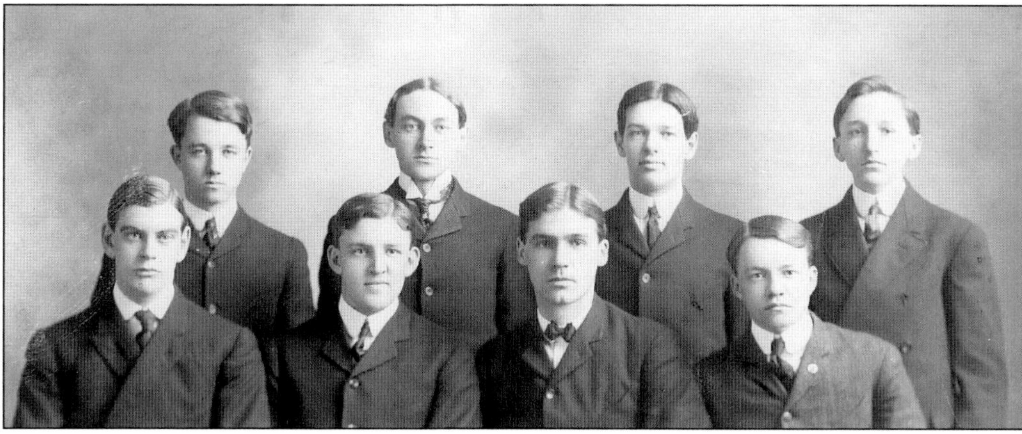

Phi Gamma Delta Brothers, Posing for a House Picture on January 21, 1905. Shown in this picture, from left to right, are as follows: (front row) Owen Dow, Otis Mcans, Bert Young, and Raymond Fellows; (back row) Raymond Smith, William Hill, Robert Steward, and Robie Mitchell.

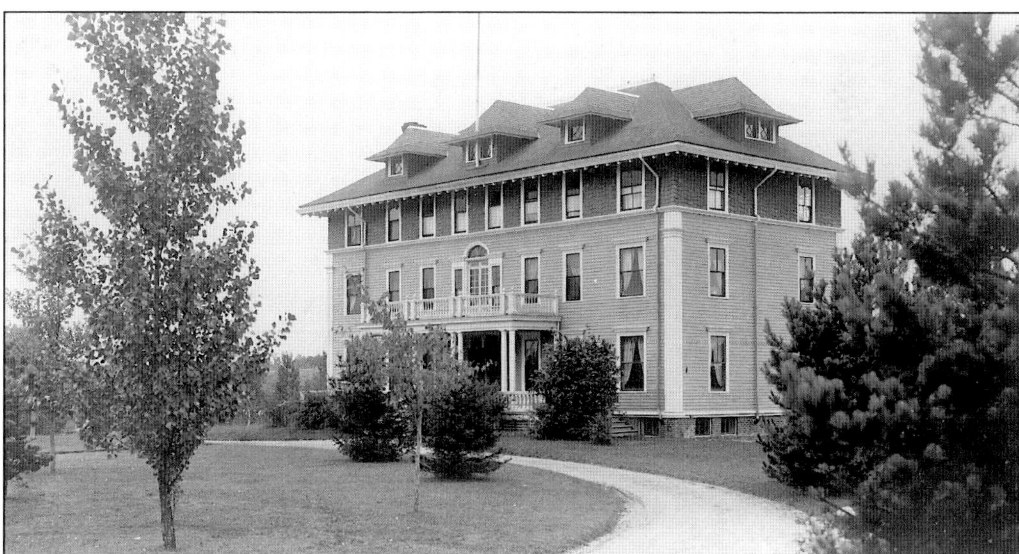

The Phi Gamma Delta Fraternity House, c. 1905.

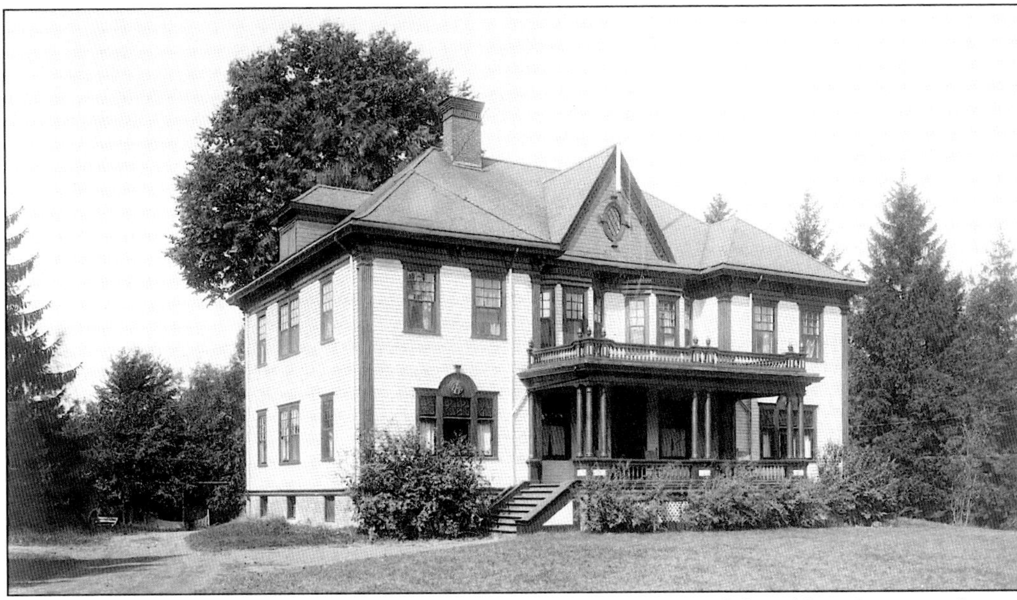

THE SIGMA ALPHA EPSILON FRATERNITY HOUSE, C. 1910. One of the oldest fraternity houses on campus, this house was built in 1904.

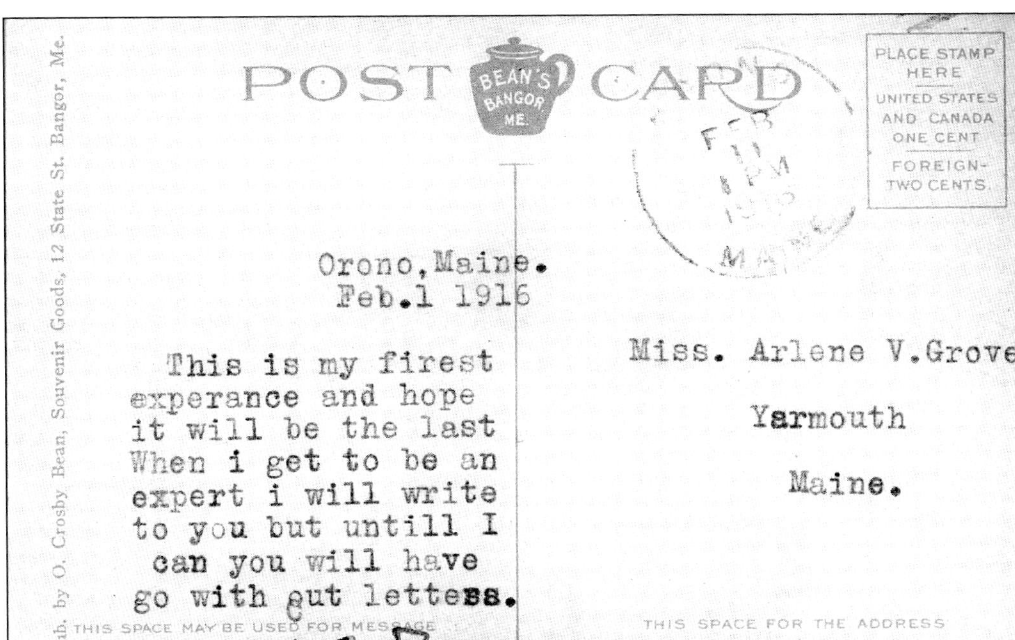

READING YOUR MAIL. A brother or visitor from Alpha Tau Omega sent this revealing note in February of 1916.

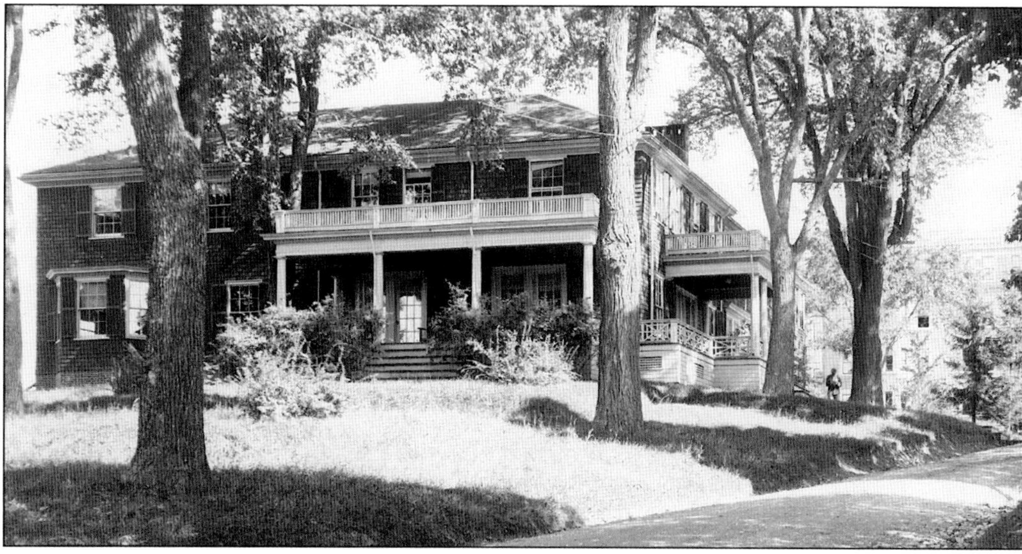

The Beta Theta Pi Fraternity House, c. 1910. The brothers built this house with help from Beta alumni in 1905, after having previously occupied the historic Frost Farmhouse. Lacking permanent residences, many of the early fraternities rented facilities on campus or hired rooms and halls in Orono.

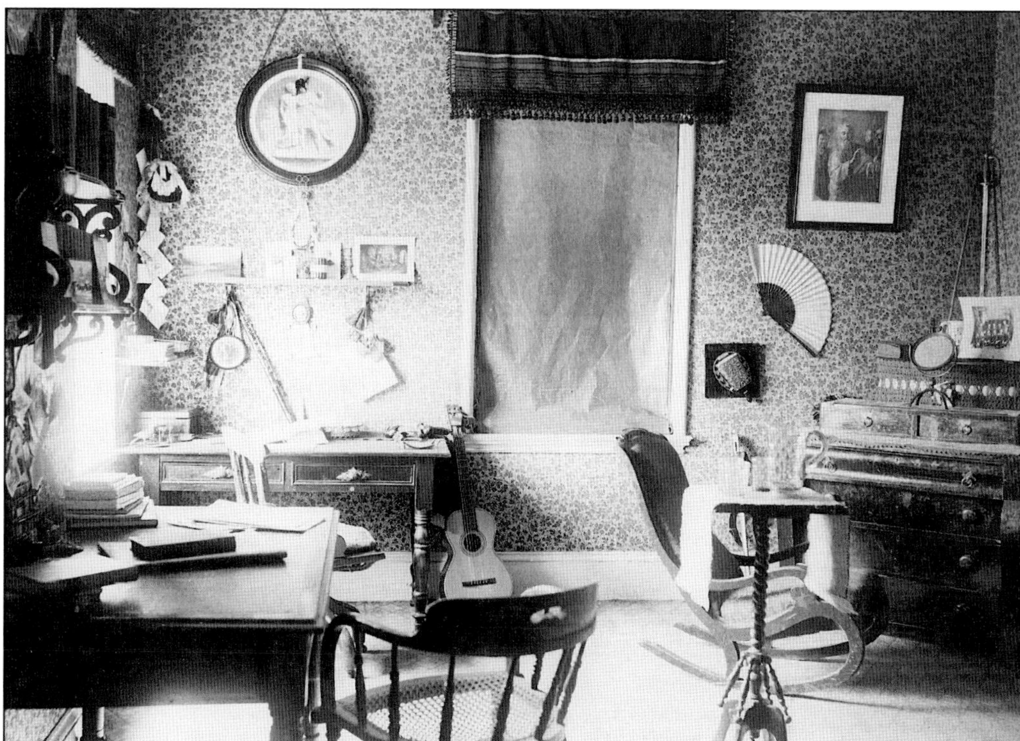

Room of Beta Theta Pi Brother Donald W. Colby, c. 1890. One might assume this person is a scholar, musician, and photographer with classical interests. Note the nightstand with the glass and pitcher.

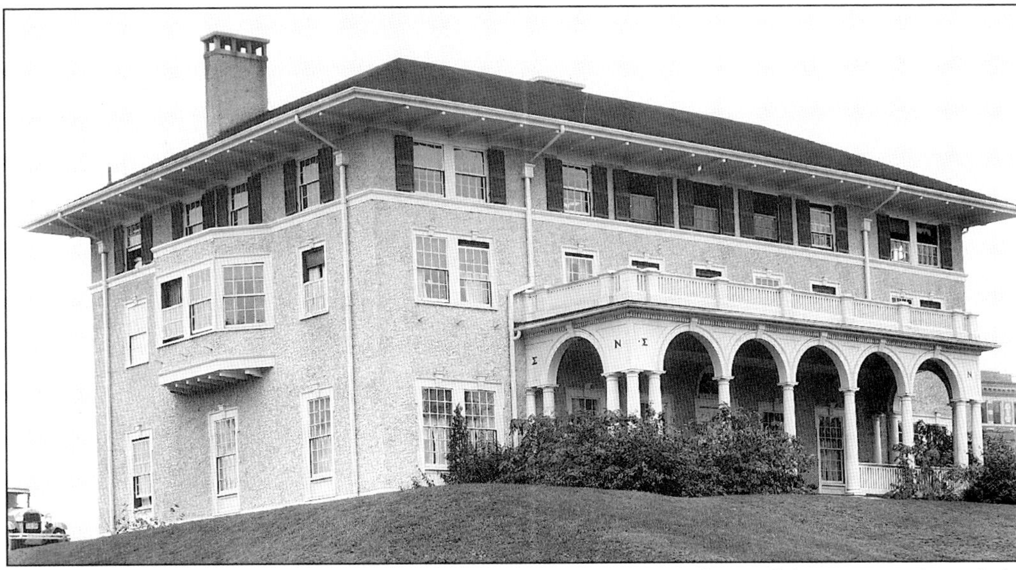

OUTSIDE THE SIGMA NU FRATERNITY HOUSE, C. 1925. Note the well-kept grounds and the automobile in the driveway. The house was built in 1916.

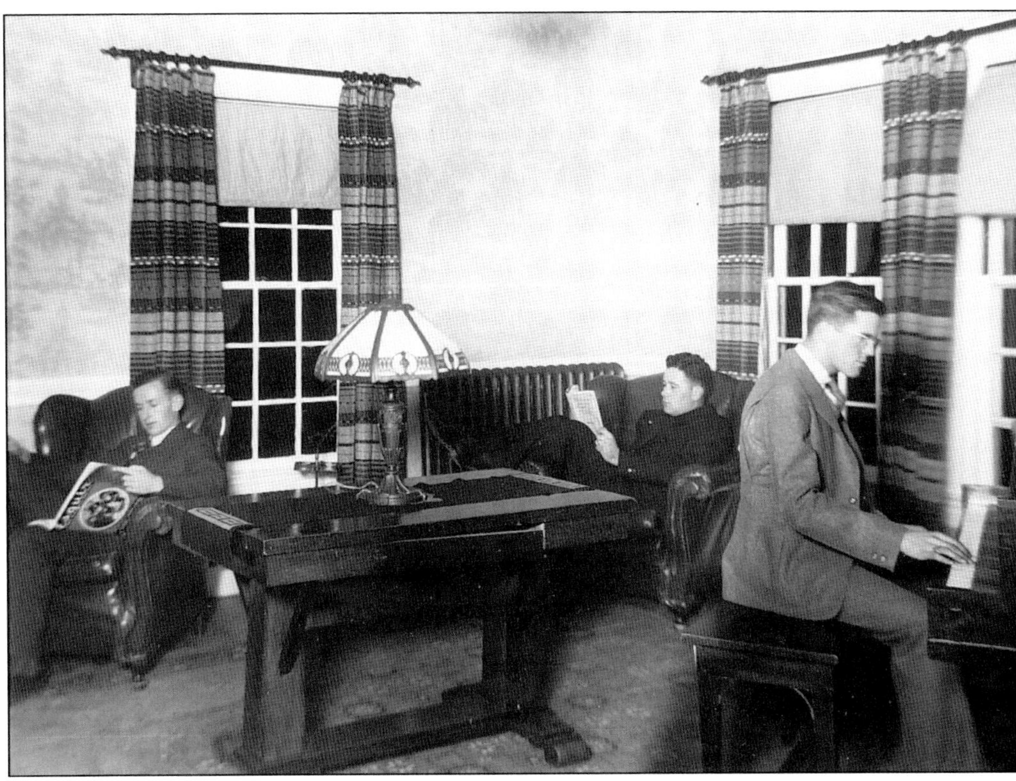

A GLIMPSE OF FRATERNITY LIFE INSIDE THE SIGMA NU HOUSE, C. 1920. The brothers are engaged in a diversity of activity, mostly recreational.

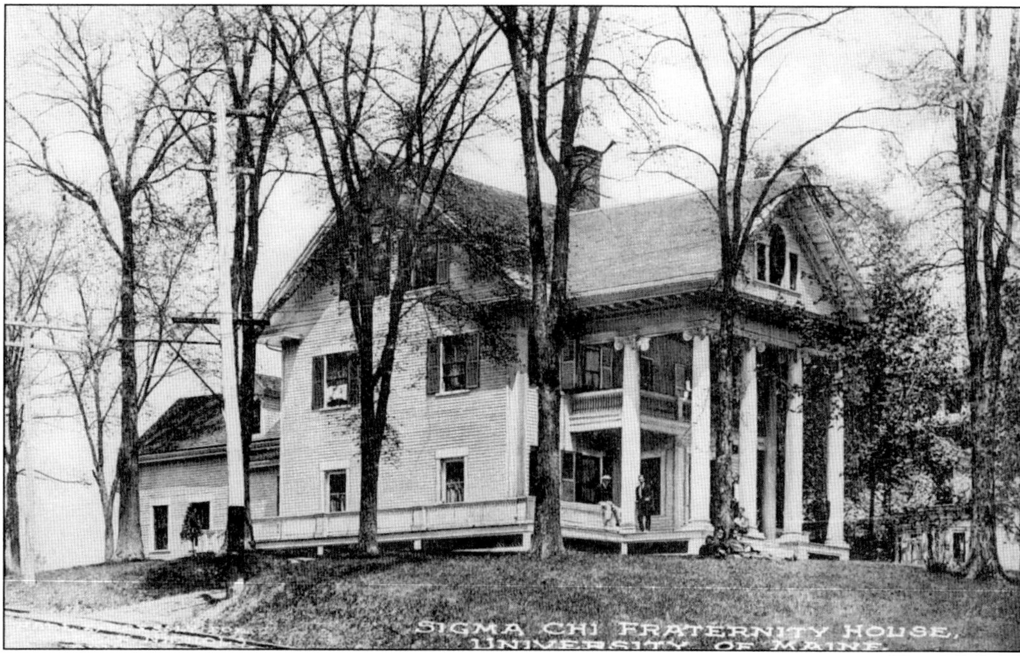

SIGMA CHI FRATERNITY HOUSE, C. 1905. Fraternity brothers bought the Joseph Treat House in 1902 and made significant renovations.

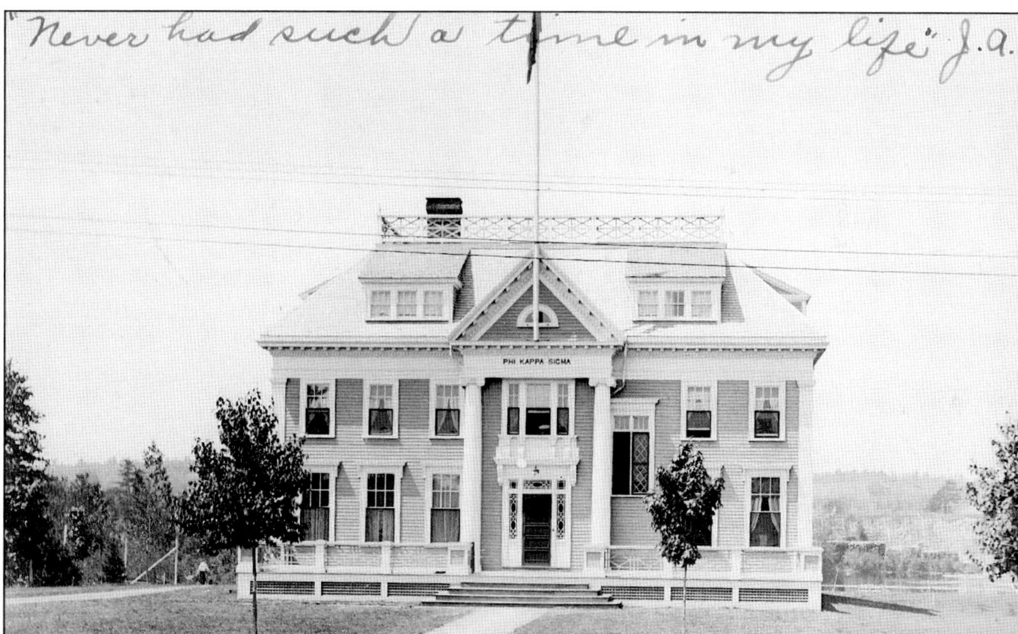

POSTCARD OF THE PHI KAPPA SIGMA HOUSE, DATED APRIL 24, 1906. The inscription reads as follows: "Never had such a time in my life."

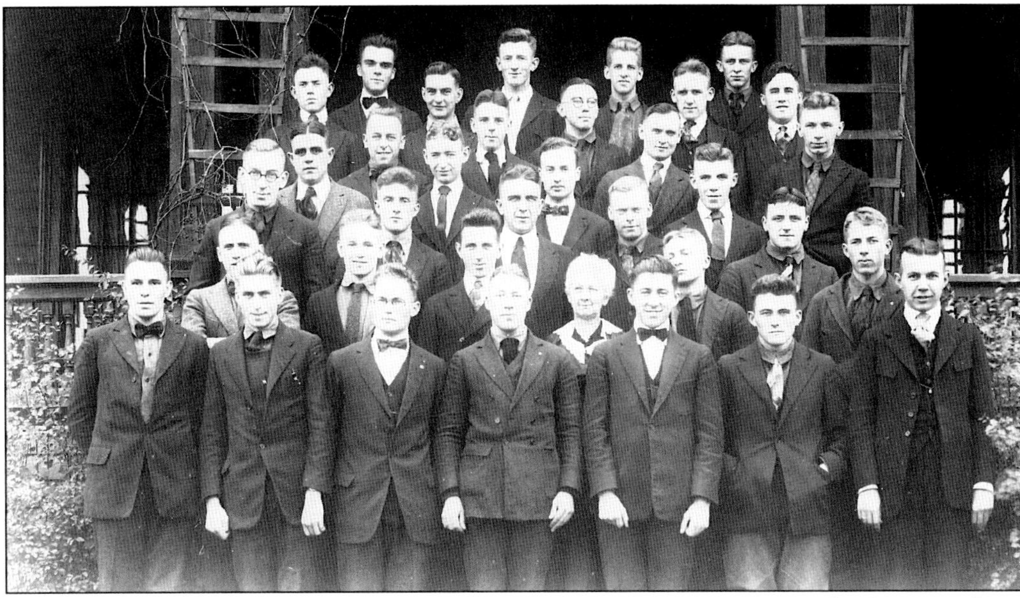

THE BROTHERS OF THETA CHI POSE OUTSIDE OF THEIR HOUSE, C. 1915. The fraternity has a tradition of almost one century at U. Maine. Brothers took advantage of guaranteed loans to build their house in 1908. The building would burn in 1956.

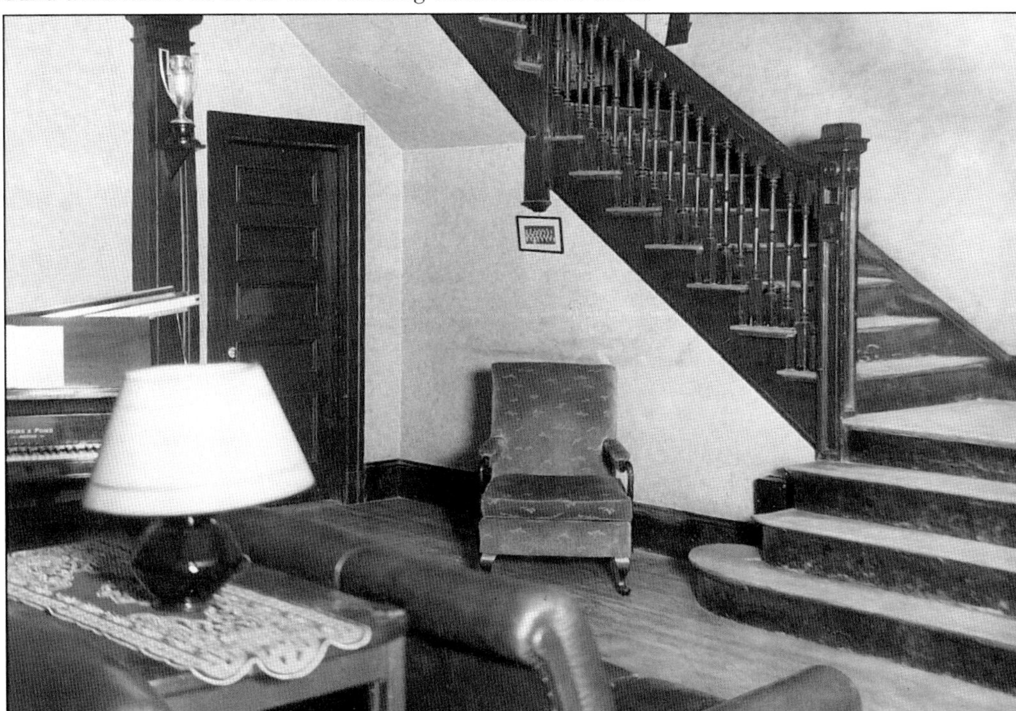

INSIDE THE THETA CHI FRATERNITY HOUSE, C. 1920. House decor could have changed from year to year, depending upon the success of pledge campaigns and the benevolence of house alumni. It appears to have been a lean year, except for the trophy on display (top left) which was probably won in an athletic event against a rival fraternity.

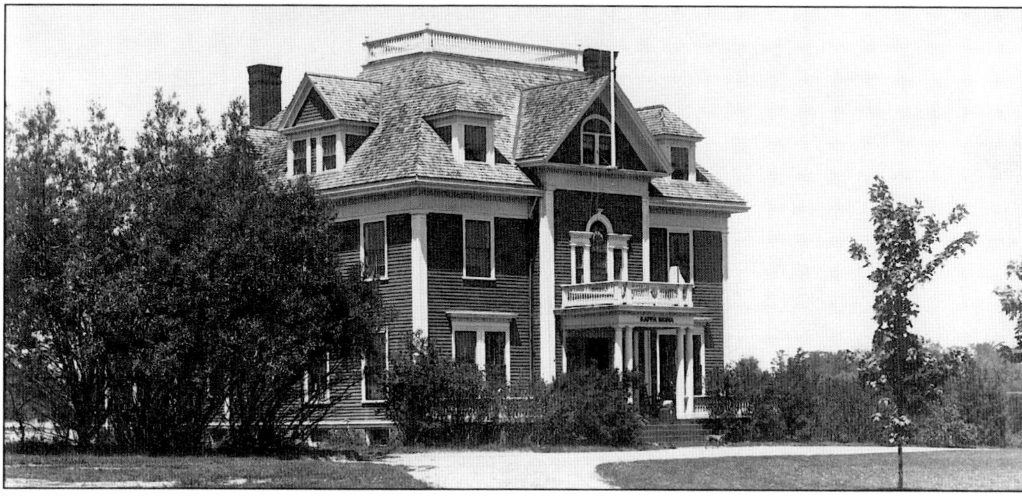

THE KAPPA SIGMA HOUSE, C. 1909.

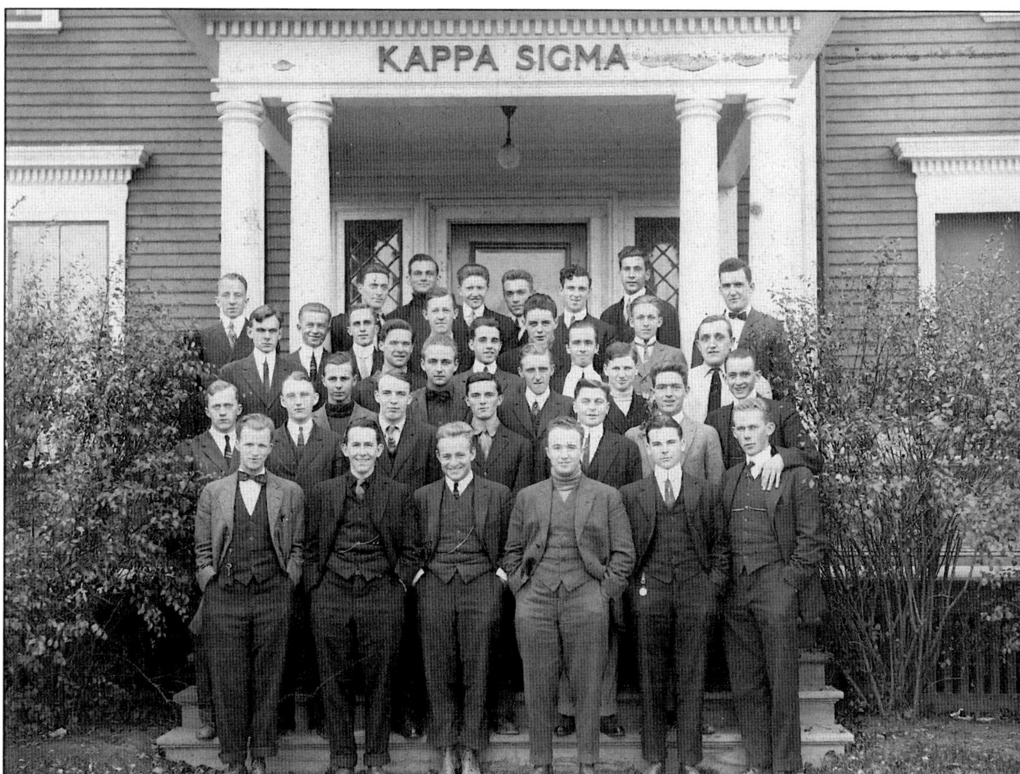

THE BROTHERS OF THE KAPPA SIGMA FRATERNITY, STANDING ON THE FRONT STEPS, NOVEMBER 12, 1913. The Kappa Sigma house, erected in 1895, holds the distinction of being the first fraternity building built on campus.

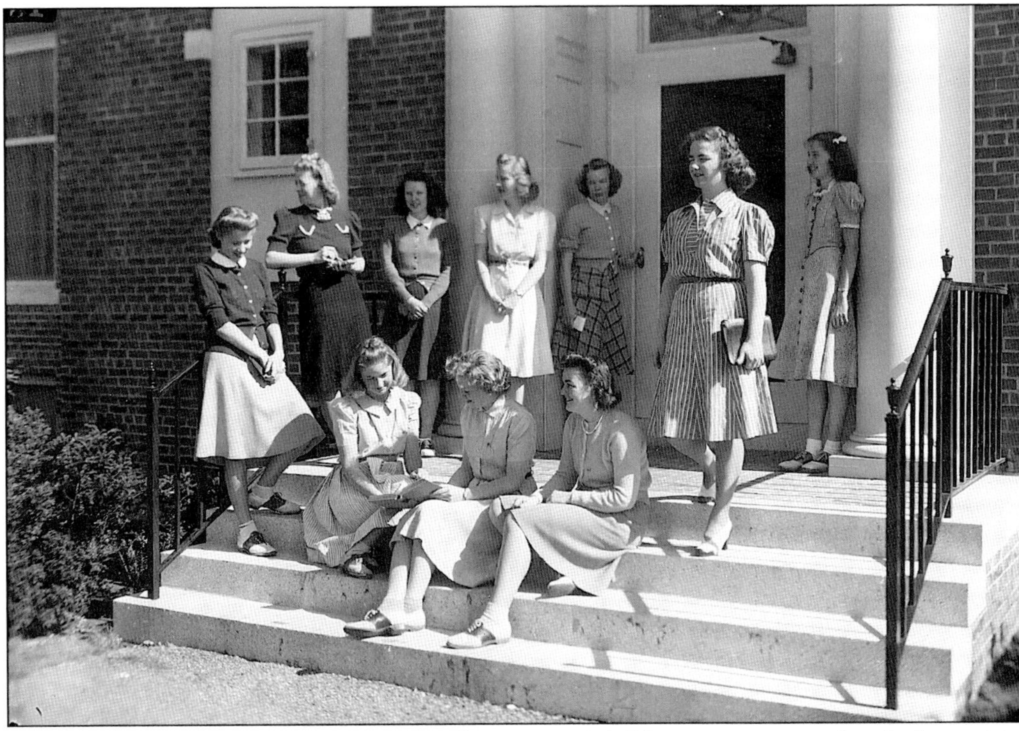

SORORITY SISTERS IN FRONT OF COLVIN HALL, C. 1935. The counterparts of male fraternities were, of course, the female sororities that began appearing on campus as early as 1896. The first sorority established was Phi Gamma, which became Delta Sigma in 1903.

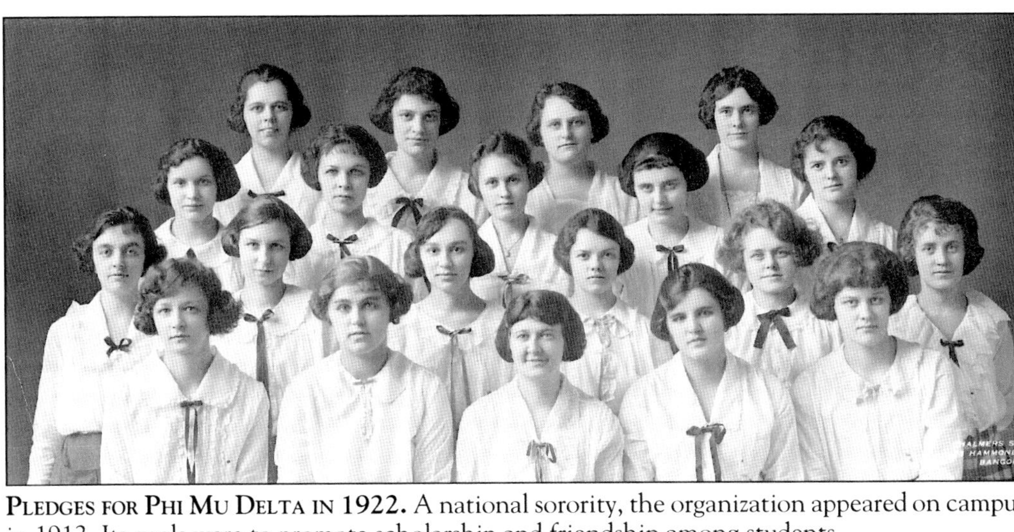

PLEDGES FOR PHI MU DELTA IN 1922. A national sorority, the organization appeared on campus in 1912. Its goals were to promote scholarship and friendship among students.

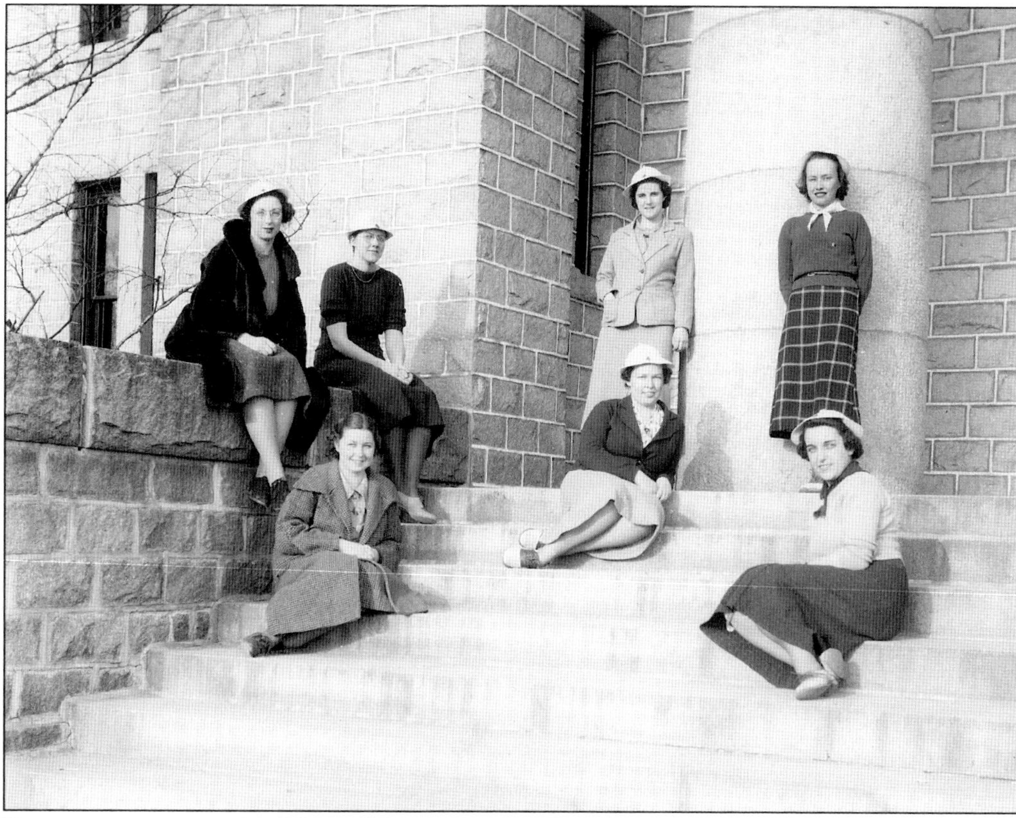

REPRESENTATIVES OF ALL MAINE WOMEN OUTSIDE CARNEGIE HALL, C. 1935. The honor society was established on campus in 1925 by President Little and Dean Caroline Colvin to recognize distinguished leadership, scholarship, and character.

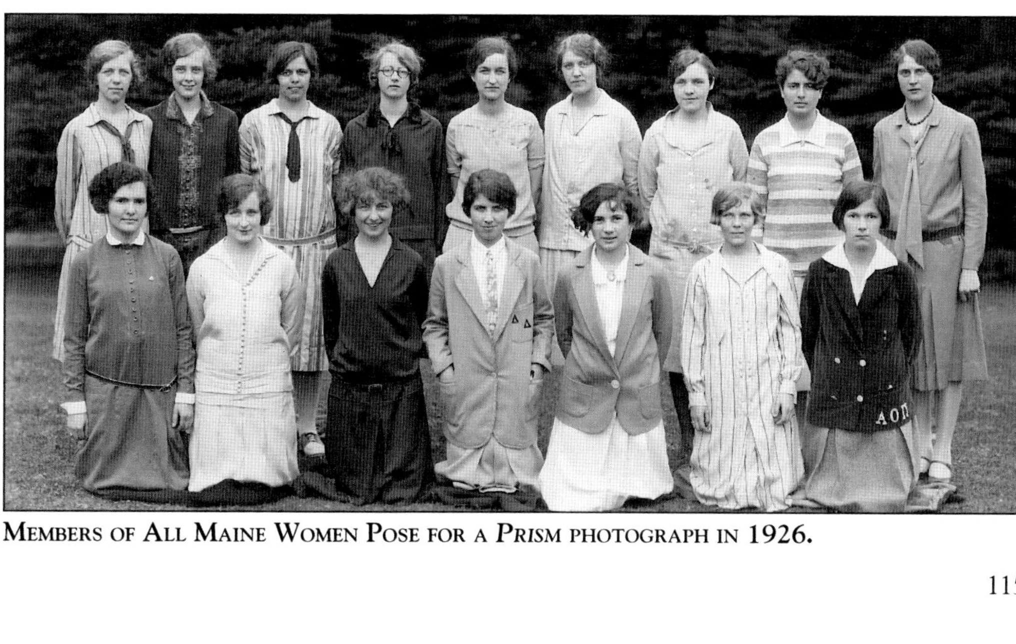

MEMBERS OF ALL MAINE WOMEN POSE FOR A *PRISM* PHOTOGRAPH IN 1926.

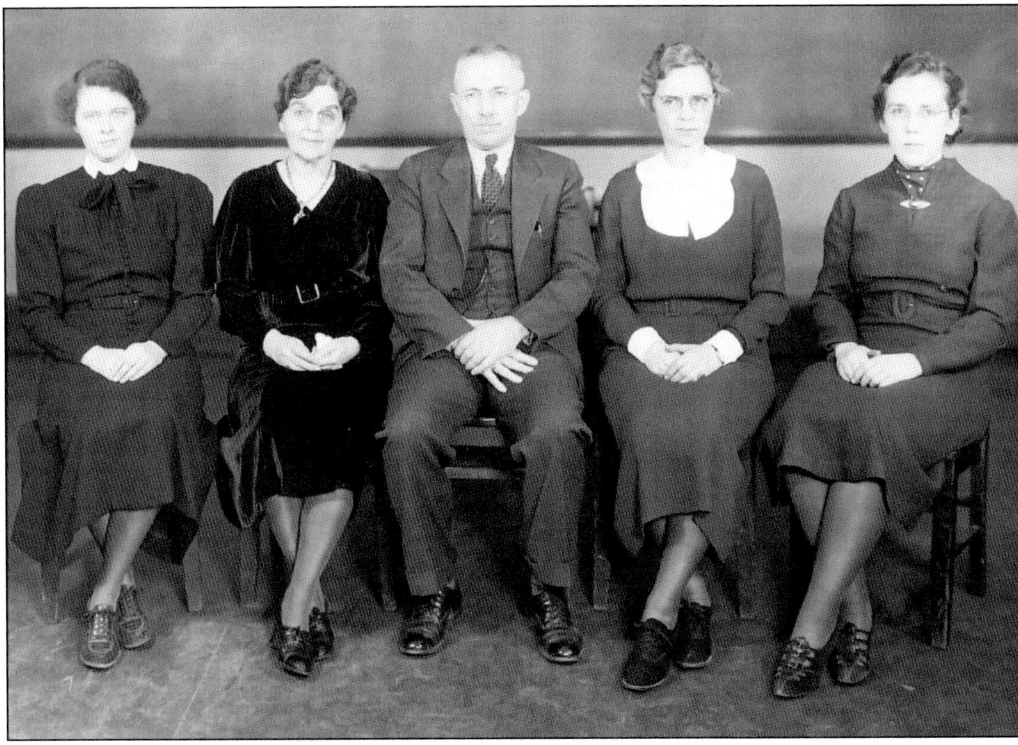

Representatives of Kappa Delta Pi Pose for a *Prism* Photograph in 1938. Shown here, from left to right, are Martha Simmons, Professor Ava Chadbourne, Dean Lutes, Dean Nilson, and Barbara Colby. The organization is an honor society for education.

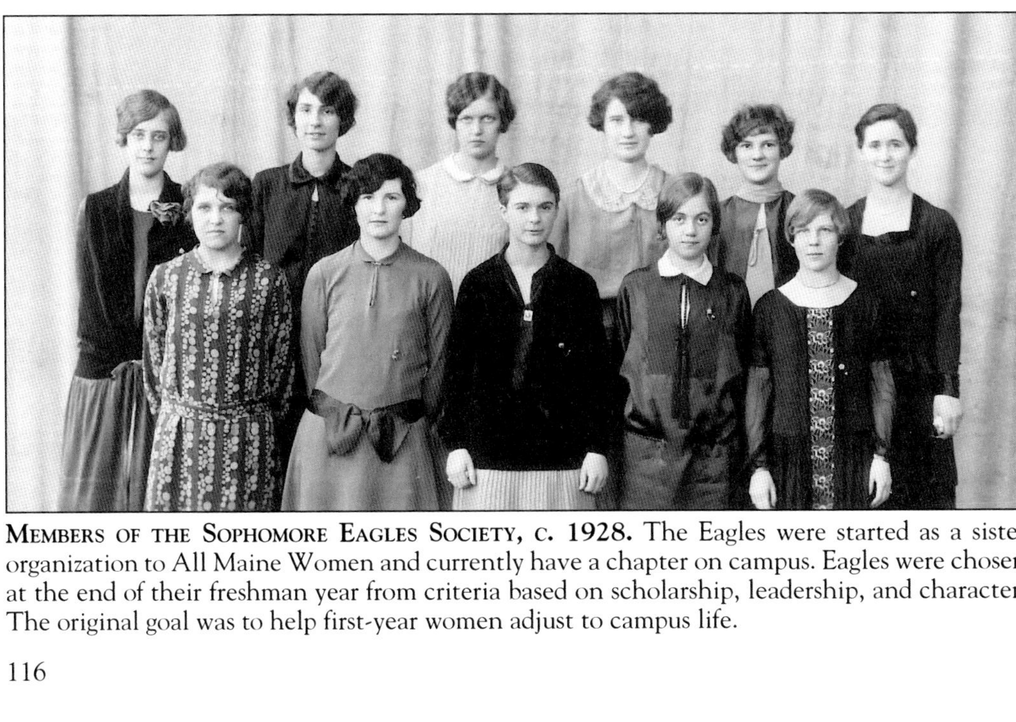

Members of the Sophomore Eagles Society, c. 1928. The Eagles were started as a sister organization to All Maine Women and currently have a chapter on campus. Eagles were chosen at the end of their freshman year from criteria based on scholarship, leadership, and character. The original goal was to help first-year women adjust to campus life.

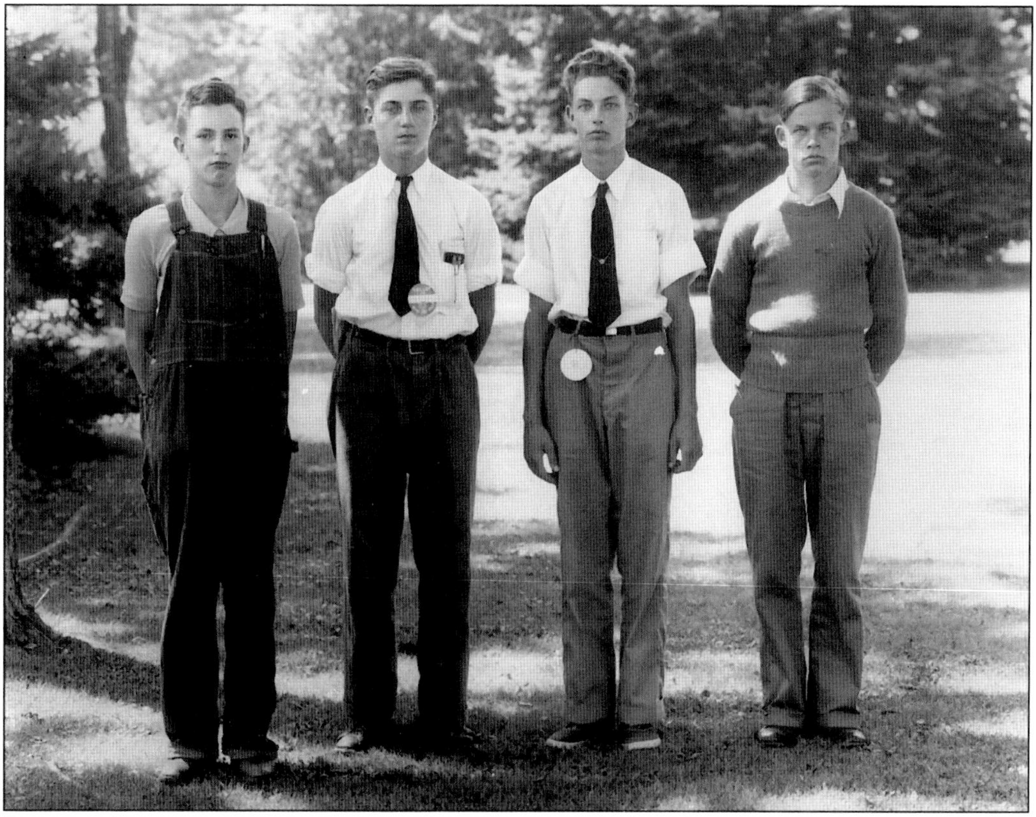

STUDENT PARTICIPANTS IN THE 4-H CLUB, c. 1930. This photograph is most likely not of university students but rather students brought by the statewide program for activities held on campus. For many, it was their first taste of college life and some would make return visits as university students.

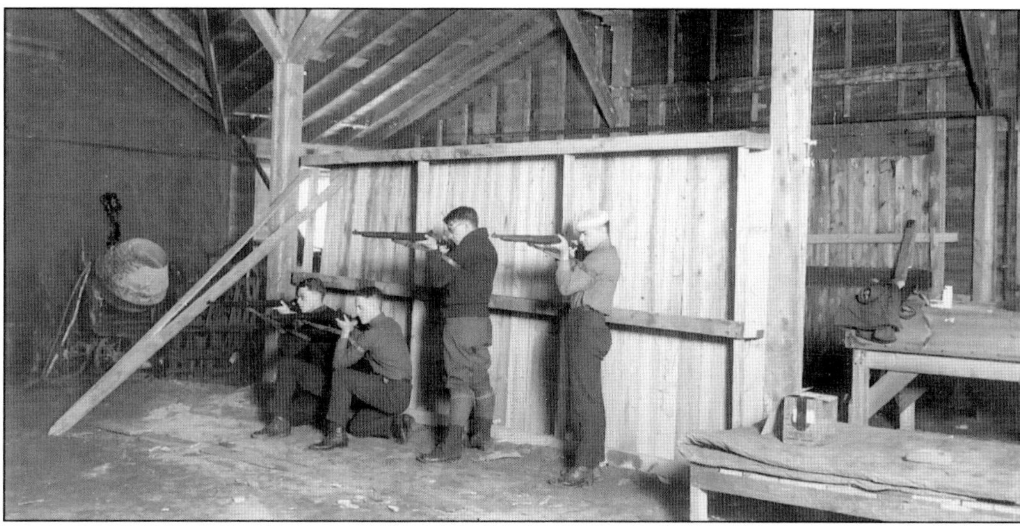

READY, AIM. . . Members of the Rifle Club pose for this c. 1925 staged photograph. A space for a rifle range was later located in Memorial Gymnasium. Riflery became a varsity sport and the club boasted the highest winning percentage of any on campus.

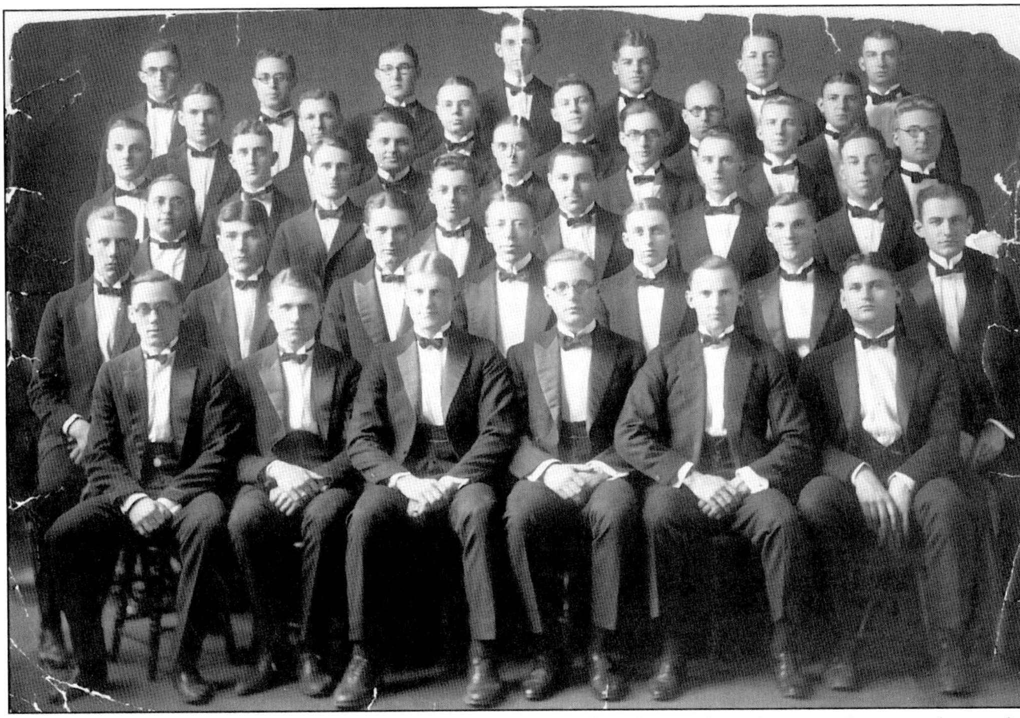

The 1923–24 Glee and Instrument Club. Music has long played a significant role in the lives and pursuits of campus residents. In 1916, Fernald wrote that music and minstrel clubs "have long held a conspicuous place in the life of the institution."

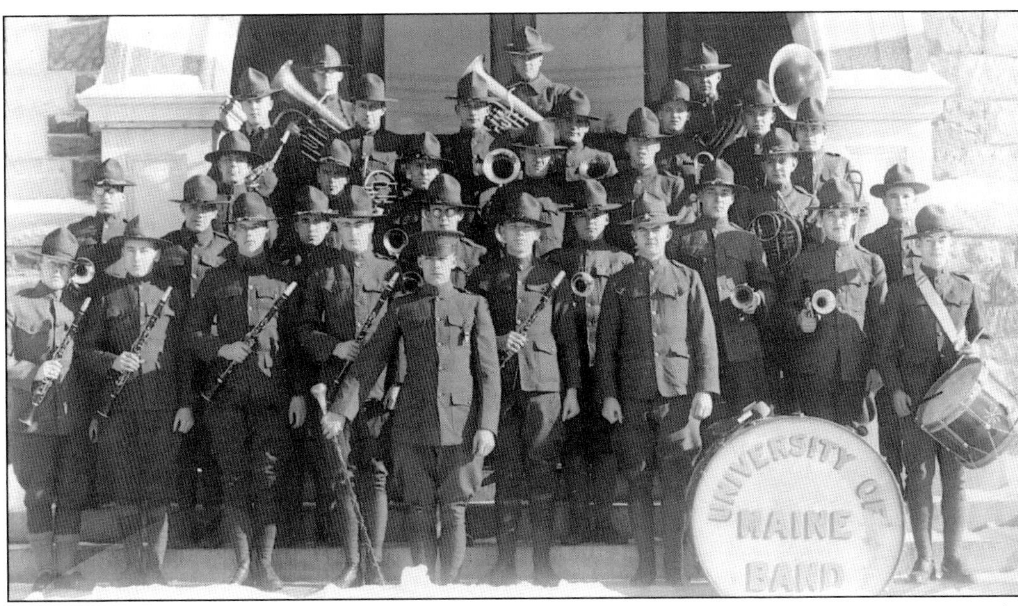

The University of Maine Marching Band, in front of Carnegie Hall, c. 1915. The two images on this page afford a contrast in the music enjoyed on campus. The university band played at football games and political rallies, while the glee club often entertained coat-and-tie gatherings at Alumni Hall and the Bangor Opera House.

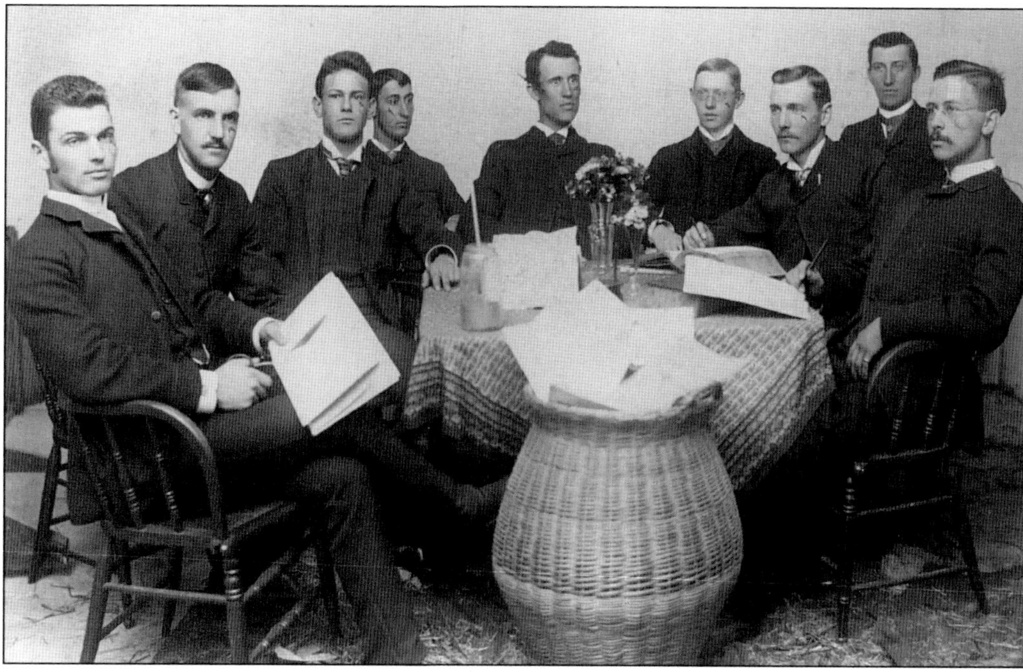

THE EDITORIAL BOARD OF THE 1887–88 *CADET*. From 1883 to 1920 there were 13 student publications on campus written by fraternities and honor societies, in addition to several attempts at a college newspaper. In 1873, the *Crucible* was issued as the first student newspaper, but it was short-lived and was replaced by the *College Reporter*. In 1885, the *Cadet* appeared as a monthly journal about student and campus life. It was later renamed the *Campus*, and in 1904 it became the *Maine Campus*.

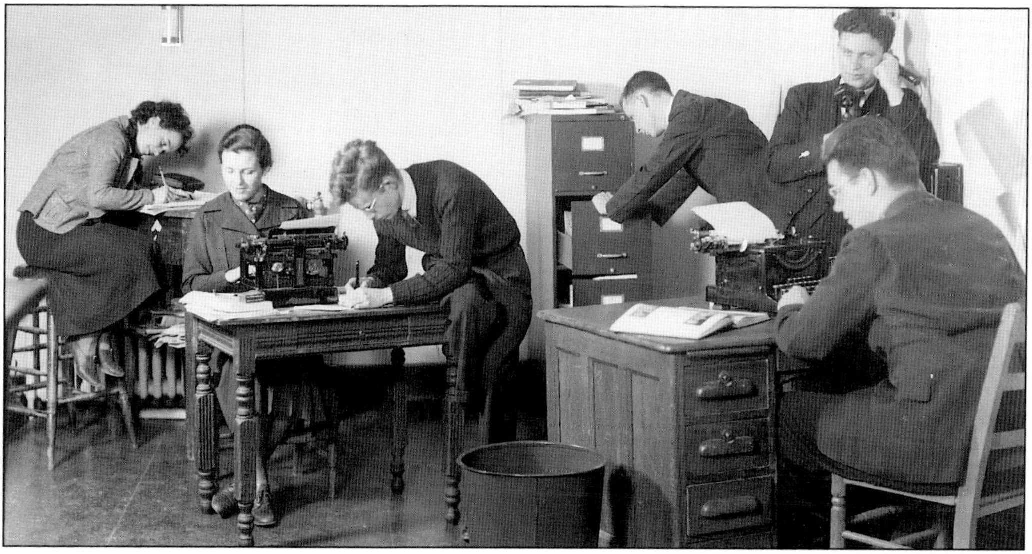

STAFF AND EDITORS WORKING ON THE *PRISM* YEARBOOK, C. 1928. The first edition of the *Prism* came out in 1894. It was a publication that chronicled student activities, campus life, and took satirical jabs at faculty and administration. The 1912 *Prism* defined itself as: "Prism—a beacon of light where the staff gets burned." The yearbook, which had a tradition of over a century, has recently been discontinued.

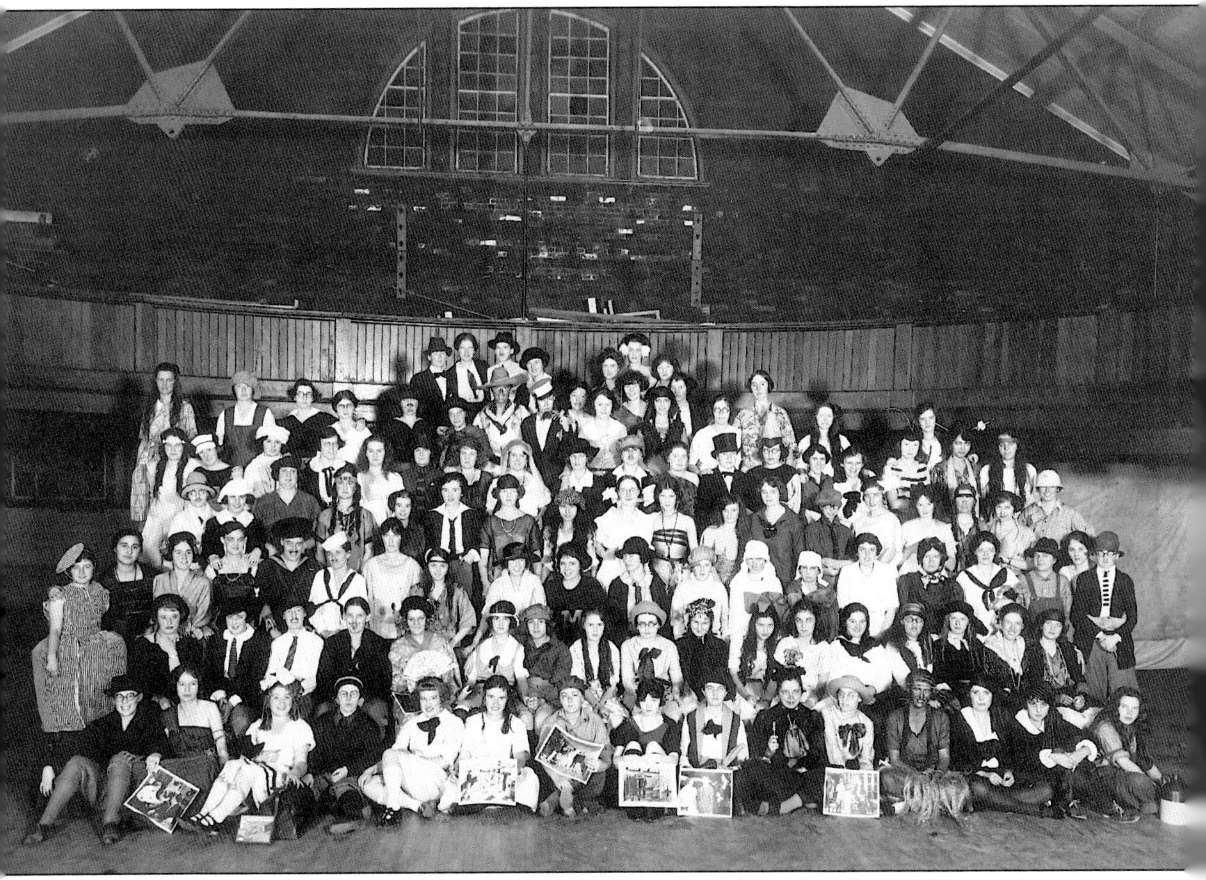

A Cast Photograph Taken in Alumni Hall, c. 1910. This could have been a theatrical performance or perhaps an event held during Maine Night, a pep rally popular on campus from 1902 to the beginning of WW I. The annual event occurred on the eve of the football game against archrival Bowdoin. Held in the gymnasium at Alumni Hall, Maine Night featured drama, singing, and exhortations from faculty and students. The event was usually followed by a bonfire and the singing of the Maine Stein Song or the University Hymn.

THE CAST OF *DUMDORA*, A PRODUCTION OF THE MAINE MASQUE IN 1915. First known as the dramatic club, the group appeared on campus around 1900. It was founded by Professor Windsor P. Daggett, who, along with student Lincoln Colcord, composed the Maine Stein Song. Daggett also founded the university orchestra, the glee club, and the marching band in his long tenure at the university.

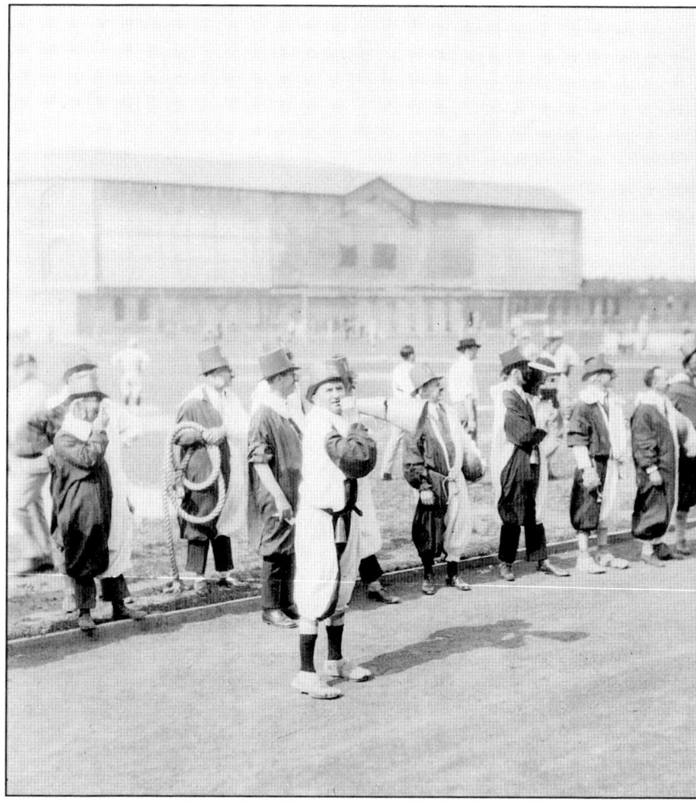

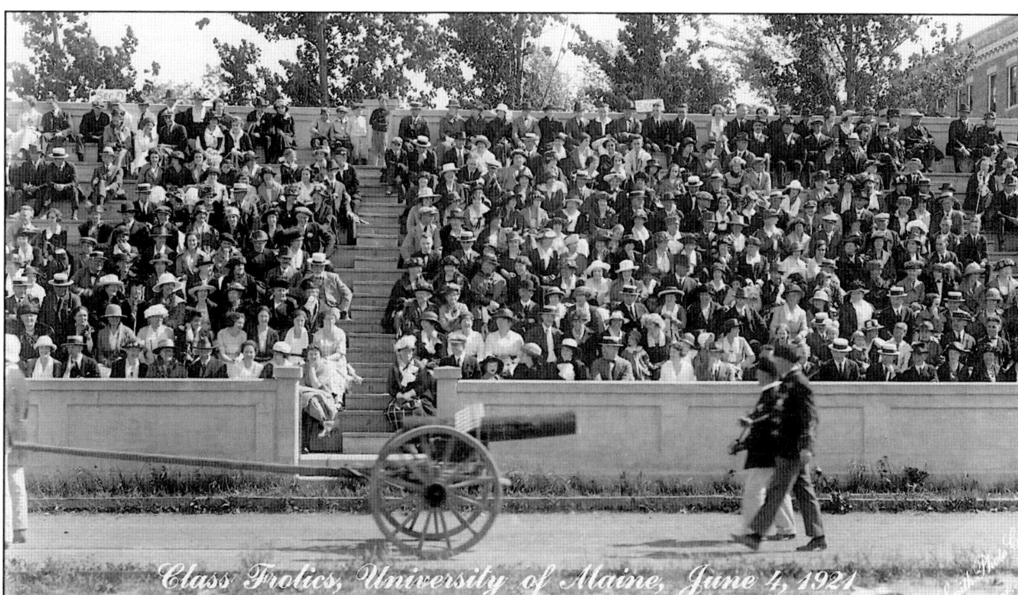

CLASS DAY ACTIVITIES, JUNE 4, 1921. Participants in the event are shown marching around the track at Alumni Field.

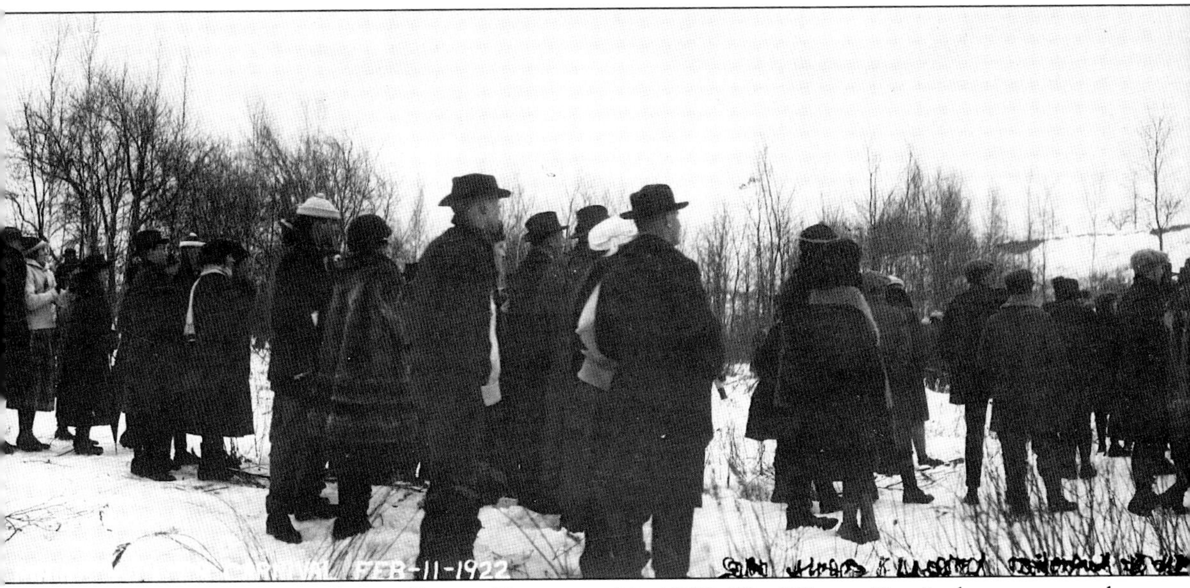

A Winter Carnival Scene, Dated February 11, 1922. The Winter Carnival was a natural tradition for students surviving the long Maine winter. This event appears to be a ski

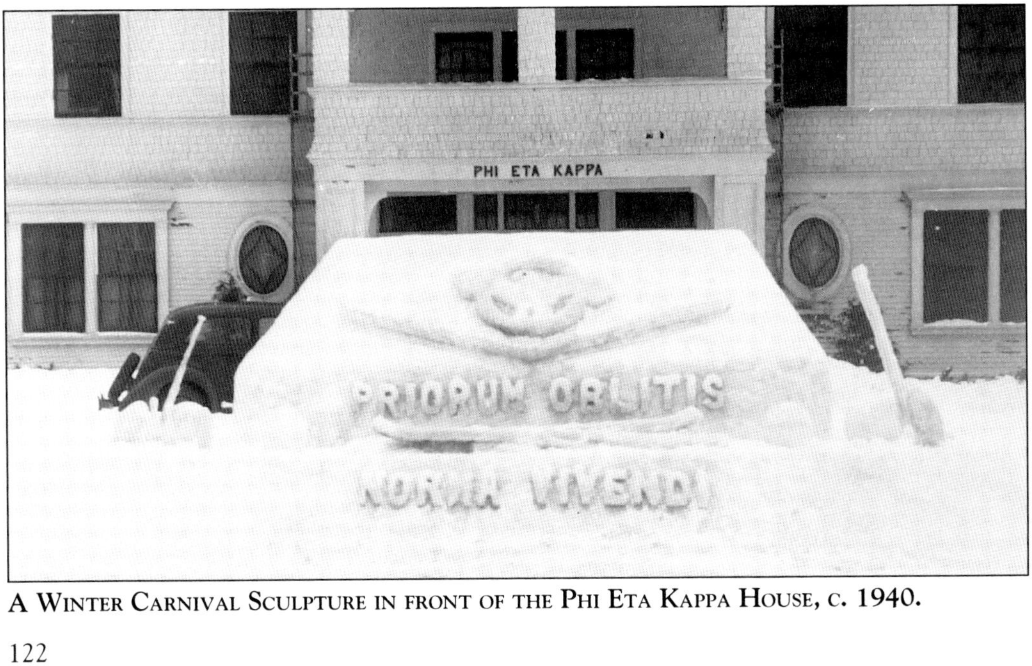

A Winter Carnival Sculpture in front of the Phi Eta Kappa House, c. 1940.

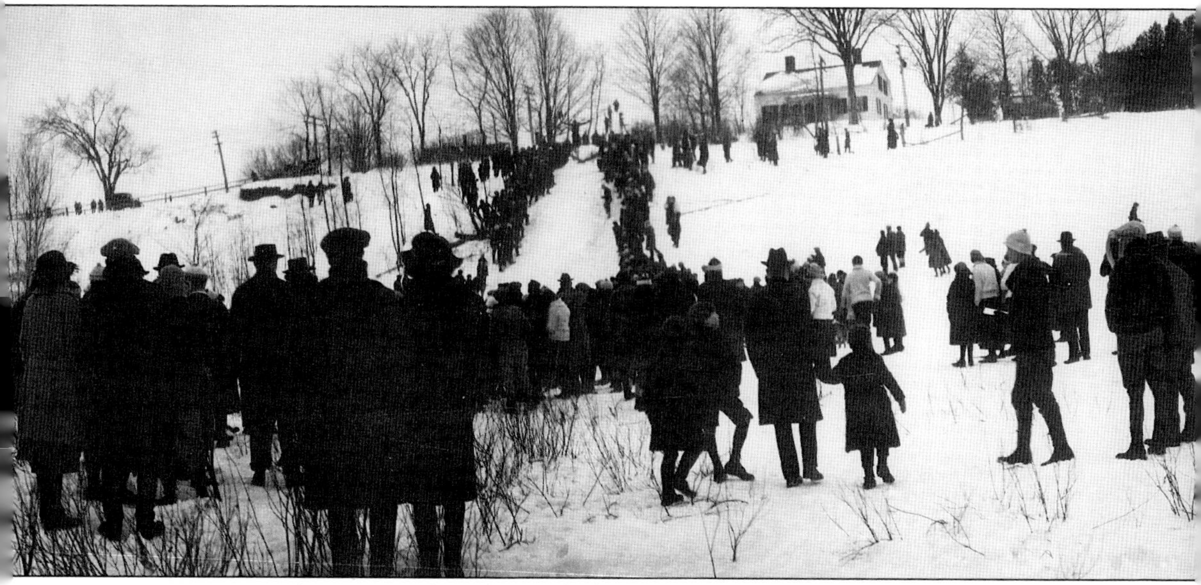

jump competition that occurred on the south shore of the Stillwater River.

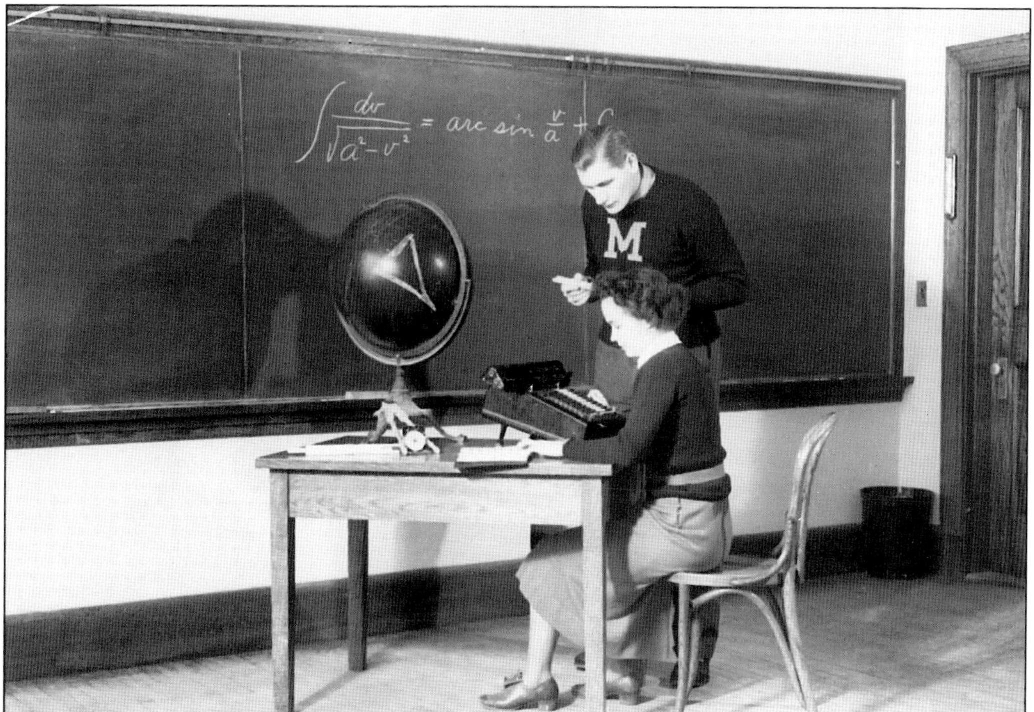

UNIVERSITY STUDENTS WALLACE GLEASON AND NANCY HENNINGS, INSIDE THE CLASSROOM IN 1938. The "M" on Gleason's sweater signifies his involvement in the M Club. As far back as 1902, M sweaters were awarded to members of the football, baseball, track, and tennis teams. An organization known as the "Wearers of the M" was founded in 1904 to promote and raise money for athletics at the university. In 1912, the group's name was changed to the M Club. In 1927, the club gave recognition to women involved in sports.

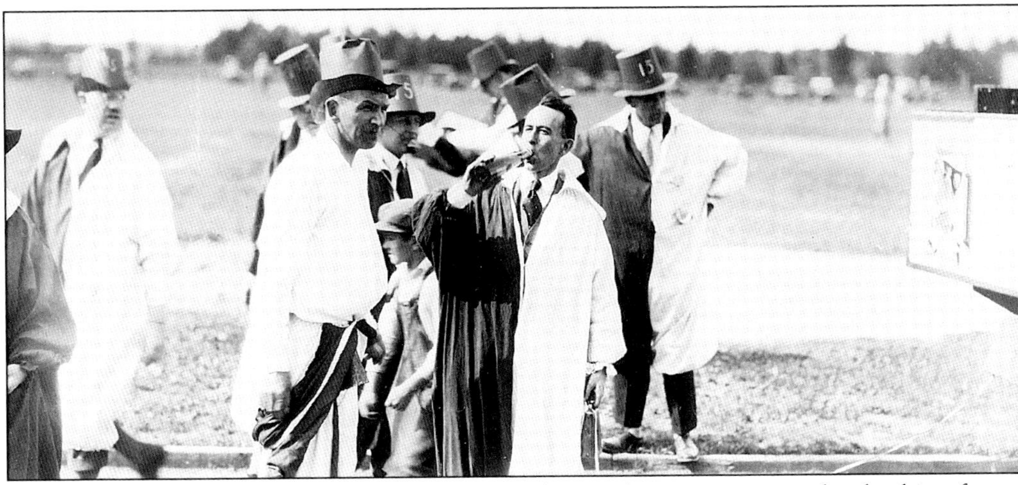

A Commencement Exercise Event, c. 1929. The gentleman appears to be drinking from a bottle in a brown bag, which may indicate a Prohibition-period date. Hats worn by returning alumni signify that they were members of the class of 1915.

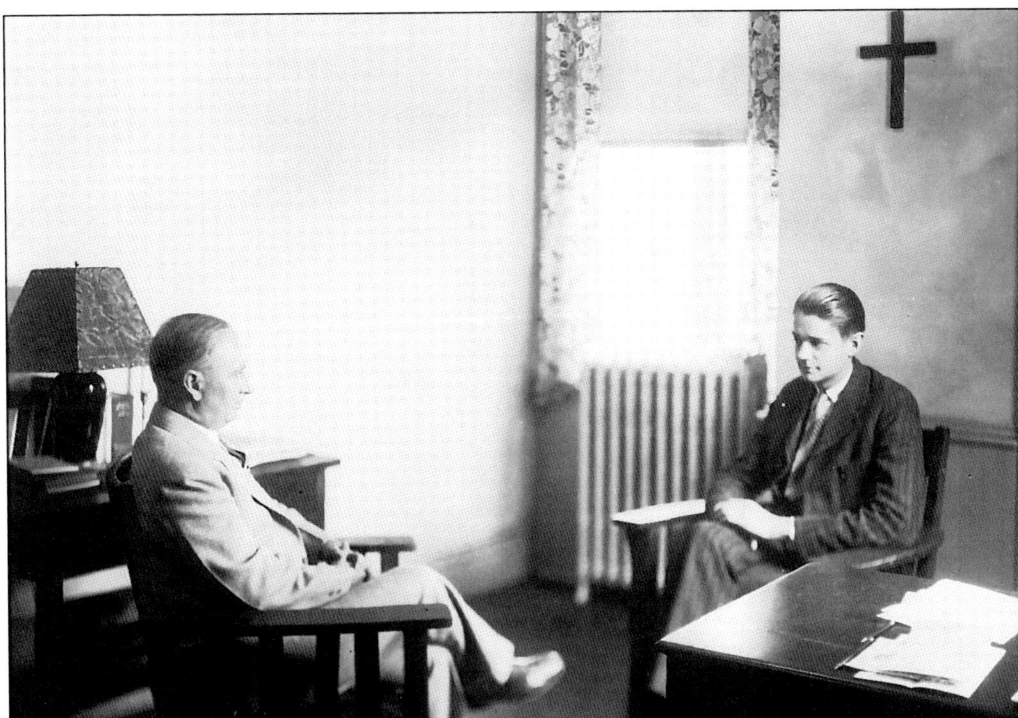

A Student Conferring with A Maine Christian Association Advisor, c. 1920. A debate that had been ongoing on campus from its beginning was whether religious training should be a province of the college. In 1917, the results of a poll among students were split over the institution of chapel and the necessity of religious instruction. The faculty maintained that it should remain a part of student life but not be compulsory.

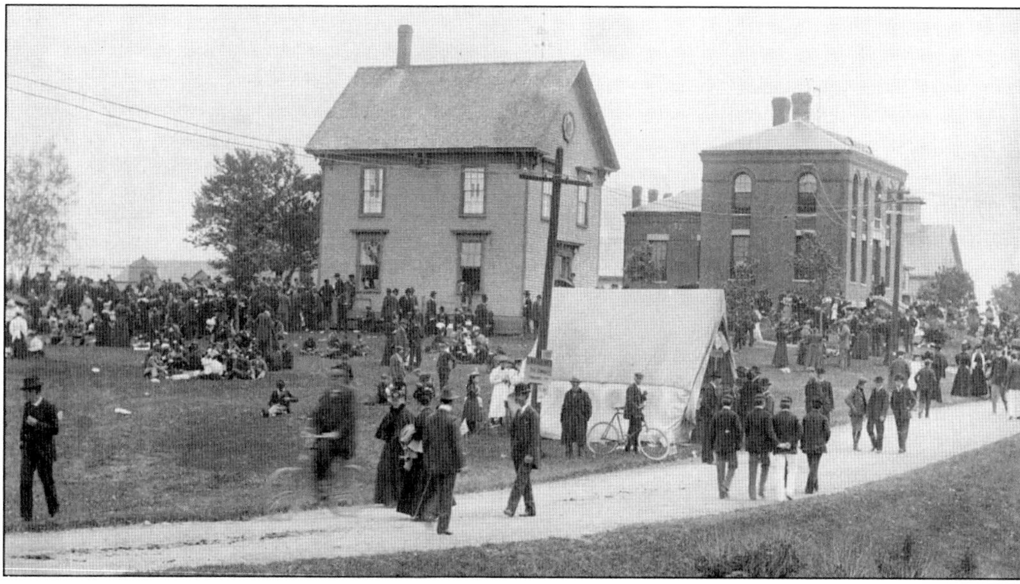

A CROWD ON CAMPUS FOR COMMENCEMENT ACTIVITIES, C. 1890. Seen in the photo are the QTV fraternity house and the experiment station. From 1885 to 1911, commencement week had its heyday with scaled-down versions occurring afterwards. In 1894, caps and gowns were worn by graduates for the first time.

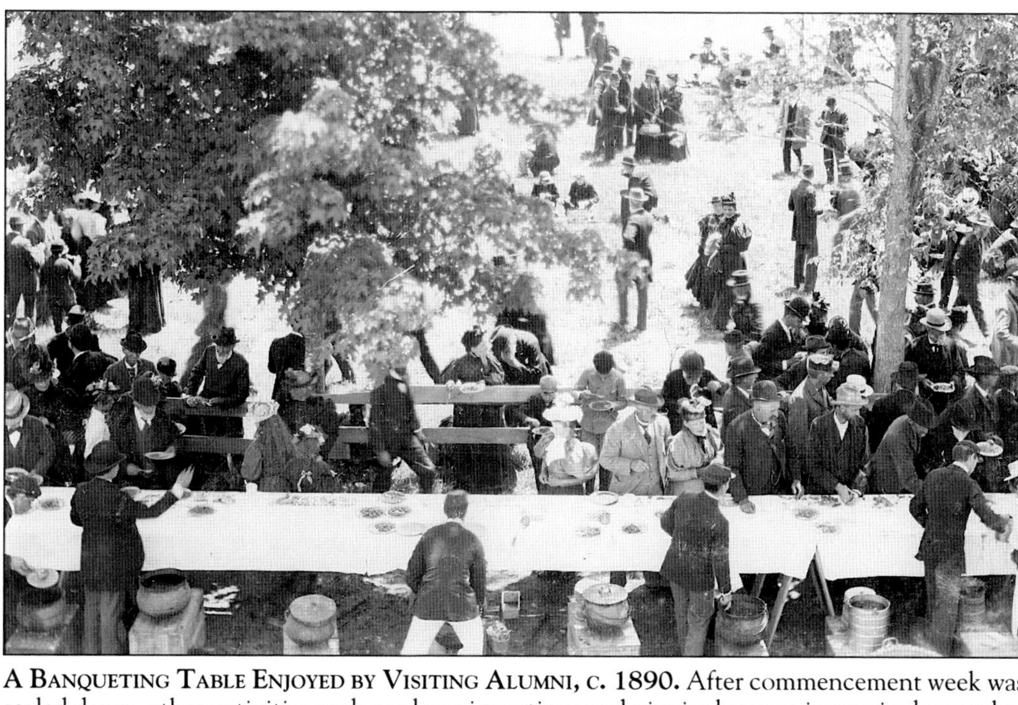

A BANQUETING TABLE ENJOYED BY VISITING ALUMNI, C. 1890. After commencement week was scaled down, other activities such as alumni meetings and picnics became increasingly popular.

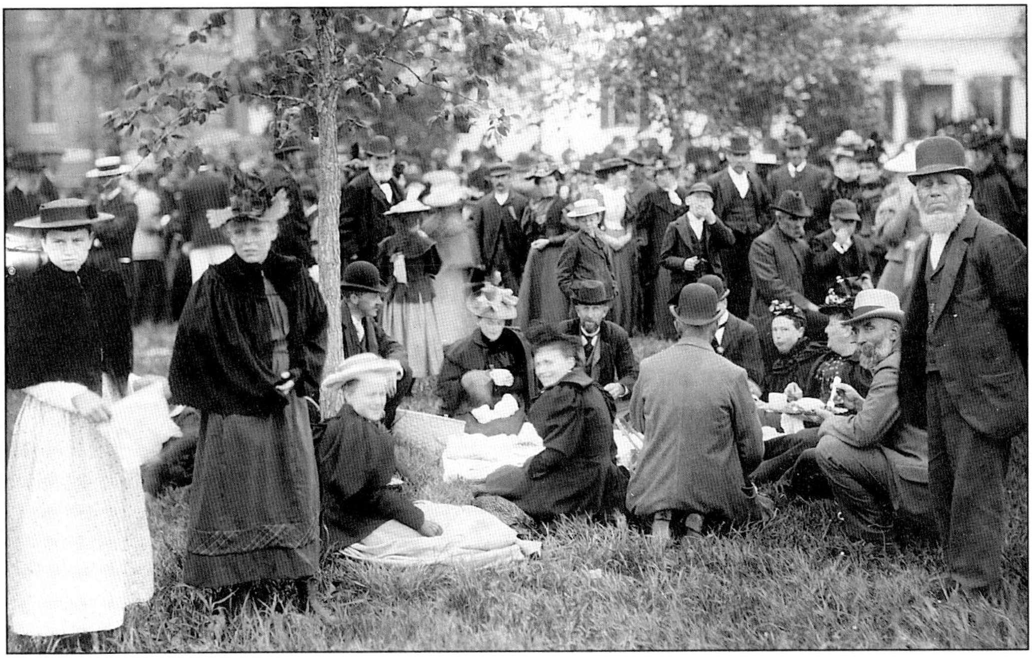

An Alumni Picnic Event, c. 1890. Alumni members are gathered here to participate in a campus picnic. This photograph depicts the old Estabrooke Hall, in the background (right), and Oak Hall is on the left. Alumni associations were created to extend the influence of the university and to renew old acquaintances.

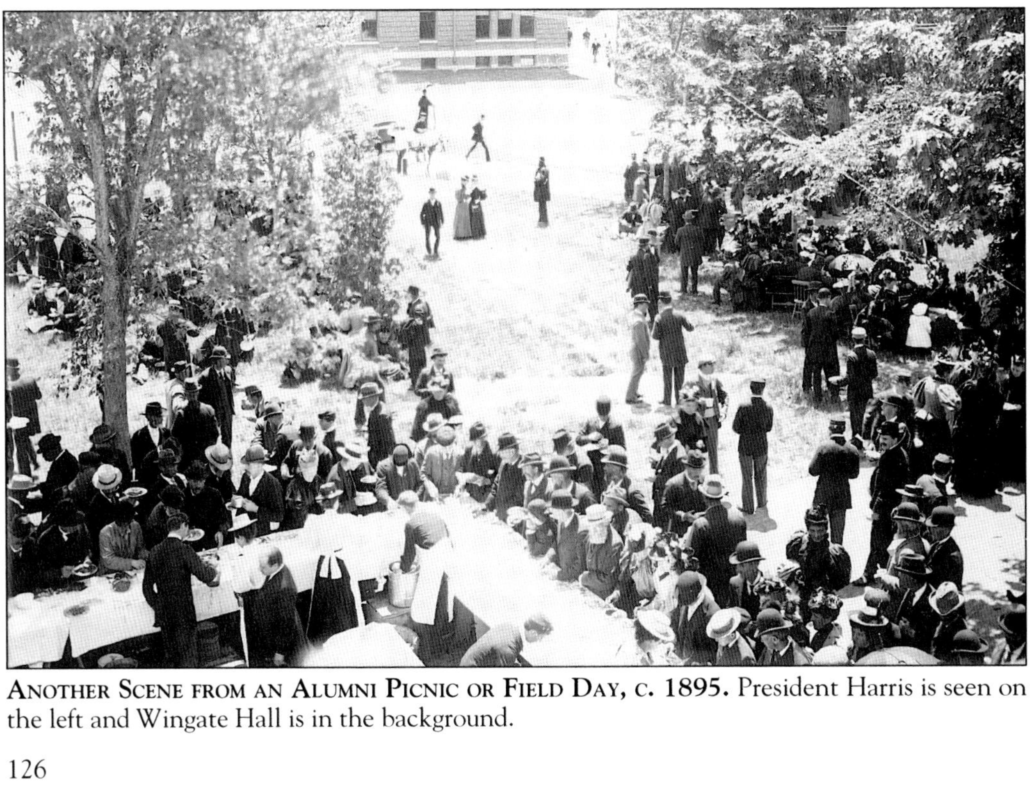

Another Scene from an Alumni Picnic or Field Day, c. 1895. President Harris is seen on the left and Wingate Hall is in the background.

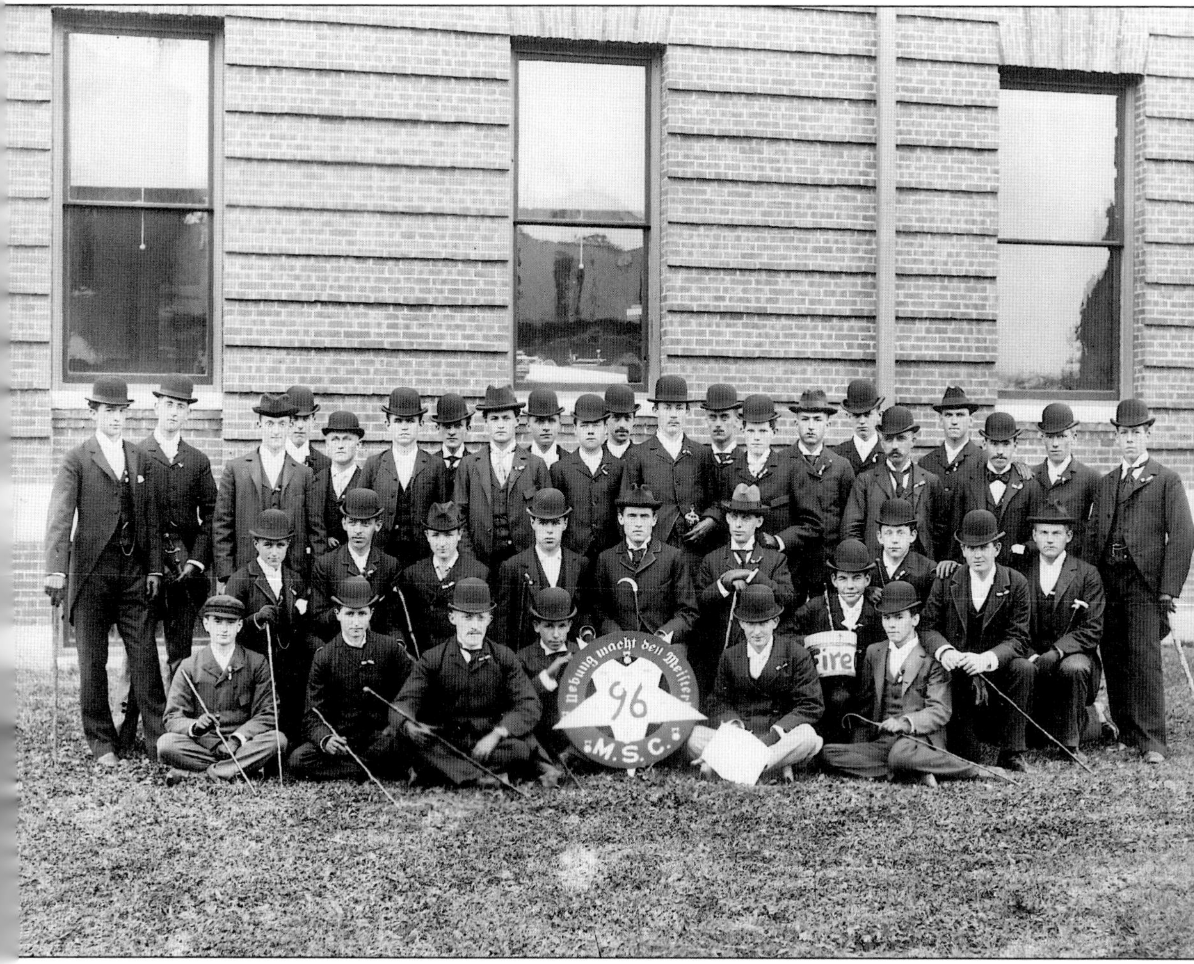

MAINE STATE COLLEGE STUDENTS, GATHERING FOR IVY DAY COMMEMORATION IN THE SPRING OF 1894. Ivy Day was established at the college to plant the vines that are prominently seen on buildings in many of the early photographs of the campus. It stemmed from the passage of the Forest Commission Act of 1889, an early environmental protection legislation. Ivy Day was also the day classes formally moved up to the next year.

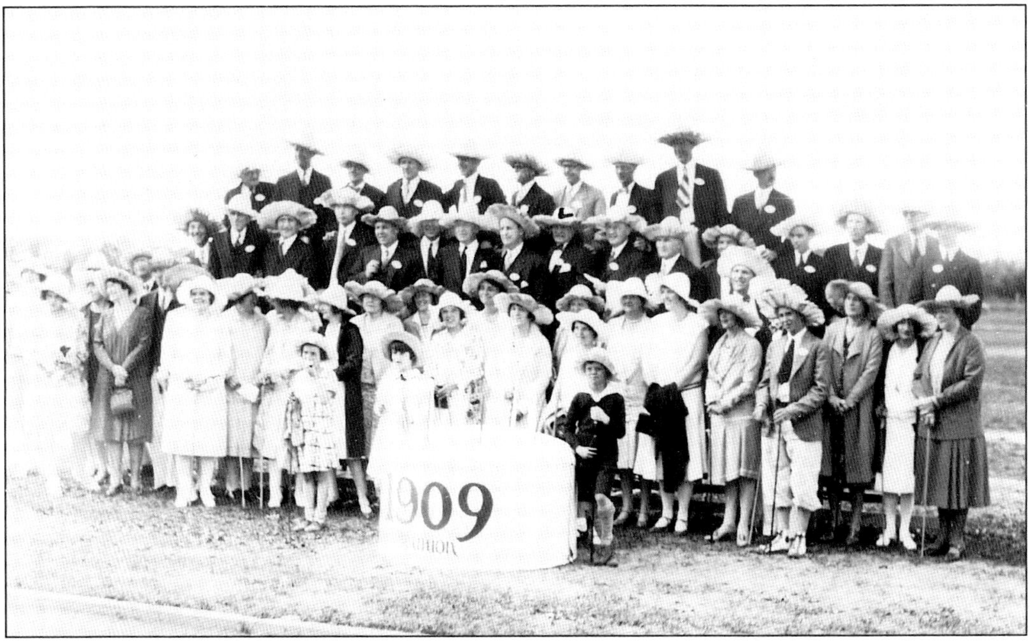

The Class of 1909 Poses for a reunion Photograph, with Mates and Children, at the 1929 Commencement. Commencement week was well established by the 1880s, with an activity scheduled for each day of the week. Major concerts were held with students giving addresses and cadets doing drills. Area ministers also provided a baccalaureate service for graduates.

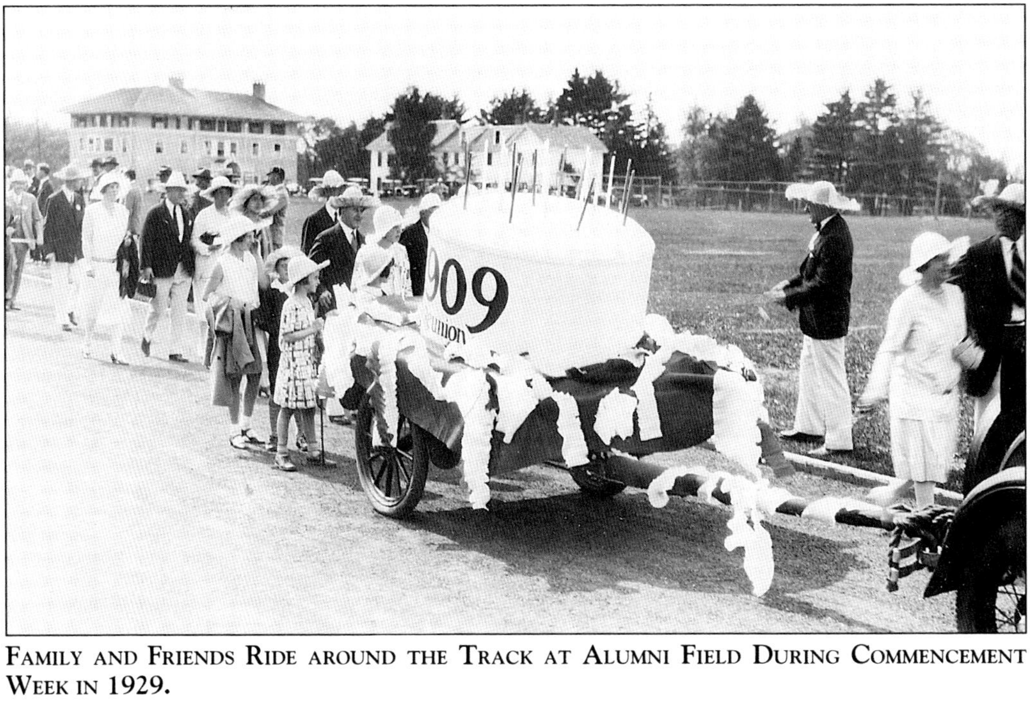

Family and Friends Ride around the Track at Alumni Field During Commencement Week in 1929.